llins

The Sha Maths Project

For the English National Curriculum

Series Editor: Professor Lianghuo Fan
UK Curriculum Consultant: Jo-Anne Lees

Practice Book

William Collins' dream of knowledge for all began with the publication of his first book in 1819. A self-educated mill worker, he not only enriched millions of lives, but also founded a flourishing publishing house. Today, staying true to this spirit, Collins books are packed with inspiration, innovation and practical expertise. They place you at the centre of a world of possibility and give you exactly what you need to explore it.

Collins. Freedom to teach.

Published by Collins
An imprint of HarperCollins*Publishers* Ltd.
The News Building
1 London Bridge Street
London SE1 9GF

Browse the complete Collins catalogue at
www.collins.co.uk

10 9 8 7 6 5 4 3 2 1

ISBN: 978-0-00-814469-2

The Shanghai Maths Project (for the English National Curriculum) is a collaborative effort between HarperCollins, East China Normal University Press Ltd. and Professor Lianghuo Fan and his team. Based on the latest edition of the award-wining series of learning resource books, *One Lesson One Exercise*, by East China Normal University Press Ltd. in Chinese, the series of Practice Books is published by HarperCollins after adaptation following the English National Curriculum.

Practice book Year 8 is translated and developed by Professor Lianghuo Fan with assistance of Ellen Chen, Ming Ni, Jing Xu, Dr. Yan Zhu and Dr. Haiyue Jin, with Jo-Anne Lees as UK curriculum consultant.

British Library Cataloguing in Publication Data
A Catalogue record for this publication is available from the British Library.

Series Editor: Professor Lianghuo Fan
UK Curriculum Consultant: Jo-Anne Lees
Commissioned by Katie Sergeant
Project Managed by Fiona McGlade and Alexander Rutherford
Design by Kevin Robbins and East China Normal University Press Ltd.
Typesetting by East China Normal University Press Ltd.
Cover illustration by Steve Evans
Production by Rachel Weaver
Printed by Grafica Veneta S. p. A

Contents

Chapter 1   Real numbers

1. 1   The concept of real numbers / 1

1. 2   Square roots: concept and evaluation (1) / 3

1. 3   Square roots: concept and evaluation (2) / 5

1. 4   Cube roots / 7

1. 5   *n*th roots / 9

1. 6   Representing real numbers on a number line / 11

1. 7   Approximation and significant figures / 13

Unit test 1 / 15

Chapter 2   Intersecting and parallel lines

2. 1   Adjacent, supplementary and vertically opposite angles / 18

2. 2   Perpendicular lines (1) / 21

2. 3   Perpendicular lines (2) / 24

2. 4   Corresponding angles and alternate angles / 27

2. 5   Properties of parallel lines (1) / 30

2. 6   Properties of parallel lines (2) / 32

2. 7   Properties of parallel lines (3) / 35

2. 8   Properties of parallel lines (4) / 38

2. 9   Properties of parallel lines (5) / 41

Unit test 2 / 44

Chapter 3   Trapezia

3. 1   What is a trapezium? / 49

3. 2   Areas of trapezia (1) / 52

3. 3   Areas of trapezia (2) / 54

3. 4   Areas of composite figures / 57

Unit test 3 / 59

Chapter 4   Triangles

4. 1   Concepts of triangles (1) / 62

4. 2   Concepts of triangles (2) / 64

4. 3   Sum of the interior angles of a triangle (1) / 66

4. 4   Sum of the interior angles of a triangle (2) / 68

4. 5   Sum of the interior angles of a triangle (3) / 71

4. 6   Congruent triangles: concepts and properties (1) / 73

4. 7   Congruent triangles: concepts and properties (2) / 76

4. 8   Testing for congruent triangles (1) / 80

4. 9   Testing for congruent triangles (2) / 83

4. 10 Testing for congruent triangles (3) / 86

4. 11 Testing for congruent triangles (4) / 89

4. 12 Testing for congruent triangles (5) / 92

Contents

4.13 Testing for congruent triangles (6) / 95

4.14 Properties of isosceles triangles / 99

4.15 Identifying isosceles triangles (1) / 102

4.16 Identifying isosceles triangles (2) / 105

4.17 Equilateral triangles / 108

Unit test 4 / 111

Chapter 5　The co-ordinate plane

5.1 Introduction to the co-ordinate plane (1) / 116

5.2 Introduction to the co-ordinate plane (2) / 118

5.3 Point movement on the co-ordinate plane (1) / 120

5.4 Point movement on the co-ordinate plane (2) / 123

5.5 Point movement on the co-ordinate plane (3) / 126

Unit test 5 / 129

Chapter 6　Direct proportion, inverse proportion and their functions

6.1 Variables and functions / 133

6.2 Direct proportion and direct proportional functions / 135

6.3 Graphs of direct proportional functions / 138

6.4 Properties of direct proportional functions / 141

6.5 Inverse proportion and inverse proportional functions / 144

6.6 Graphs of inverse proportional functions / 147

6.7 Properties of inverse proportional functions / 151

6.8 How to express functions (1) / 155

6.9 How to express functions (2) / 159

Unit test 6 / 162

Chapter 7　Introduction to proof in geometry

7.1 Statement and proof (1) / 167

7.2 Statement and proof (2) / 170

7.3 Practice and exercise in proof (1) / 172

7.4 Practice and exercise in proof (2) / 175

7.5 Practice and exercise in proof (3) / 177

7.6 Practice and exercise in proof (4) / 179

7.7 Perpendicular bisector of a line segment / 182

7.8 Angle bisectors (1) / 185

7.9 Angle bisectors (2) / 188

Unit test 7 / 190

Chapter 8　Right-angled triangles and Pythagoras' theorem

8.1 Congruence testing for right-angled triangles / 193

8.2 Properties of right-angled triangles (1) / 196

8.3 Properties of right-angled triangles (2) / 199

8.4 Properties of right-angled triangles (3) / 202

8.5 Pythagoras' theorem / 205

8.6 Applications of Pythagoras' theorem / 208

8.7 The converse of Pythagoras' theorem / 211

8.8 Applications of Pythagoras' theorem and its converse theorem / 213

8.9 The formula for distance between two points / 216

Unit test 8 / 219

Chapter 9   Statistics (I)

9.1 Organising and presenting data (1) / 222

9.2 Organising and presenting data (2) / 225

9.3 Measuring central tendency of data (1): Mean / 228

9.4 Measuring central tendency of data (2): Mode and median / 232

9.5 Measuring central tendency of data (3): Mode and median / 235

Unit test 9 / 238

End of year test / 242

Answers / 252

Chapter 1   Real numbers

1.1   The concept of real numbers

Learning objective

Recognise rational and irrational numbers

A. Multiple choice questions

1 Read these statements. The correct one is (   ).

A. A terminating decimal must be a rational number.

B. A rational number must be a terminating decimal.

C. The sum of two irrational numbers must be an irrational number.

D. The product of two irrational numbers must be an irrational number.

2 Look at these real numbers. The irrational number is (   ).

A. 0   B. -3.5

C. $\sqrt{3}$ D. $\sqrt{9}$

3 Look at these real numbers. The rational number is (   ).

A. $\sqrt{7}$ B. $\dfrac{1}{7}$

C. $7 + \pi$ D. $0.070\,070\,007\,000\,07\ldots$

4 Read these statements. The incorrect one is (   ).

A. An infinite decimal has infinitely many digits after the decimal point.

B. An infinite decimal is an irrational number.

C. Any decimal must be either a terminating decimal or an infinite decimal.

D. The sum of an infinite decimal and a terminating decimal is an infinite decimal.

B. Fill in the blanks

5 Real numbers can be classified into two categories: rational numbers and _____

_____.

6 Real numbers can also be classified into terminating decimals and _____

_____ .

7 When written as a decimal, an irrational number has _____ many non-repeating digits after the decimal point.

8 The irrational numbers in the set: $\dfrac{8}{25}$, -0.25, $0.\overset{..}{2}\overset{..}{5}$, $\dfrac{25}{8}$, π, $\sqrt{8}$ and $\sqrt{25}$ are

_____ .

9 The integer that is nearest to $\sqrt{8}$ is _____ .

10 An irrational number between 3 and 4 could be _____ .

11 a is a positive integer no greater than 10 and $\sqrt{a}$ is an irrational number. The possible values of a are _____ .

C. Questions that require solutions

12 A big square of side length 3 is divided into 9 smaller squares and a point is taken on each side to form square $ABCD$, as shown in the diagram.

(a) Calculate the area of square $ABCD$.

(b) Calculate the side length of square $ABCD$.

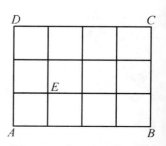

Diagram for question 12

13 The diagram shows a rectangle divided into 12 squares, each with side length 1 unit. Joining the vertices of these small squares gives diagonals of different lengths; for example, the longest diagonal is AC. One of the shortest ones is AE.

(a) Find a diagonal with a length that is rational. Use letters to represent the diagonal and find its length.

(b) Find two diagonals with lengths that are irrational. Again, use letters to represent the diagonals and find their lengths.

Diagram for question 13

1.2 Square roots: concept and evaluation (1)

 Learning objective

Recognise and calculate with square roots; solve simple quadratic equations

 A. Multiple choice questions

1 Read these statements. The incorrect one is (   ).

A. Since the square of -2 is 4, -2 is a square root of 4.

B. If one of the square roots of a number is $\dfrac{2}{5}$, then the number is $\dfrac{4}{25}$.

C. The positive square root of 0.9 is 0.3.

D. The square root of zero is zero.

2 If $a \neq 0$, then the product of the two square roots of a^2 is equal to (   ).

A. 0 B. $-a^2$ C. a^4 D. $-a^4$

3 A square root of $\sqrt{25}$ is (   ).

A. 5 or -5 B. 5 C. $\sqrt{5}$ or $-\sqrt{5}$ D. $\sqrt{5}$

 B. Fill in the blanks

4 If the _____ of a number is a, then the number is a square root of a.

5 The two square roots of a positive number a can be represented by _____ , with _____ representing the positive square root of a and _____ representing the negative square root of a.

6 The square roots of $\dfrac{1}{49}$ are _____ and the positive square root of $\dfrac{1}{49}$ is _____ .

7 One square root of _____ is $-\sqrt{5}$ and the other square root is _____ .

8 Evaluate: (a) $\sqrt{169} =$ _____   (b) $\pm\sqrt{1.69} =$ _____ .

9 Evaluate: (a) $-\sqrt{(0.25)^2} = $ _____ (b) $\sqrt{(-0.25)^2} = $ _____

(c) the square roots of $(-0.25)^2$ are _____.

10 Evaluate: $\sqrt{25} - \sqrt{16} + \sqrt{25-16} = $ _____.

C. Questions that require solutions

11 Calculate: $\sqrt{0.0009} + \sqrt{2\frac{14}{25}} + \sqrt{90\,000}$.

12 Find the value of x in each equation.

(a) $\frac{1}{3}x^2 - 12 = 0$

$x = $ _____

(b) $\frac{1}{5}x^2 + 2 = 3\frac{4}{5}$

$x = $ _____

(c) $(x+2)^2 = 25$

$x = $ _____

13 Given that $1 - x$ has two square roots and $(3x - 4)^2 = 15$, find the square roots of $6x + 3$.

14 Given that $4 - a$ and $2a + 1$ are the two different square roots of the same real number, find the value of a.

4

1.3 Square roots: concept and evaluation (2)

Learning objectives

Recognise and calculate with square roots

Solve simple quadratic equations

A. Multiple choice questions

1. Read these statements. The correct one is (   ).

    A. Only a positive number has a square root.

    B. A square root of the square of a positive number a is just a.

    C. The square roots of a non-negative number add up to zero.

    D. A real number a must have a square root.

2. Read these statements. The correct one is (   ).

    A. The positive square root of a^2 is a.

    B. Zero does not have a square root.

    C. A square root of a positive number a is $\sqrt{a}$.

    D. The square roots of the square of $-a$ are $\pm a$.

3. Read these statements. The incorrect one is (   ).

    A. $\sqrt{12}$ is the positive square root of 12.

    B. $-\sqrt{12}$ is the positive square root of -12.

    C. $\sqrt{12}$ is an irrational number.

    D. $3 < \sqrt{12} < 4$ (That is: $\sqrt{12}$ is greater than 3 but less than 4.)

B. Fill in the blanks
(Use a calculator for questions 4 to 7; give your answers correct to four decimal places.)

4. Evaluate: $\sqrt{2014} \approx$ _____.

5. Evaluate: $\sqrt{2.014} \approx$ _____.

6. The square roots of $3\dfrac{5}{6}$ are _____.

7 The square roots of $3\dfrac{5}{6}$ are _____ .

8 If $1 \leqslant a \leqslant 50$ and $\sqrt{a}$ is an integer, then there are _____ possible values of a.

9 If a is a positive integer and $a < \sqrt{2015} < a + 1$, then $a =$ _____ .

10 If $3x - 2$ has a square root, then the range of the possible value of x is _____ .

C. Questions that require solutions

11 Given that $a = \sqrt{11} - 1$, $b = \sqrt{2} + 1$ and $c = \sqrt{5} - \sqrt{3}$, compare the values of a, b and c.

12 Given that $\sqrt{x - 2} + \sqrt{y - 3} = 0$, find the square roots of $y^x + x^y$.
(Use a calculator for the final result, giving it correct to four decimal places.)

13 Given that the integer part of $\sqrt{12}$ is a and its decimal part is b, find the value of $(b - a)(b + 3a)$.

1.4   Cube roots

Learning objective

Solve problems and equations involving cube roots

A. Multiple choice questions

1. The number with square roots that equal the number itself is (   ).

   A. -1 B. 1   C. 0   D. 0 or 1

2. There are (   ) real numbers of which the cube root equals itself.

   A. 0   B. 1   C. 2   D. 3

3. Read these statements. The incorrect one is (   ).

   A. The square of -1 is 1.   B. The square root of -1 is -1.

   C. The cube of -1 is -1.   D. The cube root of -1 is -1.

B. Fill in the blanks

4. A positive number has _____ square roots, the square root of zero is _____ and a _____ number does not have square roots.

5. Calculate: (a) $\sqrt[3]{5^6}$ = _____   (b) $\sqrt[3]{-5^6}$ = _____

   (c) $\sqrt[3]{(-5)^6}$ = _____ .

6. Calculate: (a) $\sqrt[3]{12^3}$ = _____   (b) $\sqrt[3]{3^{12}}$ = _____ .

7. Calculate: (a) $\sqrt[3]{-12^3}$ = _____   (b) $\sqrt[3]{(-3)^{12}}$ = _____ .

8. Use a calculator to evaluate (correct to four decimal places):

   (a) $\sqrt[3]{20\,142\,015}$ ≈ _____

   (b) $\sqrt[3]{-2014.2015}$ ≈ _____ .

9 If $(x + 2)^3 = -8$, then $x = $ _____ .

10 If $a < 0$, then $\sqrt{a^2} - \sqrt[3]{a^3} = $ _____ .

C. Questions that require solutions

11 Three identical cubic containers have sides of length 2. Their total capacity is the same as that of a larger cubic container with sides of length a. Find the value of a. (Use a calculator to evaluate and give your answer correct to two decimal places.)

12 The formula for finding the volume of a sphere is $V = \dfrac{4}{3}\pi r^3$. If the volume of a sphere is 1234 cm^3, find its radius r. (Take π as 3. 14; give your answer correct to two decimal places.)

13 Given that the cube root of $3x - 7$ is -1, find the square root(s) of $\dfrac{4x + 1}{3x - 2}$.

14 The positive square root of a positive number a is x and its cube root is y.
Write an algebraic expression in x to represent y.

1.5 nth roots

Learning objective

Solve problems and equations involving nth roots

A. Multiple choice questions

1 If both $\sqrt{a}$ and $\sqrt{-a}$ are meaningful, then (   ).

A. $a \geqslant 0$ B. $a \leqslant 0$

C. $a = 0$ D. $a \neq 0$

2 Read these statements. The incorrect one is (   ).

A. When n is odd, a real number a has one and only one nth root.

B. When n is a positive integer, the nth root of a^n is a.

C. If $\sqrt[n]{a} = \sqrt[m]{a}$ where n is odd and m is even, then a must be zero.

D. When $a < 0$, the 6th root of $-a$ is $\pm \sqrt[6]{-a}$.

3 n is a positive integer. If $\sqrt[n]{a}$ and $\sqrt[n]{-a}$ are meaningful for all real numbers a, then (   ).

A. n is an odd number.

B. n is an even number.

C. n can be either odd or even.

D. There is no such n that satisfies the condition.

B. Fill in the blanks

4 When n is even and a is positive, a has _____ nth roots, and their sum is _____. When n is even, a negative number has _____ nth roots. When n is odd, a real number has _____ nth roots. For any integer n, the nth root of zero equals _____.

5 (a) Calculate: $\sqrt[6]{-(-4)^3}$ = _____.

(b) The 6th roots of $-(-4)^3$ are _____.

6 (a) Calculate: $\sqrt[5]{7\dfrac{19}{32}}$ = _____.

(b) The 5th root of $7\dfrac{19}{32}$ is _____.

7 Use a calculator to evaluate (correct to two decimal places):

(a) $\sqrt[4]{98\ 765} \approx$ _____.

(b) $\sqrt[5]{-98.76} \approx$ _____.

8 Use a calculator to evaluate (correct to two decimal places):

(a) the 4th roots of $\dfrac{65}{987}$ _____.

(b) the 5th root of $9\dfrac{65}{87}$ _____.

9 The integer that is nearest to $\sqrt[6]{1000}$ is _____.

10 Calculate: $\sqrt[3]{0.027} - \sqrt[10]{\left(-\dfrac{1}{2}\right)^{20}}$ = _____.

C. Questions that require solutions

11 Given that $\sqrt{x-5} + (x+2y-1)^4 = 0$, find the value of $\sqrt[3]{x+y^x}$.

12 (a) If $3x+5$ and $x+7$ are the square roots of the same number, find the value of x.

(b) If $3x+5$ and $x+7$ are the cube root of the same number, find the value of x.

13* Find the least possible positive integer n so that $\sqrt[5]{80n}$ is a positive integer.

_____

* This is a very challenging question (optional).

1.6 Representing real numbers on a number line

Learning objective

Position and compare rational and irrational numbers on a number line

A. Multiple choice questions

1 The numbers represented by all the points on a number line are (   ).

  A. All the rational numbers

  B. All the irrational numbers

  C. All the real numbers

  D. All the positive numbers and all the negative numbers

2 Given that $a^2 < b^2$, then the correct statement below is (   ).

  A. a must be greater than b.

  B. a must be less than b.

  C. On a number line, a is nearer to the origin than b is.

  D. On a number line, a and b must be on the same side of the origin.

3 Read these statements. The correct one is (   ).

  A. $-\sqrt{2}$ is less than $-\sqrt{3}$.

  B. The cube root of 8 is 2 or -2.

  C. The square roots of -4 are ± 2.

  D. The distance between two points on a number line representing $\sqrt{4}$ and $\sqrt{9}$ is 1.

B. Fill in the blanks

4 On a number line, the distance of a point representing a real number, x, from the origin is _____ to the distance of the point representing its opposite number, $-x$, from the origin.

5 Mark the approximate positions of $-\sqrt[3]{6}$ and $\sqrt{6}$ respectively on the number line below.

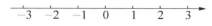

Diagram for question 5

6 Compare: (a) π _____ $2\sqrt{3}$.

(b) $-\sqrt{15}$ _____ $-\sqrt{17}$. (Write $>$ or $<$.)

7 Calculate: (a) $\sqrt{(2\sqrt{3}-5)^2} + \sqrt{3}$ = _____

(b) $\sqrt{(\sqrt{10}-3)^2} - \sqrt{10}$ = _____.

8 On a number line, points A and B represent $\sqrt{2}$ and $\sqrt{6}$ respectively. The distance between A and B is _____.

9 If $\sqrt{-(x-2)^2}$ is a real number, then $(x-3)^2$ = _____.

C. Questions that require solutions

10 The diagram shows the positions of a, b and c on a number line.

Calculate: $\sqrt{a^2} + \sqrt{(a+b)^2} - \sqrt{(a-c)^2} + \sqrt{(b+c)^2}$.

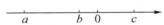

Diagram for question 10

11 On a number line, point A represents 1, point B lies to the right of point A and the distance from point B to point A is 2. The distance from point C to point A is 3. Find the distance between points B and C.

12 Without using a calculator, compare the values of $\sqrt{2} + \sqrt{3}$ and $\sqrt{5}$.

13 Find the value of $\sqrt{(3.14-\pi)^2} \div (\pi - 3.14)$.

1.7 Approximation and significant figures

Learning objective

Round and approximate numbers to a given number of decimal places or significant figures

A. Multiple choice questions

1 In the approximate values below, (   ) has one significant figure, (   ) has two significant figures, (   ) has three significant figures and (   ) has four significant figures[1].

   A. 0.005　　　　B. 50.05　　　　C. 0.050　　　　D. 0.0500

2 The correct statement below, is (   ).

   A. Approximate value 1.20 and approximate value 1.2 have the same degree of accuracy.

   B. Approximate value 1.20 and approximate value 1.2 have the same number of significant figures (or s.f.).

   C. Approximate value 12 million and approximate value 1.2 million have the same degree of accuracy.

   D. Approximate value 12.0 and 1.2 have the same degree of accuracy.

3 The approximate value of 0.596 correct to 0.01 is (   ).

   A. 0.59　　　　B. 0.6　　　　C. 0.60　　　　D. 0.600

4 The approximate value of 20 456, rounded to 2 significant figures, is (   ).

   A. 20 500　　　　B. 2.0×10^4　　　　C. 2.1×10^4　　　　D. 2.05×10^4

---

[1] In general, the number of significant figures in an approximate value is the total number of all the digits starting from the first non-zero digit, counting from left to right, to the last non-zero digit (although it may be a zero, if required by the stated number of significant figures) obtained by approximation by rounding.

B. Fill in the blanks

5 The approximate value 3. 1415 is correct to _____ decimal places, and it has _____ significant figures.

6 The approximate value 14 100 is at least correct to the nearest _____ and has _____ significant figures.

7 Rounding 1. 7320 to the nearest 0. 01 gives its approximate value as _____.
It has _____ significant figures.

8 Rounding $2. 236 \times 10^4$ to the nearest thousand gives its approximate value as _____.
It has _____ significant figures.

9 The population in a region is 16. 72 million. Expressing this number in standard form gives _____ (to 3 s.f.).

10 Use a calculator to evaluate: $\sqrt[3]{2} \approx$ _____ (to 3 s.f.).

11 Use a calculator to evaluate: $\sqrt[3]{2} \approx$ _____ (to the nearest thousandth).

C. Questions that require solutions

12 A square has the same area as a circle with diameter 1. Find the side length of the square. (Use a calculator to evaluate and give your answer correct to 0. 01.)

13 Let the integer part of $4 - \sqrt{3}$ be a and its decimal part be b. Find the approximate value of $\dfrac{b}{a} + 1$. (Use a calculator to evaluate and give your answer correct to 0. 01.)

14 Given that the approximate value of a precise number a rounded to the nearest 0. 01 is 23. 45, find the range of possible values of a.

Unit test 1

A. Multiple choice questions

1 In the set of real numbers $\sqrt{2}$, $0.\overset{..}{3}\overset{.}{4}$, $0.787\,887\,888\,788\,88\ldots$, π and $5\dfrac{1}{6}$, there are ( ) irrational numbers.

A. 1   B. 2   C. 3   D. 4

2 On a number line, the point representing -3 is A and the point representing $-\sqrt{10}$ is B. The distance between points A and B is ( ).

A. $3 - \sqrt{10}$ B. $\sqrt{10} - 3$ C. $3 + \sqrt{10}$ D. $-3 - \sqrt{10}$

3 The square root(s) of $\sqrt[3]{64}$ is (are) ( ).

A. ± 2 B. 2   C. $\pm 2\sqrt{2}$ D. $2\sqrt{2}$

B. Fill in the blanks

4 The square roots of $\sqrt{9}$ are _____.

5 The positive square root of $\sqrt[3]{125}$ is _____.

6 Given the cube root of a real number x is -3, the square roots of $9 - x$ are _____.

7 Given the square of a real number x is 49, the 4th roots of $9 + x$ are _____.

8 On a number line, point A represents $\sqrt{3}$ and the distance between A and B is $2\sqrt{3}$. Then the number represented by point B is _____.

9 If $a < -2$, calculate: $\sqrt[4]{(-a)^4} + \sqrt{(a+2)^2} = $ _____.

10 Calculate: $\sqrt{5} - \sqrt[3]{6} \approx$ _____ (to the nearest thousandth).

11 Calculate: $\dfrac{\sqrt[3]{9}}{\sqrt{3}} \approx$ _____ (to 3 s.f.).

12 If $\sqrt[3]{5x-1} + \sqrt[3]{4y+1} = 0$, then $\dfrac{x}{y} =$ _____ .

13 When x _____ , $x + \sqrt{(x-2)^2} = 2$.

14 If $x^2 - 36 = 0$ and $y^3 = 8$, then $x + y =$ _____ .

 C. Questions that require solutions (Show your working.)

15 Calculate: $2 \times \sqrt[3]{27} - \sqrt{\dfrac{1}{9} + \dfrac{1}{16}} + \sqrt{(0.1-7)^2} \div \sqrt{(0.77-1)^2}$

16 The diagram shows a large square of area 70 cm^2. A small square of area 5 cm^2 is cut from each of its four corners and then the sides are folded up along the dotted lines to form an open rectangular box. Find the volume of the rectangular box. (Give your answer correct to 0.1 cm^3.)

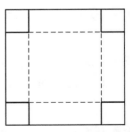

Diagram for question 16

17 Given the lengths of the two shorter sides of a right-angled triangle, one way to find the length of the hypotenuse is to place four identical right-angled triangles together into a large square, as shown in the diagram, and find the length through calculation of areas.

(a) The diagram shows a right-angled triangle with the lengths of its two shorter sides being 6 and 8 respectively. Find x, the length of the hypotenuse.

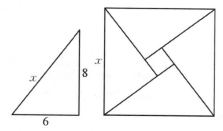

Diagram for question 17(a)

(b) Use the method from part (a) to find x, the length of the hypotenuse in a right-angled triangle where the lengths of the two shorter sides are a and b ($a \geqslant b$), as shown in the diagram.

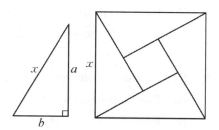

Diagram for question 17(b)

Chapter 2   Intersecting and parallel lines

2.1   Adjacent, supplementary and vertically opposite angles

Learning objective

Recognise and solve problems involving vertically opposite, adjacent and supplementary angles

A. Multiple choice questions

1. Read these statements. The correct one is (   ).

    A. Two angles sharing the same vertex are opposite angles.

    B. Vertically opposite angles must be equal.

    C. Two equal angles must be vertically opposite angles.

    D. Vertically opposite angles are not necessarily equal.

2. Read these statements. The correct one is (   ).

    A. Two angles sharing a common side are adjacent angles.

    B. Two supplementary angles must be adjacent angles.

    C. If two angles are adjacent as well as supplementary, then their non-common sides form a straight line.

    D. Two intersecting lines form a pair of adjacent angles that are equal.

3. In the diagram, there are (   ) pairs of vertically opposite angles.

    A. 2

    B. 3

    C. 4

    D. 5

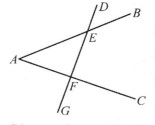

Diagram for question 3

4 In the diagram, $\angle AOF$ is an adjacent supplementary angle to (   ).

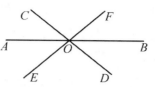

Diagram for question 4

   A. $\angle EOB$

   B. $\angle AOE$ and $\angle AOC$

   C. $\angle AOE$ and $\angle FOB$

   D. $\angle AOC$ and $\angle FOB$

B. Fill in the blanks

5 In the diagram, two intersecting lines, AB and CD, form four angles.

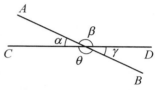

Diagram for question 5

  (a) Then α is vertically opposite angle to _____ and α is the adjacent angle to _____.

  (b) If $\beta = 155°$, then $\theta =$ _____ and $\gamma =$ _____.

6 The diagram shows two lines, AD and BC, intersecting at point O. If $\angle AOB$ is increased by $10°$, $\angle COD$ is increased by _____.

Diagram for question 6

7 In the diagram, two lines AB and CD intersect at point O. If OA bisects $\angle EOC$ and $\angle EOC = 70°$, then $\angle BOD =$ _____.

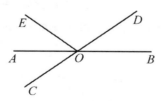

Diagram for question 7

8 Given that two angles α and β are supplementary to each other and $\alpha = \beta$, then $\alpha =$ _____.

9 If the two angles α and β add up to $90°$, the two angles β and γ are supplementary angles and $\alpha = 63°$, then $\gamma = $ _____ .

C. Questions that require solutions

10 In the diagram, three lines AB, CD and EF intersect at point O, $\alpha = 75°$ and $\beta = 60°$.
Find the size of $\angle EOC$.

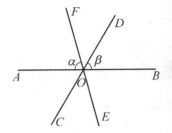

Diagram for question 10

11 The diagram shows two walls. Ian wants to measure $\angle AOB$, formed on the ground inside the walls.
He can only measure from outside the walls.
How can he measure the angle?

Diagram for question 11

12 In the diagram, lines AB and CD intersect at point O and $\angle DOE = \angle BOF = 90°$. Write down all the angles that are equal, explaining why they are equal.

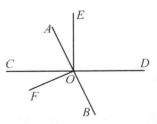

Diagram for question 12

2.2   Perpendicular lines (1)

 Learning objective

Recognise and solve problems involving perpendicular lines

 A. Multiple choice questions

1 In the diagram, $\angle AOC$ is opposite to an angle of (   ).

   A. 160°

   B. 20°

   C. 160° or 20°

   D. All of the above.

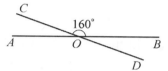

Diagram for question 1

2 Read these statements. The correct one is (   ).

   A. Through any point, there exist infinitely many lines perpendicular to a given line.

   B. Any line through a point is perpendicular to a given line.

   C. On a plane, there is one and only one line perpendicular to a given line.

   D. On a plane, there is one and only one line through a given point perpendicular to a given line.

3 Only one of these statements is correct. The correct one is (   ).

   A. A line passing through the midpoint of a line segment is called the perpendicular bisector of the line segment.

   B. If line segment AB is the perpendicular bisector of line segment CD, then CD is also the perpendicular bisector of AB.

   C. The perpendicular bisector of line segment AB divides it into two equal parts.

   D. There are infinitely many perpendicular bisectors of line segment AB.

4 Read these statements. The incorrect one is (   ).

   A. If the four angles formed by two intersecting lines are equal, then these two lines are perpendicular to each other.

   B. If two lines intersect and a pair of the adjacent angles formed are equal, then these two lines are perpendicular to each other.

   C. If two lines intersect and a pair of the vertically opposite angles formed are equal, then these two lines are perpendicular to each other.

D. Four angles are formed by two intersecting lines. If any two of them are equal, then these two lines are perpendicular to each other.

B. Fill in the blanks

5 In the diagram, lines AB and CD intersect at point O. If $\angle AOD = 90°$, then AB and CD are _____ to each other, and AB is _____ to CD.

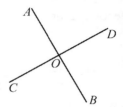

Diagram for question 5

6 In the diagram, two lines AB and CD pass through point O. If $\alpha = 35°$ and $\beta = 55°$, then OE and AB are _____ _____ to each other.

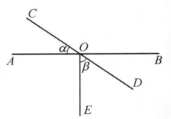

Diagram for question 6

7 In the diagram, lines AB and CD intersect at point O, $OE \perp CD$, $OF \perp AB$ and $\angle BOD = 25°$. Therefore $\angle AOC = $ _____, $\angle BOE = $ _____.

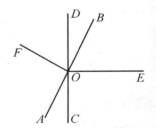

Diagram for question 7

8 In the diagram, $OA \perp OB$, $OD \perp OC$ and O is the foot of the perpendicular. If $\angle AOC = 35°$, then $\angle BOD = $ _____.

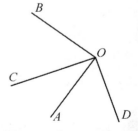

Diagram for question 8

9 In the diagram, lines AB and CD intersect at point O. If $\angle EOD = 40°$ and $\angle BOC = 130°$, then OE and AB are _____ to each other.

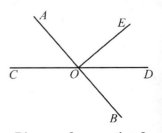

Diagram for question 9

10 The diagram shows lines AB and CD intersecting at point O. $\angle DOB = \angle DOE$ and OF bisects $\angle AOE$. If $\angle AOC = 36°$, then $\angle EOF = $ _____ .

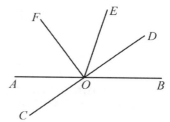

Diagram for question 10

C. Questions that require solutions

11 In the diagram, point P is inside $\angle AOB$, point M is outside $\angle AOB$ and point Q is on OB. Use a ruler and compasses to construct:
(a) from point P, a perpendicular to OA and then a perpendicular to OB
(b) from point Q, a perpendicular to OB
(c) from point M, a perpendicular to OA.

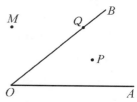

Diagram for question 11

12 In the diagram, $OE \perp OF$ and $\angle EOD$ and $\angle FOH$ are supplementary angles. Find $\angle DOH$.

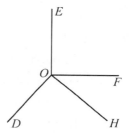

Diagram for question 12

13 In the diagram, lines AB, CD and EF intersect at point O, OG bisects $\angle BOF$, $CD \perp EF$ and $\angle AOE = 70°$. Find $\angle DOG$.

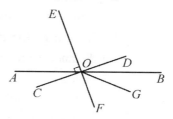

Diagram for question 13

14 In the diagram, point O lies on line AB, $\angle AOC = \dfrac{1}{3}\angle BOC$ and OC is the bisector of $\angle AOD$.
(a) Find $\angle COD$.
(b) State the relationship between OD and AB. Give reasons.

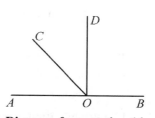

Diagram for question 14

2.3   Perpendicular lines (2)

Learning objectives

Describe, sketch and draw points, lines and perpendicular lines; solve related real life and construction problems

A. Multiple choice questions

1 The diagram shows $\triangle ABC$. $\angle BAC = 90°$ and D is the foot of the perpendicular from A to BC.

The incorrect statement of the following is (   ).

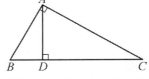

Diagram for question 1

  A. The distance from point B to AC is the length of line segment BC.
  B. The distance from point B to AD is the length of line segment BD.
  C. The distance from point C to AD is the length of line segment CD.
  D. The distance from point C to AB is the length of line segment AC.

2 Read these statements. The correct one is (   ).
  A. Through a point not on a given line, draw a line segment perpendicular to the line. The line segment is called the distance from the point to the line.
  B. The distance from a given point not on a given line to a point on the line is called the distance from the given point to the line.
  C. The length of the perpendicular line from a point to a given line is called the distance from the point to the line.
  D. The length of the perpendicular line segment from a point to a given line is called the distance from the point to the line.

3 Points A, B and C all lie on line l. Point M is not on the line. If $MA = 1.5$ cm, $MB = 3$ cm and $MC = 4$ cm, the perpendicular distance from M to line l is (   ).
  A. equal to 3 cm   B. equal to 4 cm
  C. not greater than 1.5 cm   D. greater than 4 cm

4 In the diagram, $AD \perp BD$ and $BC \perp CD$. If $AB = a$ cm and $BC = b$ cm, then the length of BD is (   ).
  A. greater than a cm   B. less than b cm
  C. greater than a cm or less than b cm
  D. greater than b cm but less than a cm

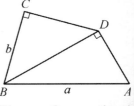

Diagram for question 4

B. Fill in the blanks

5 The diagram shows part of a water canal. It is necessary to feed water from the canal to a place represented by point C. On a plan, the engineer draws a perpendicular line segment through point C to AB, with D being the foot of the perpendicular, and decides to build a watercourse along CD. Explain why this watercourse is the shortest one that could be built _____

_____ .

Diagram for question 5

6 The diagram shows $\triangle ABC$. Given $AC \perp BC$ and $CD \perp AB$, write the lengths of AB, AC and CD in order, starting from the shortest. Use $<$ to compare them _____

_____ .

Diagram for question 6

7 The diagram shows a point P not on line l. Copy the diagram, drawing lines PA, PB, PC, ... , through point P to intersect the line l at points A, B, C, ... Use a protractor to measure α, β, γ, ... and a ruler to measure the lengths of PA, PB, PC, ...
The rule that you find is _____ .

Diagram for question 7

8 A non-fixed point O moves on line AB. P is a fixed point that is not on line AB. When the distance of the line segment PO is the shortest, $\angle POA =$ _____ degrees and hence the distance of point P to line AB is the length of line segment _____ .

9 In the diagram, the length of line segment _____ is the distance of point D to line BC and the length of line segment _____ is the distance of point A to line BC.

Diagram for question 9

10 The diagram shows points A, B and C, all on line l. The point P is not on line l. $PA = 3$ cm, $PB = 4$ cm and $PC = 6$ cm. Then the distance of point P to line l is _____ cm.

Diagram for question 10

C. Questions that require solutions

11 In the diagram, OC is the bisector of $\angle AOB$ and M lies on OC.

(a) Construct $MP \perp OA$, where P is the foot of the perpendicular.

(b) Construct $MQ \perp OB$, where Q is the foot of the perpendicular.

(c) Measure the distances of point M to OA and OB.

What conclusion can you draw?

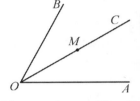

Diagram for question 11

12 In a school games day, a Year 7 athlete broke the school's record in the long jump on his fifth attempt. In the diagram, points A and B are his landing footprints and the line CD is the take-off line. Draw appropriate lines on the diagram to explain how to measure his result.

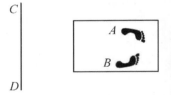

Diagram for question 12

13 The diagram shows a village, A, and a water supply factory, B, on the same river bank l. A pumping station, D, is to be built on bank l to transport water from the river to the factory and then to the village. To save costs, the pipeline to be laid should be as short as possible. Where should the pumping station be built and along what route should the pipeline be laid? Draw lines on the diagram to show your answer.

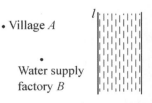

Diagram for question 13

2.4　Corresponding angles and alternate angles

Learning objective

Recognise and solve problems involving corresponding and alternate angles

A. Multiple choice questions

1 In the diagram, α is the corresponding angle to (　　).

A. β　　　　　　　　　　B. γ

C. θ　　　　　　　　　　D. ϕ

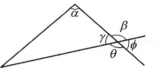

Diagram for question 1

2 In which diagrams are α and β corresponding angles? (　　)

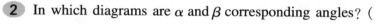

①　　　　　　②　　　　　　③　　　　　　④

A. ① and ②　　　B. ② and ③　　　C. ① and ③　　　D. ② and ④

3 In the diagram, which pair of angles are alternate angles? (　　)

A. α and β　　　B. γ and θ　　　C. β and γ　　　D. α and θ

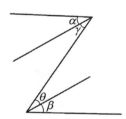

Diagram for question 3

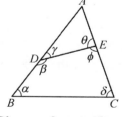

Diagram for question 4

4 The diagram shows six angles marked α, β, γ, θ, ϕ and δ. One of these statements is incorrect. The incorrect one is (　　).

A. There are 2 pairs of corresponding angles.

B. There are 5 pairs of co-interior angles.

C. There are 4 pairs of alternate angles.

D. α and θ are not alternate angles.

> **Co-interior angles** are the angles between a pair of lines on the same side of the transversal. When the two lines are parallel, co-interior are supplementary.

B. Fill in the blanks

5 In the diagram, there are _____ pairs of corresponding angles. They are _____.

6 In the diagram, there are _____ pairs of alternate angles. They are _____.

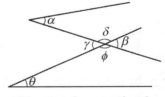

Diagram for questions 5 – 7

7 In the diagram, there are _____ pairs of co-interior angles. They are _____.

8 In the diagram, $\angle FDB$ is the alternate angle to _____ and $\angle DFB$ is the co-interior angle to _____.

Diagram for question 8

9 In the diagram, α is a corresponding angle to _____ , β is a corresponding angle to _____ , γ is an alternate angle to _____ and ϕ is the co-interior angle to _____ .

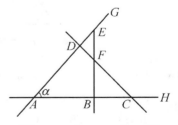

Diagram for question 9

C. Questions that require solutions

10 Write all the angles that are corresponding angles to α in the diagram.

Diagram for question 10

11 In the diagram, point A lies on line EF. List all the alternate angles and all the co-interior angles.

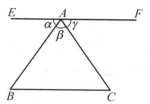

Diagram for question 11

12 Look at the diagram. How many angles are corresponding angles to the angle labelled α? Mark all of them in the diagram.

Diagram for question 12

2.5 Properties of parallel lines (1)

Learning objective

Recognise and solve problems involving angles between parallel lines and transversals

A. Multiple choice questions

1 The diagram shows $AB \parallel CD$. There are (   ) angles that are equal to α (excluding itself).

A. 5   B. 4

C. 3   D. 2

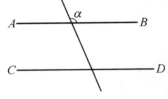

Diagram for question 1

2 If two parallel lines are cut by a third line, then the bisectors of two corresponding angles are (   ).

A. perpendicular   B. parallel   C. coincident   D. intersecting

3 In the diagram, if $AB \parallel CD$, then (   ).

A. $\alpha = \theta$

B. $\alpha = \gamma$

C. $\beta = \gamma$

D. $\alpha = \phi$

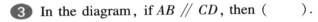

Diagram for question 3

4 In the diagram, if $l_1 \parallel l_2$ and $\gamma = 60°$, then β is (   ).

A. 60°

B. 120°

C. 70°

D. 50°

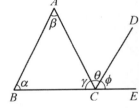

Diagram for question 4

B. Fill in the blanks

5 In the diagram, if $AB \parallel CD$ and $\alpha = 40°$, then $\angle C =$ _____ degrees.

6 In the diagram, if $AB \parallel CD$ and $\beta = 130°$, then $\angle D =$ _____ degrees.

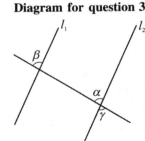

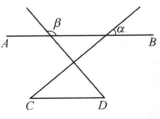

Diagram for questions 5 and 6

7 In the diagram, if $a /\!/ b$, $\alpha = (5x - 12)°$ and $\beta = (3x + 18)°$, then $\alpha =$ _____ °.

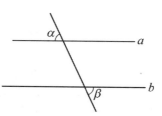

Diagram for question 7

8 In the diagram, $\alpha = 42°$, $AB /\!/ CD$ and DE bisects $\angle CDN$. Therefore, $\angle CDB =$ _____ ° and $\angle EDN =$ _____ °.

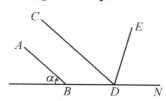

Diagram for question 8

9 In the diagram, if $AB /\!/ CD$, then $\angle B = \angle$ _____ .
Reason: _____ .

10 In the diagram, if $AD /\!/ EF$, then the equal angles are

_____ .

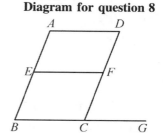

Diagram for questions 9 and 10

C. Questions that require solutions

11 In the diagram, if $AB /\!/ CD$, $\alpha = (3x + 80)°$ and $\beta = (2x + 70)°$, find γ.

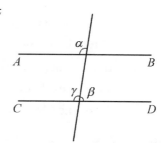

Diagram for question 11

12 In the diagram, given that $AB /\!/ CD$, EG bisects $\angle BEF$ and $\angle EFG = 40°$, find $\angle FEG$.

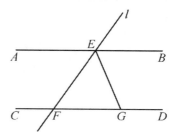

Diagram for question 12

2.6 Properties of parallel lines (2)

Learning objective

Recognise and solve problems involving angles between parallel lines and in closed shapes

A. Multiple choice questions

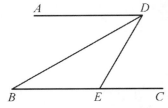

Diagram for question 1

1 In the diagram, $AD /\!/ BC$, $\angle B = 30°$ and DB bisects $\angle ADE$. $\angle DEC$ is (   ).

  A. 30°   B. 60°

  C. 90°   D. 120°

2 The diagram shows a parallelogram $ABCD$. Point E is on BA where it is extended beyond A. Equation (   ) is not necessarily true.

  A. $\alpha + \beta = 180°$ B. $\beta + \gamma = 180°$

  C. $\gamma + \theta = 180°$ D. $\beta + \theta = 180°$

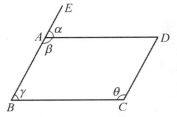

Diagram for question 2

3 One of these statements is incorrect. The incorrect one is (   ).

  A. If two lines are parallel, the corresponding angles formed with a third line are equal.

  B. If two lines are parallel, the alternate angles formed with a third line are equal.

  C. Two lines that are each perpendicular to the same line are perpendicular to each other.

  D. Two lines that are each parallel to the same line are parallel to each other.

B. Fill in the blanks

4 In the diagram, if $AB /\!/ EF$ and $BC /\!/ DE$, then $\angle E + \angle B =$ _____.

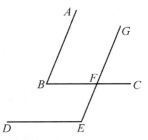

Diagram for question 4

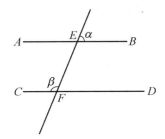

Diagram for question 5

5 In the diagram, if $AB /\!/ CD$ and $\beta = 2\alpha$, then $\beta =$ _____.

6 In the diagram, $l_1 \,/\!/\, l_2$, $AB \perp l_1$ at D, and BC and l_2 intersect at point E. If $\alpha = 45°$, then $\beta =$ _____°.

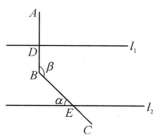

Diagram for question 6

7 In the diagram, if $AB \,/\!/\, EF \,/\!/\, CD$ and $EG \,/\!/\, BD$, then _____ angles are equal to α (excluding itself).

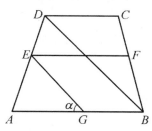

Diagram for question 7

8 The diagram shows $AB \,/\!/\, CD$, $\angle B = 40°$ and $\angle D = 10°$. $\angle B + \angle E + \angle F + \angle D =$ _____°.

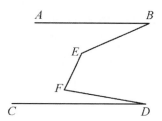

Diagram for question 8

9 The diagram shows $MA \,/\!/\, NB$, $\angle A = 70°$ and $\angle B = 40°$. $\angle P =$ _____°.

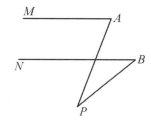

Diagram for question 9

C. Questions that require solutions

10 Follow the instructions to answer the question.

Question

In the diagram, $AB \,/\!/\, CD$, $\angle A = 130°$ and $\angle C = 110°$. Find $\angle APC$.

Solution

Method 1: Through point P, draw $PQ \,/\!/\, AB$.

Then $\angle A + \alpha =$ _____° (_____)

Since $\angle A = 130°$, $\alpha =$ _____°

Since $PQ /\!/ AB$ and $AB /\!/ CD$, $PQ /\!/ CD$. (Note: Two lines both parallel to a third line are parallel to each other.)

Therefore _____ (_____)

Since $\angle C = 110°$ (_____)

then $\beta =$ _____ °

Therefore $\angle APC =$ _____ + _____ = _____ °.

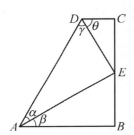

Diagram for question 10

Method 2: Extend AP beyond P so it intersects the extension of DC at point M. Can you continue to write down the solution? Have a go.

11 In the diagram, $AB /\!/ CD$, AE bisects $\angle DAB$ and DE bisects $\angle ADC$.

Explain why $DE \perp AE$. (Hint: the three interior angles in a triangle add up to 180°.)

Diagram for question 11

12 The diagram shows $AD /\!/ BC$ and $\angle ADE = \angle CBF$. Explain why $\angle E = \angle F$.

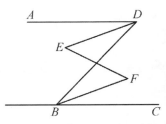

Diagram for question 12

2.7　Properties of parallel lines (3)

Learning objective

Recognise and solve problems involving angles between parallel lines and in closed shapes

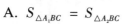

A. Multiple choice questions

1 The diagram shows $l_1 /\!/ l_2$. The incorrect equation about the areas of triangles is (　　).

(Note: In this book, S is used to stand for area, unless otherwise stated.)

A. $S_{\triangle A_1BC} = S_{\triangle A_2BC}$

B. $S_{\triangle BA_1A_2} = S_{\triangle CA_1A_2}$

C. $S_{\triangle A_1BO} = S_{\triangle A_2CO}$

D. $S_{\triangle A_1OA_2} = S_{\triangle BOC}$

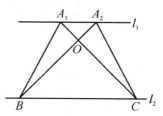

Diagram for question 1

2 One of these statements is incorrect. The incorrect one is (　　).

A. Given $a /\!/ b$, then the perpendicular distances from any points on line a to line b are equal.

B. Given $a /\!/ b$, then the perpendicular distances from any points on line a to line b are not equal.

C. Given $a /\!/ b$, then the perpendicular distances from any points on line a to line b are a fixed value.

D. Given $a /\!/ b$, then the perpendicular distances from all the points on line a to line b are equal.

3 In the diagram, $a /\!/ b$ and $BC = \dfrac{3}{2}AD$.

The ratio of $S_{\triangle ABC} : S_{\triangle BAD}$ is equivalent to (　　).

A. $\dfrac{2}{3}$

B. 2

C. 3

D. $\dfrac{3}{2}$

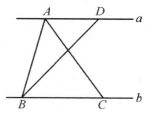

Diagram for question 3

4 Three lines a, b and c are on the same plane and $a /\!/ b /\!/ c$. The perpendicular distance between lines a and b is 3 cm and the perpendicular distance between lines a and c is 5 cm. Therefore the perpendicular distance between lines b and c is (   ).

A. 2 cm   B. 8 cm   C. 2 cm or 8 cm   D. uncertain

B. Fill in the blanks

5 In the diagram, $AD \mathbin{/\mkern-5mu/} BC$ and $AB \mathbin{/\mkern-5mu/} DC$. By drawing lines on the diagram, work out the distances between AD and BC and between AB and DC. The perpendicular distance between AD and BC is _____ and that between AB and DC is _____ .

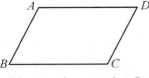

Diagram for question 5

6 In the diagram, $a \mathbin{/\mkern-5mu/} b$ and $AC = BD = EG$. There are _____ triangles that have the same area as $\triangle AEG$.

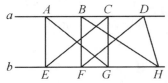

7 In the diagram, $a \mathbin{/\mkern-5mu/} b$ and $AC = BD = EG$. Given that $S_{\triangle ACE} = 1$, the area of the quadrilateral $AEGC$ is _____ .

Diagram for questions 6 and 7

8 The diagram shows a parallelogram $ABCD$. Point E is any point on AD.
If $S_{ABCD} = 20 \text{ cm}^2$, then $S_{\triangle EBC} =$ _____ cm^2.

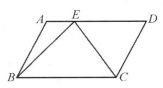

Diagram for question 8

9 The diagram shows $\triangle ABC$. D lies on side BC and $BD : DC = 2 : 3$. If the area of $\triangle ABD$ is 16, then the area of $\triangle ACD$ is _____ .

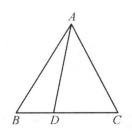

Diagram for question 9

C. Questions that require solutions

10 The diagram shows a parallelogram $ABCD$. Point E lies on side AB and point F lies on side AD.
Explain why $S_{\triangle ECD} = S_{\triangle FBC}$.

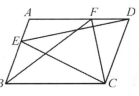

Diagram for question 10

11 The diagram shows quadraliteral $ABCD$ with $AD \parallel BC$.

Explain why $S_{\triangle ABO} = S_{\triangle DCO}$.

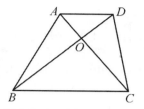

Diagram for question 11

12 In the diagram, $AB \parallel DC$, $AD \parallel BC$, E is a point on side BC and the extension of DE intersects the extension of AB at point F. Explain why $S_{\triangle ABE} = S_{\triangle CFE}$.

(Hint: draw segment DB and observe how the areas of the three triangles $\triangle ABE$, $\triangle DBE$ and $\triangle CEF$ are related.)

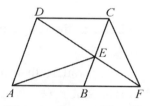

Diagram for question 12

2.8 Properties of parallel lines (4)

Learning objective

Recognise and solve problems involving angles between parallel lines and in closed shapes

A. Multiple choice questions

1 In the diagram, $AB \parallel CD$, $CD \parallel EF$, $\alpha = 30°$ and $\beta = 70°$.

$\angle BCE$ is (　　).

A. 40°

B. 100°

C. 140°

D. 130°

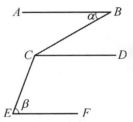

Diagram for question 1

2 Look at the diagram. Only statement (　　) is correct.

A. Since $AB \parallel CD$, $\alpha = \angle D$. Reason: If two lines are parallel, then the alternate angles are equal.

B. Since $AB \parallel CD$, $\gamma = \angle \theta$. Reason: If two lines are parallel, then the corresponding angles are equal.

C. Since $AB \parallel CD$, $\gamma = \angle \theta$. Reason: If two lines are parallel, then the alternate angles are equal.

D. Since $AB \parallel CD$, $\alpha = \angle \beta$. Reason: If two lines are parallel, then the alternate angles are equal.

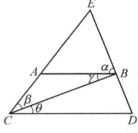

Diagram for question 2

3 The diagram shows that $AD \parallel BC$ and point E is on the BD extended beyond D.

If $\angle ADE = 155°$, then $\angle DBC$ is (　　).

A. 155°　　　　　　　　B. 35°

C. 45°　　　　　　　　D. 25°

Diagram for question 3

4 The diagram shows a rectangular piece of paper $ABCD$ folded along EF so that EM intersects BF at G. If $\angle EFG = 55°$, the $\angle BGE$ is (　　).

A. 105°　　　　　　　　B. 110°

C. 125°　　　　　　　　D. 115°

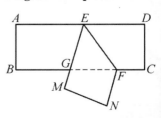

Diagram for question 4

B. Fill in the blanks

5 In the diagram, if $FE \parallel AB$, then $\beta =$ _____ .

Reason: _____

_____ .

6 In the diagram, if $AB \parallel DC$, then $\gamma =$ _____ .

Reason: _____

_____ .

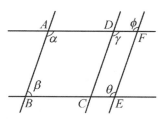

7 In the diagram, if $AF \parallel BE$, then $\alpha + \beta =$ _____ .

Reason: _____

Diagram for questions 5 – 8

_____ .

8 In the diagram, if $AF \parallel BE$ and $\alpha = 120°$, then $\gamma =$ _____ .

Reason: _____

_____ .

9 A girl started from point A and walked in the direction of $60°$ east of north for 10 m to reach point B. She then walked from point B for 10 m in the direction of $15°$ west of south to reach point C. $\angle ABC =$ _____ °

10 In the diagram, $a \parallel b$. $\alpha + \gamma - \beta =$ _____ °

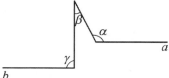

Diagram for question 10

C. Questions that require solutions

11 The diagram shows a window $ABCD$, with $AD \parallel BC$. The glass was broken and, for the replacement, the angles were measured.

$\angle A = 125°$ and $\angle D = 110°$. Find $\angle B$ and $\angle C$.

Diagram for question 11

12 In the diagram, $DE \parallel BC$ and $\angle BDE - \angle B = 20°$.
Find $\angle ADE$.

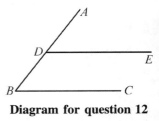

Diagram for question 12

13 In the diagram, $AB \parallel CD$, EF intersects AB and CD at points M and N respectively, $\angle EMB = 50°$, MG bisects $\angle BMF$ and MG intersects CD at G. Find α.

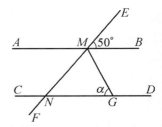

Diagram for question 13

2.9　Properties of parallel lines (5)

Use properties of parallel lines to solve geometry problems

 A. Multiple choice questions

1 The diagram shows $\triangle ABC$ with $\angle C = 90°$. If $BD \parallel AE$ and $\angle DBC = 20°$, then $\angle CAE$ is (　　).

　A. 40°

　B. 60°

　C. 70°

　D. 80°

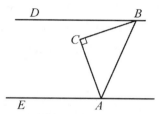

Diagram for question 1

2 The diagram shows a set square and two parellel lines a and b. Given that $\alpha = 55°$, then β is (　　).

　A. 45°

　B. 35°

　C. 55°

　D. 125°

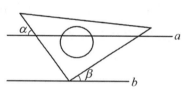

Diagram for question 2

3 In the diagram, $AB \parallel CD$ and $AD \parallel BC$. One of these conclusions is incorrect. The incorrect one is (　　).

　A. $\alpha + \beta = 180°$

　B. $\beta + \gamma = 180°$

　C. $\gamma + \theta = 180°$

　D. $\alpha + \gamma = 180°$

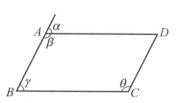

Diagram for question 3

4 In the diagram, $AB \parallel CD$. α is (　　).

　A. 75°

　B. 80°

　C. 85°

　D. 95°

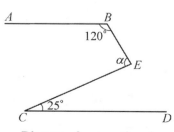

Diagram for question 4

B. Fill in the blanks

5 In the diagram, given that $AB \parallel CD$ and $\alpha = 70°$, then $\beta =$ _____.

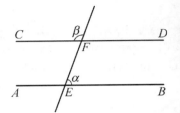

Diagram for question 5

6 Two rectangular pieces of paper are placed as shown in the diagram, so that a vertex of one piece lies on a side of the other piece. Then $\alpha + \beta =$ _____.

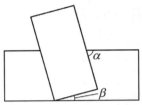

Diagram for question 6

7 The diagram shows $\triangle ABC$ with its three vertices lying on lines a and b and $a \parallel b$. Given that $\alpha = 120°$ and $\beta = 80°$, then γ is _____.

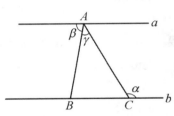

Diagram for question 7

8 In the diagram, $a \parallel b$, $AC \perp AB$ at A and $\alpha = 65°$. β is _____.

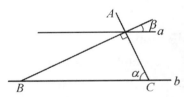

Diagram for question 8

9 In the diagram, CD bisects $\angle ACB$, $DE \parallel AC$ and $\alpha = 30°$. β is _____.

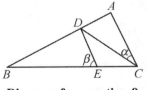

Diagram for question 9

10 A pair of set squares are placed as shown in the diagram, with point A lying on ED and $BC \parallel ED$. Then $\angle AFC$ is _____.

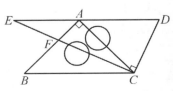

Diagram for question 10

C. Questions that require solutions

11 In the diagram, $\alpha = \beta$ and $\angle C = \angle D$. Explain why $\angle A = \angle F$.

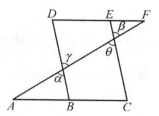

Diagram for question 11

12 In the diagram, $AB \parallel CD$, BE and DE intersect at E.
Explain why $\angle ABE = \angle D + \angle E$.

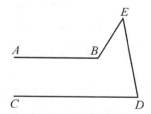

Diagram for question 12

13 In the diagram, $a \parallel b$. Study the relationship between α, β, γ, θ and ϕ. What is your conclusion? Give reasons. (Note: Two lines both parallel to a third line are parallel to each other.)

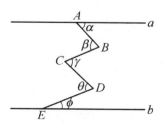

Diagram for question 13

Unit test 2

A. Multiple choice questions

1 Look at the diagram. One of these statements is incorrect. The incorrect one is (　　).

A. α and ϕ are corresponding angles.

B. γ and θ are supplementary angles.

C. α and δ are corresponding angles.

D. γ and ϕ are alternate angles.

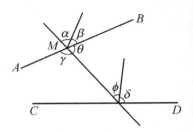

Diagram for question 1

2 Two parallel lines are cut by a third line, forming eight angles. The bisectors of (　　) are perpendicular to each other.

A. alternate angles   B. co-interior angles

C. corresponding angles   D. alternate angles and corresponding angles

3 Four lines on a plane intersect at the same point. They form (　　) pairs of vertically opposite angles.

A. 4   B. 8   C. 10   D. 12

4 In the diagram, given that $AD \parallel EF \parallel BC$, $AB \parallel CD$ and $\angle ABD = \angle ADB$, then in addition to $\angle ADB$, there are (　　) other angles equal to $\angle ABD$.

A. 2

B. 3

C. 4

D. 12

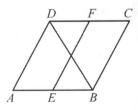

Diagram for question 4

5 As shown in the diagram, l_1 and l_2 are cut by l_3 at points A and B, and $AC \parallel BD$. If $\alpha = 20°$, then β is (　　).

A. 20°

B. 160°

C. 30°

D. uncertain

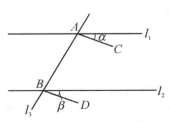

Diagram for question 5

6 P and Q are points on sides OA and OB of $\angle AOB$ respectively. Diagram (   ) shows the correct drawing of the perpendicular line segment PM from P to OB and the perpendicular line segment QN from Q to OA.

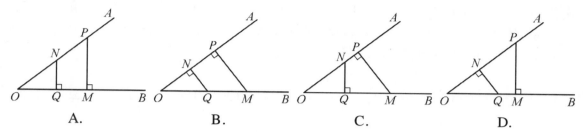

A.   B.   C.   D.

Diagram for question 6

B. Fill in the blanks

7 In the diagram, _____ angles are corresponding angles to α, and _____ angles are alternate angles to α.

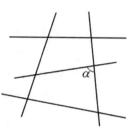

Diagram for question 7

8 The diagram shows that A, B and C lie on the same line. Among all the angles marked, there are _____ pairs of alternate angles.

9 In the diagram, A, B and C all lie on the same line. Among all the angles marked, there are _____ pairs of corresponding angles.

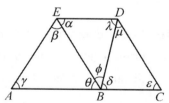

Diagram for questions 8 – 13

10 In the diagram, A, B and C all lie on the same line.
If _____ // _____ , then $\beta = \phi$.
Reason: _____ .

11 In the diagram, A, B and C all lie on the same line.
If _____ // _____ , then $\delta = \lambda$.
Reason: _____ .

12 In the diagram, A, B and C all lie on the same line.

If _____ // _____ , then $\theta = \varepsilon$.

Reason: _____ .

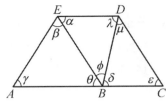

13 In the diagram, A, B and C all lie on the same line. If AE // BD and AB // ED, then among all the angles marked, the pairs of equal angles are _____ .

Diagram for questions 8 – 13

14 In the diagram, AB // CD, $\beta = 100°$ and $\gamma = 120°$. Then $\alpha = $ _____°.

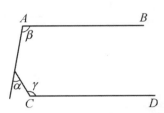

Diagram for question 14

15 The diagram is a sketch of a traditional letter opener. In the handle (the shaded area), the top left corner is a right angle, and the top and bottom sides are parallel (a small semicircle was removed from its bottom side). The long sides of the blade are also parallel. α and β are formed when the blade is rotated. $\alpha + \beta = $ _____ .

Diagram for question 15

16 In the diagram, a // b, points B and C lie on line b and point A lies on line a. If $BC = 5$ and $S_{\triangle ABC} = 10$, then the distance between lines a and b is _____ .

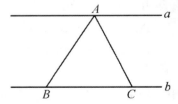

Diagram for question 16

17 The diagram shows a quadrilateral $ABCD$ and AB // CD. If $S_{\triangle ADM} = 0.8$ and $S_{\triangle BNC} = 1$, then $S_{\text{quadrilateral } MFNE} = $ _____ .

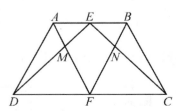

Diagram for question 17

18 The diagram shows the shape formed by folding a rectangular piece of paper $ABCD$ along a line MN. If $\angle AMD = 36°$, then $\angle BNC =$ _____ °.

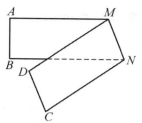

Diagram for question 18

C. Questions that require solutions

19 In the diagram, $AB \parallel EF$ and $BC \parallel DE$. What is the relationship between $\angle ABC$ and $\angle DEF$? Give reasons.
(Note: Two lines both parallel to a third line are parallel to each other.)

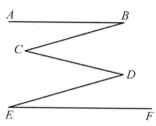

Diagram for question 19

20 In the diagram, AE bisects $\angle BAD$ and $CF \parallel AE$. Given that $\angle BAC = 70°$ and $\angle B = 30°$, find $\angle BCF$.

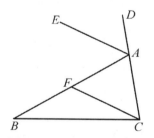

Diagram for question 20

21 In the diagram, $AD \parallel BC$ and $AD = 2BC$. Given that $S_{\triangle ABC} = 3$, find $S_{\triangle CAD}$.

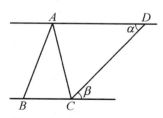

Diagram for question 21

22 In all the four diagrams, $AB \ /\!/ \ CD$. Look at each diagram carefully and study the relationships of $\angle APC$, $\angle PAB$ and $\angle PCD$. Write four conclusions and then select any one of them and explain why it is true.

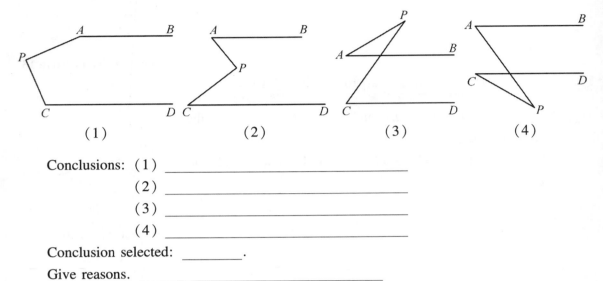

Conclusions: (1) _____

(2) _____

(3) _____

(4) _____

Conclusion selected: _____.

Give reasons. _____

23 Figure 1 shows a rectangular piece of paper. Figure 2 shows the result of folding the paper down along EF. Figure 3 shows the result of folding the paper again, up along BF.

(a) Given that $\angle DEF = 20°$, then in Figure 3, what is $\angle CFE$?

(b) Given that $\angle DEF = \alpha$, express $\angle CFE$ in Figure 3 in terms of α.

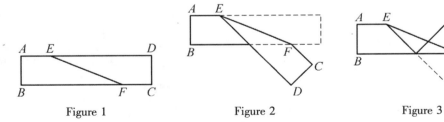

| Figure 1 | Figure 2 | Figure 3 |

Diagram for question 23

Chapter 3　Trapezia

3.1　What is a trapezium?

Learning objective

Recognise and identify properties of trapezia

A. Multiple choice questions

1　A quadrilateral with exactly one pair of opposite sides parallel is called (　　).

A．a parallelogram　　B．a rectangle　　　C．a trapezium　　　D．a rhombus

2　Two identical trapezia can definitely be combined to form (　　).

A．a triangle　　　　　　　　　B．a parallelogram

C．a rectangle　　　　　　　　D．a square

3　A quadrilateral that has one line of symmetry is (　　).

A．an equilateral triangle　　　B．a parallelogram

C．a rectangle　　　　　　　　D．an isosceles trapezium

4　It is impossible to divide a trapezium into two parts to get (　　).

A．two triangles　　　　　　　B．a parallelogram and a triangle

C．two parallelograms　　　　　D．two right-angled trapezia

B. Fill in the blanks

5　A quadrilateral with only _____ pair of parallel sides parallel is a trapezium.

6　A trapezium in which one angle is a right angle is called a _____ .
A trapezium in which the lateral (non-parallel) sides are equal is called _____ .

In a trapezium, the two parallel sides may be called the bases and the two non-parallel sides may be called the lateral sides.

7 In a trapezium, the sum of two neighbouring angles along either lateral side is
_____°.

8 If you draw a perpendicular line from a point on one of the bases of a trapezium to the other base, the segment between this point and the foot of the perpendicular is the _____ of the trapezium.

9 The figure obtained by extending the two lateral sides of a trapezium so that they meet is a _____.

10 There are _____ trapezia in the diagram below.

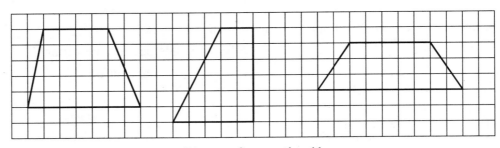

Diagram for question 10

11 The diagram represents a centimetre-squared grid, on which three trapezia of different types are drawn. Fill in the brackets according to the characteristics of each trapezium.

Diagram for question 11

The one on the left is a general trapezium. Its base on the top is _____ cm; its height (also called its **perpendicular height**) is _____ cm.

The middle one is a right-angled trapezium. Its base on the top is _____ cm; its height is _____ cm.

The right one is an isosceles trapezium. Its top base is _____ cm; its height is _____ cm.

12 True or false. (Put a tick (✓) for true and a (×) for false.)

(a) A figure that has only one pair of opposite sides parallel is called a trapezium.

_____

(b) The shorter lateral side of a right-angled trapezium is the height. _____

(c) There are infinitely many places where the height can be drawn between the parallel sides in a trapezium. _____

(d) The length of the top base of a trapezium is not equal to the length of its bottom base. _____

C. Questions that require solutions

13 Draw the height of each trapezium in the diagram below.

(a)   (b)   (c)

Diagram for question 13

14 How many trapezia are there in this figure?

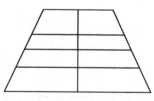

Diagram for question 14

3.2 Areas of trapezia (1)

Learning objective

Calculate the area of a trapezium

A. Multiple choice questions

1 Two trapezia with (   ) can form a parallelogram.

A. the same shape   B. the same area

C. each of their two bases and their heights being equal

D. the same shape and the same area

2 Calculate the area of the trapezium in the diagram. The correct expression is (   ).

A. $(12 + 28) \times 10$ B. $(12 + 28) \times 22 \div 2$

C. $(12 + 28) \times 14 \div 2$ D. $(12 + 28) \times 10 \div 2$

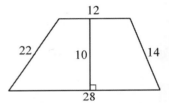

Diagram for question 2

B. Fill in the blanks

3 When a parallelogram with area 100 cm^2 is divided into two identical trapezia, the area of each trapezium is _____ cm^2.

4 One base of a trapezium is 7.5 cm, which is 3 cm shorter than the other base. Its height is 6 cm. Its area is _____ cm^2.

5 The sum of the two bases of a trapezium is 120 cm, which is twice its height. Its area is _____ cm^2.

6 The two bases of a trapezium are 6 m and 10 m. Its height is 9 m. If a maximum parallelogram is cut out from the trapezium, the remaining figure is a _____ and the area of the figure is _____ m^2.

7 In a trapezium, one base is 6.8 m, which is half the length of the other base. Its height is 3.6 m less than the longer base. The area of the trapezium is _____ m^2.

C. Questions that require solutions

8 Find the area of each trapezium in the diagram. All lengths are in centimetres.

(a)

5.5

4

3.5

(b)

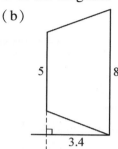

5   8

3.4

(c)

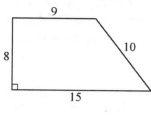

9

8   10

15

Diagram for question 8

9 A piece of farmland is in the shape of a trapezium. The two base lengths are 20 m and 15 m, and the height is 15 m. What is the area of this farmland?

10 A plot of land is in the shape of a trapezium. One base is 17 m. The other base is 1 m less than twice the first base but 3 times its height. Find the area of this plot.

11 A steel company received a batch of steel tubes, which were stacked in a trapezium-shaped pile. There were 10 tubes in the top layer and 20 tubes in the bottom layer, with a total of 11 layers. Each layer has one fewer tube than the one below it. If the price of each steel tube was £500, what was the total value of all the steel tubes?

3.3　Areas of trapezia (2)

Learning objective

Use the formula for the area of a trapezium to solve problems

A. Multiple choice questions

1　Given that the bases of a trapezium is equal to a base of a triangle, and their heights are also equal, then only statement (　　) is correct.

A. The trapezium and the triangle have the same area.

B. The area of the trapezium is twice that of the triangle.

C. The area of the trapezium must be larger than that of the triangle.

D. All of the above are incorrect.

2　Given that one of the bases of a trapezium is equal to a side of a parallelogram, and their heights are also equal, then only statement (　　) is correct.

A. The area of the trapezium must be equal to that of the parallelogram.

B. The area of the trapezium must be smaller than that of the parallelogram.

C. The area of the trapezium must be larger than that of the parallelogram.

D. All of the above are incorrect.

B. Fill in the blanks

3　Fill in the table about the area of trapezia.

First base (cm)	2.4	4	3.32	1.9
Second base (cm)	2.8	6	4.48	_____
Height (cm)	3	_____	5	3.2
Area (cm²)	_____	15	_____	7.36

4 Calculate the unknown lengths in the trapezia below. (Note: S denotes area.)

(a)

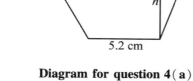

Diagram for question 4(a)

If $S = 42$ cm^2, then $h =$ _____

(b)

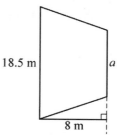

Diagram for question 4(b)

If $S = 120$ m^2, then $a =$ _____ .

C. Questions that require solutions

5 The cross-section of a canal is a trapezium. The area of the cross-section is 1.52 m^2, its depth is 0.8 m, and one base is 1.4 m. Find the length of the other base.

6 One base of a trapezium is 5.6 cm, which is 1.4 cm shorter than the other base. The area is 20.16 cm^2. Find the height of the trapezium.

7 In the diagram, the side lengths of the two squares in each figure are 4 cm and 3 cm. Find the areas of the shaded parts.

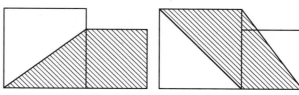

Diagram for question 7

8 The area of a trapezium is 128 cm², its height is 8 cm, and one of its bases is 4 cm longer than the other base. Find the length of the other base.

9 The diagram shows a right-angled trapezium $ABCD$, AD is 12 cm, BC is 16 cm, and the area of triangle ACD is 60 cm². Find the area of the right-angled trapezium.

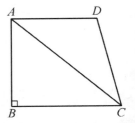

Diagram for question 9

10 In a right-angled trapezium, if one base is extended by 5 cm, the other base is extended by 2 cm, and the height remains unchanged, then the area is increased by 28 cm² and it becomes a square. Find the area of the original right-angled trapezium.

3.4   Areas of composite figures

Learning objective

Calculate the area of quadrilaterals and linear composite shapes

A. Multiple choice questions

1. A parallelogram and a trapezium have the same area and the same height. The base of the parallelogram is $2a$ and one base of the trapezium is a. The other base of the trapezium is (   ).

   A. a B. $2a$ C. $3a$ D. $5a$

2. In the diagram, $a \parallel b$ and $EA = AF$. One of these equations about the areas is incorrect. The incorrect one is (   ).

   A. $S_{\text{trapezium } EBCA} = S_{\text{trapezium } ABCF}$

   B. $S_{\triangle EBF} = S_{\triangle ECF}$

   C. $S_{\text{trapezium } EBCA} + S_{\text{trapezium } ABCF} = S_{\text{trapezium } EBCF}$

   D. $S_{\text{trapezium } EBCA} + S_{\triangle ACF} = S_{\text{trapezium } EBCF}$

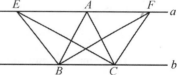

Diagram for question 2

B. Fill in the blanks

3. A trapezium can be considered as a composite figure made up of _____ triangles by connecting two opposite vertices.

4. Calculate the area of each composite figure below. All lengths are in centimetres.

   (a)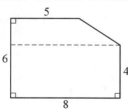

   Area = _____

   (b)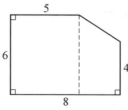

   Area = _____

   (c)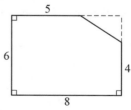

   Area = _____

   (d)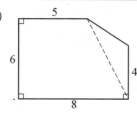

   Area = _____

   (e)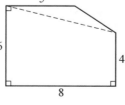

   Area = _____

C. Questions that require solutions

5 Use different ways of calculation to find the area of the composite figure below. All lengths are in centimetres.

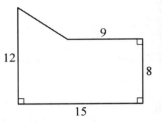

Diagram for question 5

6 Find the area of each composite figure as shown below. All lengths are in centimetres.

(a)

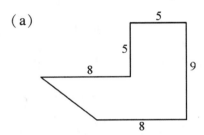

Diagram for question 6(a)

(b)

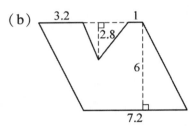

Diagram for question 6(b)

(c)

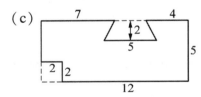

Diagram for question 6(c)

7 Find the area of the shaded part in each figure below. All lengths are in centimetres.

(a)

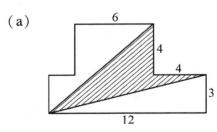

Diagram for question 7(a)

(b)

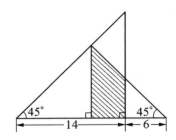

Diagram for question 7(b)

Unit test 3

A. Multiple choice questions

1 Read these statements about a trapezium. The incorrect one is (   ).

A. A trapezium has only one pair of opposite sides that are parallel to each other.

B. A trapezium must have two pairs of angles both with sum 180°.

C. It is possible for a trapezium to have three obtuse angles.

D. It is impossible for a trapezium to have only one right angle.

2 When a right-angled trapezium is divided into two parts, it is impossible for the two parts to be (   ).

A. an obtuse-angled triangle and a right-angled triangle

B. a rectangle and a triangle

C. a rectangle and a right-angled trapezium

D. a parallelogram and an obtuse-angled triangle

3 If the bases and height of a trapezium are all tripled, then the area of the enlarged trapezium is (   ) times the area of the original trapezium.

A. 3   B. 9   C. 18   D. 27

4 Look at the figure on the right. If the area of the trapezium is 4 times that of the triangle, then the other base of the trapezium is (   ).

A. 6 cm   B. 8 cm

C. 9 cm   D. 15 cm

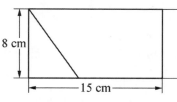

Diagram for question 4

B. Fill in the blanks

5 The area of the trapezium shown in the diagram is _____ .

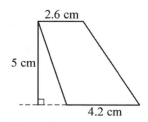

Diagram for question 5

6 The diagram shows a trapezium *ABCD* with an area of 18 cm². Given its height is 4 cm, *BC* is 5.4 cm and *E* is the midpoint of *AD*, the area of triangle *ABE* is _____ cm².

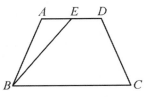

Diagram for question 6

7 If the product of one base of a trapezium and its height is 5.4 cm, and the product of its other base and its height is 8.8 cm, the area of this trapezium is _____.

C. Questions that require solutions

8 Look at the figure. If the area $S = 36$ cm², find *h*.

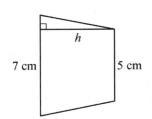

Diagram for question 8

9 The diagram shows an isosceles trapezium *ABCD* with an area of 64 cm². The two bases are 6 cm and 10 cm, and the area of $\triangle AOD$ is 15 cm².
(a) Find the height of the trapezium.
(b) Find the area of $\triangle AOB$.

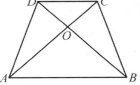

Diagram for question 9

10 Find the area of each composite figure below. All lengths are in centimetres.

(a)

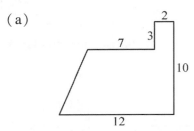

Diagram for question 10(a)

(b)

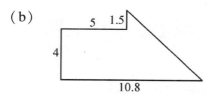

Diagram for question 10(b)

11 The diagram shows a rectangle $ABCD$. E is a point on the line AD extended beyond D. Connecting CE and BE, and given that $AB = 15$ cm, $DE = 4$ cm and the area of $\triangle DEF$ is 12 cm^2, find:

(a) the area of $\triangle CEF$

(b) the area of the trapezium $ABFD$.

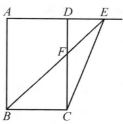

Diagram for question 11

12 A steel plate is in the shape of a trapezium. The lengths of the two bases are 120 cm and 180 cm, and the height is 160 cm. If the sale price of each square metre of the steel plate is £5, what is the total price for this piece of steel plate?

13 One base of a parallelogram is 10 m. If the length of the base is reduced by 2 m, then the area of the trapezium formed is 108 m^2. Find the area of the original parallelogram.

Chapter 4   Triangles

4.1   Concepts of triangles (1)

Learning objective

Solve problems involving side lengths and perimeters of triangles

A. Multiple choice questions

1 One of these sets of lengths of three line segments cannot form a triangle. This set is
(   ).

    A. 3, 8, 4   B. 4, 9, 6   C. 15, 20, 8   D. 9, 15, 8

2 The lengths of the sides of a triangle are 2, x and 13, where x is a positive integer. There are (   ) such triangles.

    A. 2   B. 3   C. 5   D. 13

3 In the diagram, the height (also called the **perpendicular height**) of $\triangle ABC$ from the vertex A to the side BC is (   ).

    A. AD B. BE

    C. CF D. BF

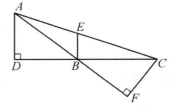

Diagram for question 3

B. Fill in the blanks

4 If the lengths of two sides of a triangle are 3 cm and 6 cm, and the length of the third side is an odd number, then the perimeter of the triangle is _____ cm.

5 The lengths of four line segments are 5, 6, 18 and 19. Using any three of them as sides to construct triangles, _____ different triangles may be constructed.

6 In the diagram, if $AH \perp BC$ and the foot of the perpendicular is H, then there are _____ triangles for which AH is a height. These triangles are _____.

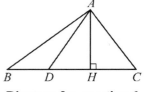

Diagram for question 6

7 The diagram shows $\triangle ABC$, where D is the midpoint of BC, $\angle BAC = 90°$ and AE and AF are the angle bisectors of $\triangle ABD$ and $\triangle ADC$ respectively.

$BD = $ _____ $= \dfrac{1}{2}$ _____ .

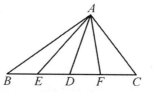

Diagram for questions 7 – 9

8 With the same given conditions as in question 6, $\angle BAE = \angle$ _____ $=$ $\dfrac{1}{2} \angle$ _____ .

9 With the same given conditions as in question 6, $\angle EAF = $ _____ degrees.

C. Questions that require solutions

10 In $\triangle ABC$, given $a = 3\,\text{cm}$ and $b = 4\,\text{cm}$, find the range of possible values of c. If c is an even number, what is the perimeter of the triangle?

11 Is the drawing of the line segment in each $\triangle ABC$ correct? Explain why.

(a)

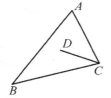

Angle bisector of $\triangle ABC$: CD

(b)

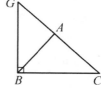

Height of $\triangle ABC$ from A to side BC: BG

12 The lengths of the sides of a triangle are a, b and c, its perimeter is $12\,\text{cm}$, $c + a = 2b$ and $c - a = 2$. Find the values of a, b and c.

13 For positive integers a, b and c, $a \leqslant b \leqslant c$ and $c = 6$. Do triangles with side lengths a, b and c exist? If so, find how many such triangles exist, and write the side lengths of each of these triangles. Otherwise, explain why.

4.2　Concepts of triangles (2)

Learning objective

Classify triangles by internal angles and side lengths and solve problems

A. Multiple choice questions

1 Given one angle of a triangle is 120°, then the triangle must be (　　).
　A. an obtuse-angled triangle　　　　B. a right-angled triangle
　C. an acute-angled triangle　　　　D. possibly any of the above

2 Given two sides in a triangle are equal, then the triangle is (　　).
　A. a non-equilateral triangle　　　　B. an equilateral triangle
　C. a right-angled triangle　　　　D. an isosceles triangle

3 The diagram shows a triangle with a part of it hidden.
The triangle must be (　　).
　A. an equilateral triangle
　B. an acute-angled triangle
　C. a right-angled triangle
　D. an obtuse-angled traingle

Diagram for question 3

4 If the three heights of a triangle intersect exactly at one vertex of the triangle, then the triangle is (　　).
　A. an acute-angled triangle　　　　B. a right-angled triangle
　C. an obtuse-angled triangle　　　　D. none of the above

B. Fill in the blanks

5 Two sides of an isosceles triangle are 4 cm and 9 cm. The third side is _____ cm.

6 Two sides of an isosceles triangle are 5 and 8. The perimeter is _____.

7 Given five line segments with lengths 1 cm, 2 cm, 3 cm, 4 cm and 5 cm, then using three of them as sides, the number of triangles that can be formed is _____.

8 The perimeter of an isosceles triangle is 5 and its three sides are all integers. The length of the two equal sides is _____.

9 The longest side of a non-equilateral triangle is 7, and the shortest side is 2. If the third side is an integer, then it must be _____.

10 The base of an isosceles triangle is 10 cm. A segment joining the midpoint of one of the two equal sides and the opposite vertex divides the triangle into two parts. If the perimeter of one part is 4 cm longer than that of the other part, the length of the two equal sides is _____ cm.

C. Questions that require solutions

11 In $\triangle ABC$, $AB = 7$, $BC = 4x$ and $AC = 3x$.
(a) Find the range of the values of x.
(b) Given that $\triangle ABC$ is an isosceles triangle, find the value of x.

12 Given that triangle ABC is an isosceles triangle, the base $BC = 8$ and the difference between AC and BC is 4, find the length of AC.

13 On the diagram, draw as many equilateral triangles as possible by using the given points as the vertices. How many can you draw?

Diagram for question 13

4.3　Sum of the interior angles of a triangle (1)

Learning objective

Solve problems involving the interior angle sum of a triangle

A. Multiple choice questions

1　Only one of these sets of angles can be the three interior angles of a triangle. That set is
(　　).
A. $100°, 50°, 20°$　B. $10°, 10°, 60°$　C. $0°, 90°, 90°$　D. $2.5°, 2.5°, 175°$

2　In a triangle, two interior angles are $30°$ and $60°$. The triangle is (　　).
A. an acute-angled triangle　　　　B. a right-angled triangle
C. an obtuse-angled triangle　　　　D. an isosceles triangle

3　In a triangle, the smallest interior angle is $46°$. The triangle is (　　).
A. an acute-angled triangle　　　　B. a right-angled triangle
C. an obtuse-angled triangle　　　　D. indeterminate

4　Read these statements. The correct one is (　　).
A. In a triangle, there are at least two interior angles that are acute angles.
B. In a triangle, there are at least two interior angles that are obtuse angles.
C. In a triangle, there is at least one interior angle that is a right angle.
D. In a triangle, there is at least one interior angle that is an obtuse angle.

B. Fill in the blanks

5　In a triangle, if two interior angles are $22.5°$ and $67.5°$, the remaining interior angle is

_____.

6　In a right-angled triangle, one acute angle is $75°$. The other acute angle is _____.

7　In $\triangle ABC$, one angle is $20°$ and $\angle B = \angle C$. Then $\angle B =$ _____.

8　In $\triangle ABC$, if $\angle A = \angle B = 4\angle C$, then $\angle C =$ _____.

9 In an isosceles triangle, one interior angle is 94°. The other two interior angles are ____

_____.

10 In an isosceles triangle, one interior angle is 40°. The other two interior angles are ____

_____.

C. Questions that require solutions

11 The diagram shows △ABC with angle bisectors BD and CE intersecting at point F. If ∠A = 50°, what is the size of ∠DFE?

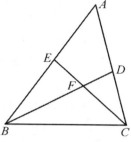

Diagram for question 11

12 In the diagram, given that $\angle A = \frac{1}{2}\angle ABC = \frac{1}{2}\angle C = \angle DBC$, find ∠ADB.

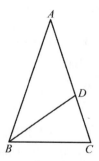

Diagram for question 12

13 The diagram shows △ABC. Angle bisectors BD and CE intersect at point F. Given that ∠EFD = n°, find ∠A.

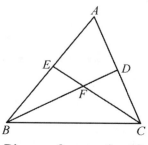

Diagram for question 13

4.4　Sum of the interior angles of a triangle (2)

Learning objective

Solve problems involving the internal and external angle sum of a triangle

A.　Multiple choice questions

1　If an exterior angle of a triangle is equal to its adjacent interior angle, then the triangle is (　　).

  A.　an acute-angled triangle
  B.　a right-angled triangle
  C.　an obtuse-angled triangle
  D.　possibly any of the above

2　In these diagrams, the one in which $\alpha > \beta$ must be true is (　　).

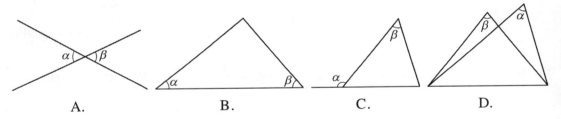

  A.　　　　　　　　B.　　　　　　　　C.　　　　　　　　D.

3　If the ratio of the three exterior angles of a triangle is $2:3:4$, then the ratio of their adjacent interior angles is (　　).

  A.　$2:3:4$　　　B.　$4:3:2$　　　C.　$5:3:1$　　　D.　$1:3:5$

4　The diagram shows $\triangle ABC$. Point D is on BC extended beyond C. Joining A and D, if $\angle BAC = \angle BCA$, $\angle B = \angle D = \alpha$ and $\angle CAD = \beta$, then the relationship between α and β is (　　).

  A.　$\alpha + \beta = 180°$
  B.　$3\alpha + 2\beta = 180°$
  C.　$\alpha = 2\beta$
  D.　$3\alpha + \beta = 180°$

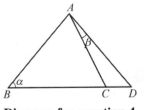

Diagram for question 4

B.　Fill in the blanks

5　In a triangle, if the sum of two exterior angles is equal to three times the third interior angle (so it is not adjacent to either of the two exterior angles), then the interior angle is _____.

6 If an exterior angle of a triangle is 72°, then its adjacent interior angle is _____ degrees.

7 In all the three exterior angles of a triangle, there is (are) at least _____ obtuse angle(s).

8 In all the three exterior angles of a triangles there is (are) at most _____ right angle(s).

9 If an exterior angle of a triangle is less than its adjacent interior angle, then the triangle must be _____ triangle.

10 The diagram shows $\triangle ABC$ with $\angle B = 25°$. Point E is on BC extended beyond C and ED is perpendicular to AC, passing through O, with D the foot of the perpendicular. If $\angle E = 40°$, then $\angle A =$ _____.

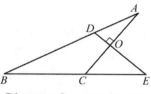

Diagram for question 10

C. Questions that require solutions

11 The diagram shows $\triangle ABC$ with $\angle B = 2\angle A$ and $\angle ACD = 120°$. Find $\angle A$ and $\angle B$.

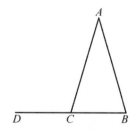

Diagram for question 11

12 In the diagram, $AB /\!/ CD$, $\alpha = \angle F$ and $\beta = \angle E$. Find $\angle EOF$.

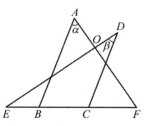

Diagram for question 12

13 The diagram shows $\triangle ABC$ with $\alpha = \beta$, $\gamma = \theta$ and $\angle BAC = 63°$. Find $\angle DAC$.

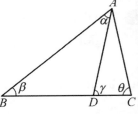

Diagram for question 13

14 The diagram shows $\triangle ABC$. BD bisects $\angle ABC$, CD bisects $\angle ACE$ and BD and CD intersect at point D.

(a) Given that $\angle A = 40°$, find the size of $\angle D$.

(b) Observing the solution above, can you see a pattern in the relationship between the sizes of $\angle A$ and $\angle D$? Write down your findings.

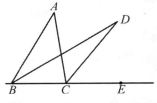

Diagram for question 14

4.5   Sum of the interior angles of a triangle (3)

Learning objective

Solve problems in triangles using facts about angle and length

A. Multiple choice questions

1 In the diagram, the correct relationship between $\angle C$, α and β is (   ).

A. $\alpha < \beta < \angle C$

B. $\beta > \alpha > \angle C$

C. $\angle C > \alpha > \beta$

D. $\alpha > \beta > \angle C$

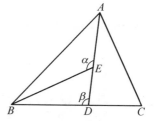

Diagram for question 1

2 In $\triangle ABC$, given that $\angle A = \dfrac{1}{2}\angle B = \dfrac{1}{3}\angle C$, then the triangle is (   ).

A. an acute-angled triangle

B. an obtuse-angled triangle

C. a right-angled triangle

D. possibly any of the above

3 The diagram shows $\triangle ABC$. The bisectors of the exterior angles adjacent to $\angle ABC$ and $\angle ACB$ intersect at point D. Of the following equations, the correct one is (   ).

A. $\angle A + \angle D = 90°$

B. $\angle A - \angle D = 90°$

C. $\dfrac{1}{2}\angle A + \angle D = 90°$

D. $\dfrac{1}{2}\angle A - \angle D = 90°$

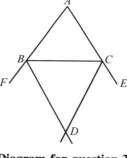

4 Of the following statements, the correct one is (   ).

Diagram for question 3

A. In a triangle, an exterior angle is larger than its adjacent interior angle.

B. In a triangle, an exterior angle is equal to the sum of two interior angles.

C. In a triangle, there is at most one interior angle not less than a right angle.

D. In a triangle ABC, the angle bisectors of two interior angles, $\angle A$ and $\angle B$, intersect at point O. $\triangle OAB$ is not necessarily an obtuse-angled triangle.

B. Fill in the blanks

5 In $\triangle ABC$, $\angle B = 64°$ and $\angle A = 31°$. $\angle C =$ _____°.

6 In a triangle, one of the interior angles is 40° and two of the angles are equal. The interior angle that is not equal to either of the two equal angles is _____.

7 If the ratio of the three exterior angles of a triangle is $2 : 3 : 4$, then the largest interior angle of the triangle is _____ degrees.

8 In $\triangle ABC$, $\angle A = 80°$. The angle bisector of $\angle B$ and the angle bisector of the exterior angle to $\angle C$ intersect at point D. Then $\angle BDC =$ _____.

9 In a triangle, if only two of the three exterior angles are obtuse, then the triangle is _____ triangle.

C. Questions that require solutions

10 The diagram shows $\triangle ABC$ with $\angle B = 65°$ and $\angle C = 45°$. AD is the height from A to side BC, and AE is the bisector of $\angle BAC$. Find $\angle DAE$.

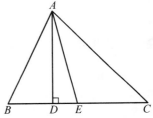

Diagram for question 10

11 The diagram shows $\triangle ABC$. Point D is on the side BC extended beyond C, $\angle A = 96°$ and the angle bisectors of $\angle ABC$ and $\angle ACD$ intersect at point E. Find the size of $\angle E$.

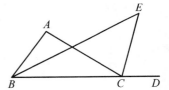

Diagram for question 11

12 The diagram shows $\triangle ABC$ in which $\angle A = 42°$ and the trisectors of $\angle ABC$ and $\angle ACB$ intersect at D and E respectively. Find $\angle D$ and $\angle E$. (Note: The trisector of an angle divides the angle into three equal parts.)

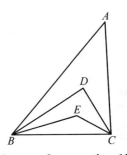

Diagram for question 12

4.6 Congruent triangles: concepts and properties (1)

Learning objective

Identify congruent triangles and understand relevant concepts

A. Multiple choice questions

1 Read these statements. The correct one is (　　).

A. Two triangles with the same shape are congruent triangles.

B. Two triangles with the same area are congruent triangles.

C. Given two congruent triangles, their perimeters and the areas, respectively, are equal.

D. All equilateral triangles are congruent triangles.

2 In the following pairs of congruent triangles, the pair that can coincide with each other through rotation is (　　).

A.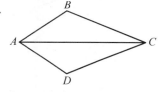

B.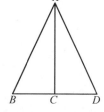

C.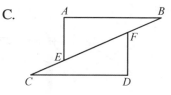

D.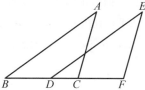

3 In the diagram, $\triangle ABC \cong \triangle DEF$, $AB = 7$, $BC = 11$ and $EC = 6$. The length of CF is (　　). (Note: the symbol $\cong$ means 'is congruent to'.)

A. 7

B. 5

C. 3

D. 1

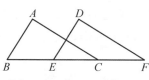

Diagram for question 3

B. Fill in the blanks

4 Look at the diagram.

In $\triangle ABC$, the angle opposite BC is _____.

In $\triangle DBC$, the angle opposite BC is _____.

In $\triangle EBC$, the angle opposite BC is _____.

In $\triangle ABD$, the side opposite $\angle A$ is _____.

In $\triangle AEC$, the side opposite $\angle A$ is _____.

Diagram for question 4

5 In the diagram, $\triangle ABC \cong \triangle ADE$. Their corresponding sides are

_____ and _____ , _____ and _____ , and

_____ and _____ . Their corresponding angles are

_____ and _____ , _____ and _____ , and

_____ and _____ .

Diagram for question 5

6 In the diagram, given that $\triangle ACE \cong \triangle BCD$, $CD = 5$ cm and $BC = 12$ cm, then $AD =$ _____ cm.

Diagram for question 6

7 In the diagram, given that $\triangle ABC$ is rotated around point B as the centre of rotation, point A is rotated to point E, and point C is rotated to point D, then _____ $\cong$ _____ .

Diagram for question 7

8 If $\triangle ABC \cong \triangle DEF$ (points A, B and C are corresponding to points D, E and F respectively), $\angle A = 68°$, $\angle B = 65°$ and $DE = 20$ cm, then $\angle F =$ _____ , $AB =$ _____ cm.

9 Given that $\triangle ABE \cong \triangle ACD$, point A is the common vertex, points B and C are corresponding points, $AB = 4$ and $AE = 6$, then the range of possible values of side CD is _____ .

C. Questions that require solutions

10 In the diagram, $\triangle ABC \cong \triangle DEF$, $\angle A = 50°$, $\angle B = 70°$ and $BC = 3$.

Find the sizes of EF, $\angle D$ and $\angle F$.

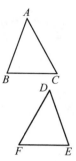

Diagram for question 10

11 In the diagram, AD, BE and CF are the heights of $\triangle ABC$. After folding $\triangle ABC$ along AD, point F coincides with point E and point B coincides with point C.

(a) Write down all the congruent triangles.

(b) Choose one pair of congruent triangles and write down their corresponding angles and sides.

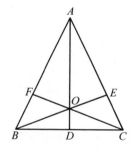

Diagram for question 11

12 In the diagram, $\triangle ACF \cong \triangle DBE$, $\angle E = \angle F$, $AD = 11$ and $BC = 7$. Find the length of AB.

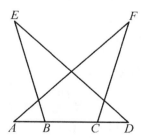

Diagram for question 12

4.7 Congruent triangles: concepts and properties (2)

Learning objective

Know the conditions for congruency in triangles

A. Multiple choice questions

1. Read these statements. The incorrect one is (   ).

   A. The lengths of all the sides in congruent triangles are equal.

   B. Given two sides of a triangle and the angle opposite one of the two sides, it is possible to construct more than one triangle.

   C. The perimeters of congruent triangles are equal and so are the areas.

   D. To determine if two triangles are congruent, at least one of the conditions needs to be about the sides of the triangles.

2. Of the following sets of conditions, the one that can uniquely determine $\triangle ABC$ is (   ).

   A. $AB = 3$, $BC = 4$ and $AC = 8$

   B. $AB = 4$, $BC = 3$ and $\angle A = 30°$

   C. $\angle A = 60°$, $\angle B = 45°$ and $AB = 4$

   D. $\angle C = 90°$ and $AB = 6$

3. In the diagram, $\triangle BAD \cong \triangle BEC$, $AB = BE$.

   There are (   ) correct conclusions in the following set.

   ① $AB = CE$ ② $AD = EC$ ③ $\alpha = \beta$ ④ $\angle A = \angle E$.

   A. 1   B. 2

   C. 3   D. 4

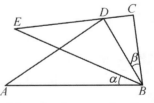

Diagram for question 3

B. Fill in the blanks

4. Given the lengths of three sides to draw a triangle, then the shape and size of the triangle _____ be uniquely determined. (Write 'can' or 'cannot'.)

5. Given $AB = 5$ cm and $AC = 2$ cm to draw isosceles $\triangle ABC$, then the shape and size of the triangle _____ be uniquely determined. (Write 'can' or 'cannot'.)

6 In the diagram Rt△ABC ≅ Rt△DEC and AC ⊥ BD. Then ∠A + ∠DEC = _____.

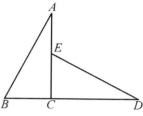

Diagram for question 6

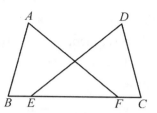

Diagram for question 7

7 In the diagram △ABF ≅ △DCE and ∠A = ∠D.
Then ∠AFB + ∠BED = _____.

8 The diagram shows Rt△ABC. Draw the angle bisectors of acute angles ∠A and ∠B, intersecting BC and AC at points D and E respectively. AD and BE intersect at point F. Then ∠AFB = _____.

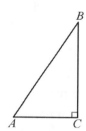

Diagram for question 8

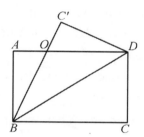

Diagram for question 9

9 In the diagram, △BDC′ is obtained by folding a rectangular playing card ABCD along BD. There are _____ pairs of congruent triangles.

C. Questions that require solutions

10 Complete the following solution and then construct △ABC with the given conditions.

(a) In the diagram, you are given the line segments a and c, and angle α. Construct △ABC so that BC = a, AB = c and ∠ABC = α.

Solution:

① Draw a line segment _____ = a.

② With B as the vertex and BC as one side, draw ∠_____ = α.

③ On side _____ take line segment _____ = c.

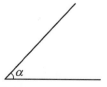

Diagram for question 10(a)

④ Join _____.

Then $\triangle ABC$ is the triangle required.

(b) In the diagram, given: angle α, angle β and line segment c. Construct $\triangle ABC$ so that $\angle A = \alpha$, $\angle B = \beta$ and $AB = c$.

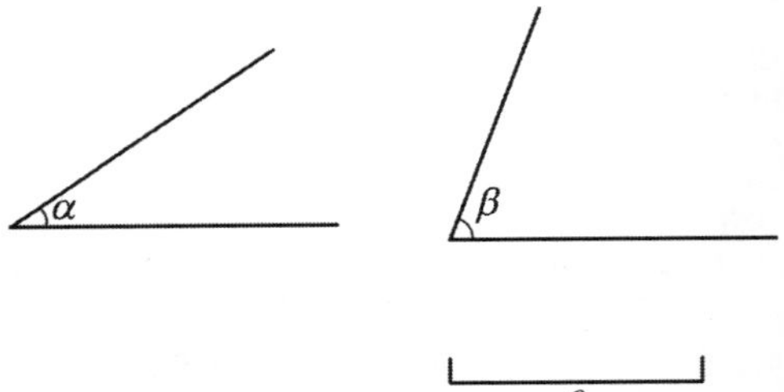

Solution:

① Draw _____ $= \alpha$.

② On side _____ take line segment _____ $= c$.

③ With _____ as the vertex and _____ as one side, draw $\angle$ _____ $= \beta$, line segment _____ intersecting _____ at point _____.

Then $\triangle ABC$ is the triangle required.

Diagram for question 10(b)

(c) As shown in the diagram, given: line segments a, b and c. Construct $\triangle ABC$, so that $AB = c$, $AC = b$ and $BC = a$.

Solution:

① Draw line segment $BC =$ _____.

② With point _____ as the centre and line segment _____ as the radius, draw an arc. Then with point _____ as the centre and line segment _____ as the radius, draw another arc. Label the interesecting point _____.

(Note: An arc is a part of the circumference of a circle.)

③ Join _____ and join _____.

Then $\triangle ABC$ is the triangle required.

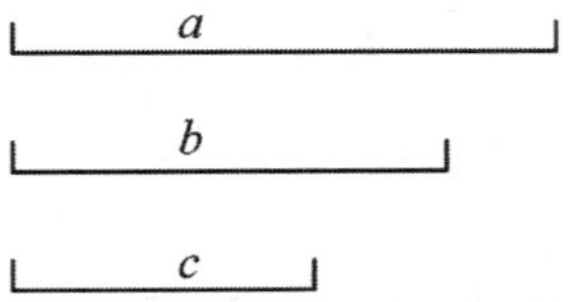

a

b

c

Diagram for question 10(c)

11 Construct $\triangle ABC$ so that $\angle A = 30°$, $\angle B = 80°$ and $AB = 3$ cm.

12 Construct $\triangle ABC$ so that $AB = 3$ cm, $BC = 4$ cm and $AC = 4$ cm.

13 Construct $\triangle ABC$ so that $AB = 3$ cm, $AC = 5$ cm and $\angle A = 45°$.

14 Construct $\triangle ABC$ so that $\angle A = 60°$, $AB = 5$ cm and $BC = 4.5$ cm. How many triangles of different shapes are there satisfying such given conditions?

4.8 Testing for congruent triangles (1)

Learning objective

Know and use the criteria for congruence in triangles to solve problems

A. Multiple choice questions

1 $\triangle ABC$ and $\triangle ADC$ share a common side AC. If (   ) , then $\triangle ABC \cong \triangle ADC$.

A. $AB = AD$ and $\angle B = \angle D$ B. $AB = AD$ and $\angle ACB = \angle ACD$

C. $AB = AD$ and $\angle BAC = \angle DAC$ D. $BC = DC$ and $\angle BAC = \angle DAC$

2 In the diagram, $AD = AE$, $BE = CD$ and $\alpha = \beta$.
If $\angle AEC = 110°$ and $\angle BAE = 60°$,
then $\angle CAE = ($ $)$.

A. $20°$

B. $30°$

C. $40°$

D. $50°$

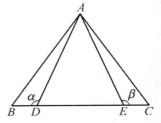

Diagram for question 2

3 In the diagram, $AD \perp AB$, $AE \perp AC$, $AD = AB$ and $AE = AC$.
Read these statements. The correct one is (   ).

A. $\triangle ABD \cong \triangle ACE$

B. $\triangle ADF \cong \triangle AEG$

C. $\triangle BMF \cong \triangle GCM$

D. $\triangle ADC \cong \triangle ABE$

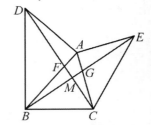

Diagram for question 3

B. Fill in the blanks

4 In the diagram, $AB = DC$ and $\angle ABC = \angle DCB$. Then
$\triangle ABC \cong \triangle DCB$, reason: _____. (Write 'SSS',
'SAS' or 'AAS'.)

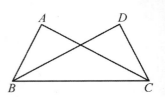

Diagram for question 4

5 In the diagram, $AD = BC$.

If _____,

then $\triangle ABC \cong \triangle CDA$.

(Write one condition only.)

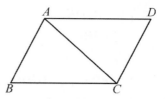

Diagram for question 5

6 In the diagram, if $AB \parallel DE$, $BC \parallel EF$, $BC = EF$ and $AB = DE$, then $\triangle ABC \cong$ _____, reason: _____. (Write 'SSS', 'SAS' or 'AAS'.)

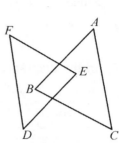

Diagram for question 6

7 In the diagram, the two triangles are _____ congruent. (Write 'definitely' or 'definitely not'.)

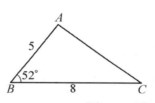 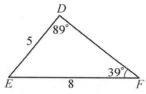

Diagram for question 7

C. Questions that require solutions

8 In the diagram, given that $AE = DB$, $BC = EF$ and $BC \parallel EF$, explain why $\triangle ABC$ and $\triangle DEF$ are congruent.

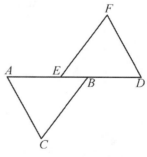

Diagram for question 8

9 In the diagram, $AB = AC$, D is the midpoint of side BC, point E is on AD extended beyond D, and $DE = AD$. Is $AC = CE$? Explain your answer.

Solution: Yes, $AC = CE$.

D is the midpoint of BC.

$BD = CD$ ( ).

In $\triangle ABD$ and $\triangle ECD$:

Diagram for question 9

$$\begin{cases} AD = DE(\qquad\qquad\qquad) \\ \angle ADB = \angle EDC(\qquad\qquad\qquad) \\ BD = CD \end{cases}$$

Therefore, $\triangle ABD \cong \triangle ECD$ (   ).

Then $AB = CE$ (   ).

Since $AB = AC$ (given):

$AC = CE$

10   In the diagram, given that C, M and N are the midpoints of AB, CE and CD respectively, $CM = CN$ and $\alpha = \beta$, explain why $AD = BE$.

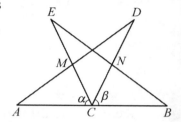

Diagram for question 10

11   The diagram shows two squares $ABDE$ and $BCGF$.
(a) Explain why $\triangle ABF \cong \triangle DBC$.
(b) Is it true that $AF = DC$? Explain.

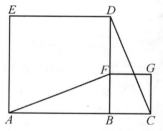

Diagram for question 11

4.9   Testing for congruent triangles (2)

Learning objective

Know and use the criteria for congruence in triangles to solve problems

A. Multiple choice questions

1 Read these statements. The incorrect one is (   ).

   A. If two angles and the included side of one triangle are equal to the corresponding angles and side of another triangle, these two triangles are congruent.

   B. If two angles and the side opposite one of the two angles of one triangle are equal to the corresponding angles and side of another triangle, these two triangles are congruent.

   C. If two sides and the included angle of one triangle are equal to the corresponding sides and angle of another triangle, these two triangles are congruent.

   D. If two sides and the angle opposite one of the two sides of a triangle are equal to the corresponding sides and angle of another triangle, these two triangles are congruent.

2 In the diagram, $\angle A = \angle D$ and $\alpha = \beta$. If $\triangle ABC \cong \triangle DEF$, the additional condition that is needed is (   ).

   A. $\angle E = \angle B$

   B. $ED = BC$

   C. $AB = EF$

   D. $AF = CD$

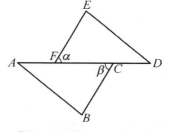

Diagram for question 2

3 In $\triangle ABC$ and $\triangle DEF$, $\angle A = 40°$, $\angle B = 80°$, $AB = 4$, $\angle D = 40°$, $\angle E = 80°$ and $EF = 4$. Then $\triangle ABC$ and $\triangle DEF$ are (   ).

   A. definitely congruent

   B. not necessarily congruent

   C. definitely not congruent

   D. none of the above

B. Fill in the blanks

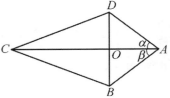

4 In the diagram, $\alpha = \beta$. If _____ ,
then $\triangle ABC \cong \triangle ADC$ (AAS).

5 In the diagram, $\alpha = \beta$. If _____ ,
then $\triangle ABO \cong \triangle ADO$ (SAS).

Diagram for questions 4 and 5

6 In the diagram, $\angle B = \angle E = 90°$ and $AD = CF$. If _____ , then
$\triangle ABC \cong \triangle DEF$.

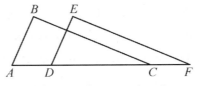

Diagram for question 6

7 The diagram shows a triangular piece of glass broken up into
three smaller pieces. If one of the smaller pieces can be
taken to a store for the replacement of the original piece,
then it should be number _____ . (Fill in with one of the
piece numbers.)

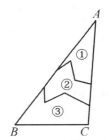

Diagram for question 7

C. Questions that require solutions

8 In the diagram, $AD = CE$, $\angle A = \angle E$ and $BC \parallel FD$.
Explain why $AB = EF$.

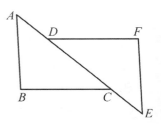

Diagram for question 8

9 In the diagram, $AE \perp AB$, $AD \perp AC$, $AB = AC$ and $\angle B = \angle C$.
Explain why $BD = CE$.

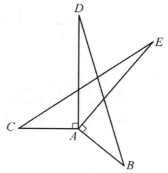

Diagram for question 9

10 In the diagram, $DF \perp AC$, $BE \perp AC$, $DF = BE$ and $\angle B = \angle D$. Give the reasons for $AB = CD$.

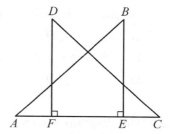

Diagram for question 10

11 In the diagram point M lies on AB, $\alpha = \beta$ and $\gamma = \theta$.
Explain why $AC = AD$.

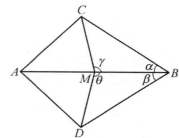

Diagram for question 11

4.10　Testing for congruent triangles (3)

Learning objective

Know and use the criteria for congruence in triangles to solve problems

A. Multiple choice questions

1 The diagram shows two triangles, $\triangle ABC$ and $\triangle DEF$. Of the following sets of conditions, the one that can be used to determine that $\triangle ABC \cong \triangle DEF$ is (　　).

A. $AB = DE$, $BC = EF$, $\angle A = \angle D$

B. $\angle A = \angle D$, $\angle C = \angle F$, $AC = EF$

C. $AB = DE$, $BC = EF$, $C_{\triangle ABC} = C_{\triangle DEF}$ ($C_{\triangle ABC}$ denotes the perimeter of $\triangle ABC$)

D. $\angle A = \angle D$, $\angle B = \angle E$, $\angle C = \angle F$

2 The diagram shows two triangles, $\triangle ABC$ and $\triangle DEF$. Given $AB = DE$, to determine $\triangle ABC \cong \triangle DEF$, two additional conditions are needed. Of the following sets of two additional conditions, the one that is not sufficient for this purpose is (　　).

A. $\angle B = \angle E$, $BC = EF$　　　　B. $BC = EF$, $AC = DF$

C. $\angle A = \angle D$, $\angle B = \angle E$　　　　D. $\angle A = \angle D$, $BC = EF$

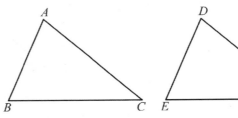

Diagram for questions 1 and 2

3 In the diagram, points E and D lie on AB and AC respectively and $AE = AD$. Join BD and CE which intersect at point O, and then join AO and BC. If $\alpha = \beta$, then there are (　　) pairs of congruent triangles in the diagram.

A. 5　　　　　　　B. 6

C. 7　　　　　　　D. 8

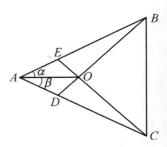

Diagram for question 3

B. Fill in the blanks

4 In the diagram, $AB = CD$ and $AD = BC$. If $\beta = 40°$ and $\gamma = 80°$, then $\angle A =$ _____.

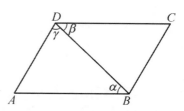

Diagram for question 4

5 In the diagram, $AB = CD$, $DE = AF$ and $CF = BE$. If $\angle AFB$ $= 60°$ and $\angle CDE = 80°$, then $\angle ABC =$ _____.

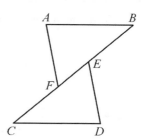

Diagram for question 5

6 In the diagram, $AB = BD$. If there is one more given condition _____ or _____, then $\triangle ABC \cong \triangle DBC$.

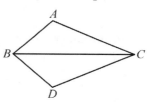

Diagram for question 6

7 The diagram shows $\triangle ABC$. Given $AB = AC$ and D is the midpoint of BC, then $\triangle ABD \cong \triangle ACD$ (reason: _____), and $\angle ADC =$ _____.

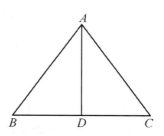

Diagram for question 7

8 In the diagram, given that $BD = CE$, $BE = CD$ and $\angle ABC = 58°$, then $\angle ACB =$ _____.

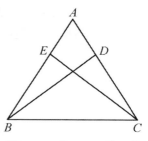

Diagram for question 8

9 In the diagram, given that $BE = DF$, $AF = CE$, then with one more condition _____ , then $\triangle ABF \cong \triangle CDE$.

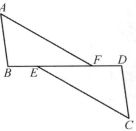

Diagram for question 9

C. Questions that require solutions

10 In the diagram, $AC = BE$, $AE = BC$ and $\angle ABC = 35°$. Find the measure of $\angle EAB$.

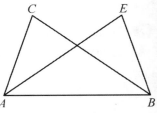

Diagram for question 10

11 In the diagram, given that $AB = DC$ and $\angle A = \angle D$, explain why $\angle ABC = \angle DCB$.

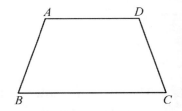

Diagram for question 11

12 In the diagram, P is a point inside square $ABCD$ and point E is outside the square, such that $BE = BP$ and $AE = CP$.
Give reasons to show that:
(a) $\triangle ABE \cong \triangle CBP$
(b) $\angle PBE$ is a right angle.

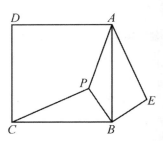

Diagram for question 12

4.11   Testing for congruent triangles (4)

Learning objective

Know and use the criteria for congruence in triangles to solve problems

A. Multiple choice questions

1 In the diagram, given $\alpha = \beta$, $\angle A = \angle D$ and $AB = DB$, then the reason that $\triangle ABC \cong$ $\triangle DBE$ is (   ).

A. AAS

B. ASA

C. SAS

D. SSS

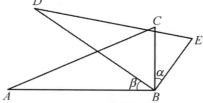

Diagram for question 1

2 Look at the triangles shown below, with the given conditions. The congruent triangles are (   ).

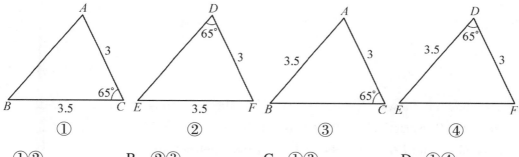

A. ①②   B. ②③   C. ①③   D. ①④

B. Fill in the blanks

3 In the diagram, given that $AB = BC$ and $\alpha = \beta$, then one more given condition is needed in order to determine that $\triangle ADB \cong \triangle CEB$.

(a) The needed condition is _____ , reason: _____ .

(b) The needed condition is _____ , reason: _____ .

(c) The needed condition is _____ , reason: _____ .

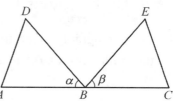

Diagram for question 3

4 In the diagram, given $BC = CE$, $AC = CD$ and $\alpha = \beta$, then $\triangle$_____ $\cong \triangle$_____ , reason: _____.

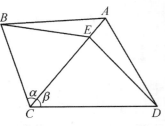

Diagram for question 4

5 In the diagram, $AB \perp DE$ with A being the foot of the perpendicular from D, $AB = AD$, C lies on AB and $AC = AE$. Then $\triangle$_____ $\cong \triangle$_____ , reason: _____.

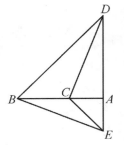

Diagram for question 5

6 The diagram shows $\triangle ABC$. If $\angle B = \angle C = 65°$, $BD = CF$ and $BE = CD$, then $\angle EDF$ is _____.

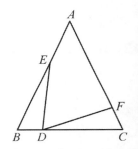

Diagram for question 6

7 The diagram shows $\triangle ABC$. D and E are the midpoints of AB and AC respectively. Point G is on the extension of BE beyond E, and $EG = BE$. Point F is on the extension of CD beyond D, and $DF = CD$. Join FA and AG. If $BC = 15$, then the distance between F and G is _____.

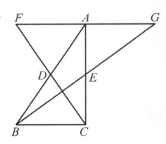

Diagram for question 7

C. Questions that require solutions

8 In the diagram, given that $CA = CB$, $AD = BD$ and M and N are the midpoints of CA and CB respectively, explain why $DM = DN$.

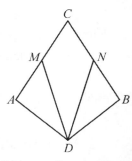

Diagram for question 8

9 In the diagram, $AB = AC$, $AD = AE$ and $\angle EAB = \angle DAC$. If $BD = 16$, find CE.

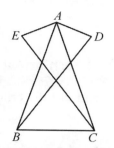

Diagram for question 9

10 The diagram shows a right-angled trapezium $ABCD$, with $AB \parallel CD$ and $AB \perp BC$. Point E lies on BC. DE and AE bisect $\angle CDA$ and $\angle DAB$ respectively.

(a) Is E the midpoint of BC? Explain your answer.

(b) Give the reasons why $DE \perp AE$.

(Note: Draw $EF \perp AD$ with F the foot of the perpendicular.)

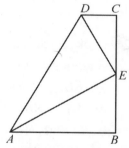

Diagram for question 10

4.12 Testing for congruent triangles (5)

Learning objective

Know and use the criteria for congruence in triangles to solve problems

A. Multiple choice questions

1 In the diagram, given that $AB = AC$ and $AD = AE$, there are
(   ) pairs of congruent triangles.

A. 3

B. 4

C. 5

D. 6

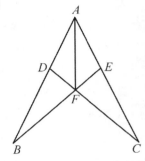

Diagram for question 1

2 Look at the diagram. In the following sets of given conditions, the one that will not necessarily lead to $\triangle ABD \cong \triangle EBC$ is (   ).

A. $AB = EB$, $\alpha = \beta$, $BD = BC$

B. $\alpha = \beta$, $AB = EB$, $\angle A = \angle E$

C. $AB = EB$, $\alpha = \beta$, $AD = EC$

D. $\alpha = \beta$, $\angle D = \angle C$, $AB = EB$

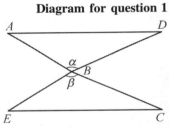

Diagram for question 2

3 In the diagram, $\alpha = \beta$ and $AC = AD$. Consider adding one of the following given conditions so that $\triangle ABC \cong \triangle AED$.

① $AB = AE$

② $BC = ED$

③ $\angle C = \angle D$

④ $\angle B = \angle E$

The number of choices is (   ).

A. 4

B. 3

C. 2

D. 1

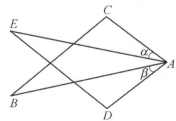

Diagram for question 3

B. Fill in the blanks

4 In the diagram, $\angle ABC = \angle DEF$ and $AB = DE$. In order to determine that $\triangle ABC \cong \triangle DEF$:

(a) if using 'SAS' as the reason, one more condition is needed, which is _____.

(b) if using 'ASA' as the reason, one more condition is needed, which is _____.

(c) if using 'AAS' as the reasons for congruence, then more condition is needed, which is _____.

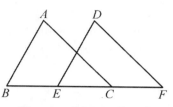

Diagram for question 4

5 In the diagram, in $\triangle ABC$, $\angle A = \angle B$, points D, E and F lie on AC, BC and AB respectively, $AD = EF$, $BE = AF$ and $DF = BF$. If $\angle A = 70°$, then $\angle DFE =$ _____.

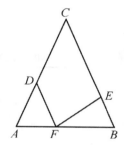

Diagram for question 5

6 The diagram shows $\triangle ABC$, in which E is the midpoint of side AC and $CN \parallel AB$. Through point E, a line from N intersects AB at M. If $MB = 6$ cm and $CN = 4$ cm, then $AB =$ _____ cm.

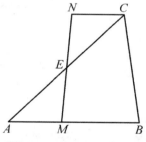

Diagram for question 6

7 The diagram shows a rectangle $ABCD$. Points E and F lie on BC and CD respectively, $AE = AD$ and $FE = FD$. If $\angle BAE = 46°$, then $\angle CEF =$ _____.

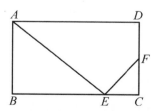

Diagram for question 7

C. Questions that require solutions

8　The diagram shows $\triangle ABC$. Two heights AD and BE intersect at H and $AD = BD$. Give the reasons for the following conclusions.

(a) $\angle DBH = \angle DAC$　　(b) $\triangle BDH \cong \triangle ADC$.

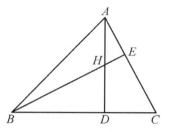

Diagram for question 8

9　The diagram shows $\triangle ABC$. D is the midpoint of side BC. Point E is on the extension of AD and $BE \perp AD$. $CF \perp AD$ with the foot of the perpendicular being point F. Give reasons why $AE + AF = 2AD$.

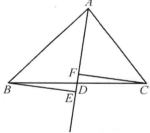

Diagram for question 9

10　The diagram shows $\triangle ABC$. D is the midpoint of AC, $BD \perp AC$ where the foot of the perpendicular is point D, $AE /\!/ BC$ and the extension of ED intersects BC at F. Give reasons why $AB = AE + BF$.

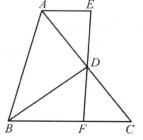

Diagram for question 10

4.13　Testing for congruent triangles (6)

Learning objective

Know and use the criteria for congruence in triangles to solve problems

A. Multiple choice questions

1 The correct statement is (　　).

A. Two equilateral triangles are congruent.

B. Two triangles of the same area are congruent.

C. If two trianges each have an angle of 30°, and two sides of one of the triangles are equal to two sides of the other triangle, then they are congruent.

D. If one side of an equilateral triangle is equal to one side of another equilateral triangle, then the two equilateral triangles are congruent.

2 In the diagram, $\angle B = \angle C$. To determine $\triangle ABE \cong \triangle ACD$, one more condition is needed. Of the following conditions, the one that is not sufficient for this purpose is (　　).

A. $AD = AE$

B. $AB = AC$

C. $BE = CD$

D. $\angle AEB = \angle ADC$

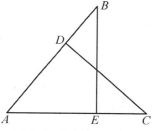

Diagram for question 2

3 The diagram shows $\triangle ABC$. If $AB = AC$, AD is the angle bisector and $BE = CF$, then (　　) of the following statements are correct.

① AD bisects $\angle EDF$　　② $\triangle EBD \cong \triangle FCD$

③ $BD = CD$　　④ $AD \perp BC$

⑤ $AE = ED$

A. 2　　　　　　B. 3

C. 4　　　　　　D. 5

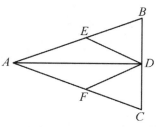

Diagram for question 3

B. Fill in the blanks

4 In the diagram, points C, B and E lie on the same line. If $\angle C = \angle E = \angle ABD = 90°$, $AB = BD$, and $CE = 10$ cm, then $DE + AC =$ _____ cm.

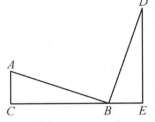

Diagram for question 4

5 In the diagram, $AD = DE$, $AB = BE$ and $\angle A = 80°$. Then $\angle CED =$ _____.

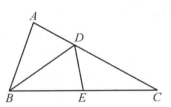

Diagram for question 5

6 In the diagram, $\angle C = \angle D$. To determine $\triangle ABC \cong \triangle ABD$, one more condition needs to be met. Write down two such conditions _____

_____.

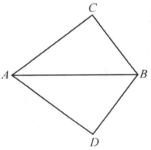

Diagram for question 6

7 The diagram shows $\triangle ABC$. D is the midpoint of BC, point E lies on AD, point F lies on AD produced, and $CE \parallel BF$. If $AF = 7$ and $AE = 4$, then $DF =$ _____.

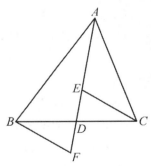

Diagram for question 7

8 The diagram shows $\triangle DEF$ on a square grid. D, E and F are the vertices of the small squares (nodes of the grid). Draw three more triangles $\triangle ABC$ with all the vertices on the nodes of the grid so that $\triangle ABC \cong \triangle DEF$.

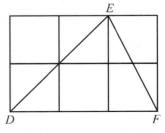

Diagram for question 8

C. Questions that require solutions

9 In the diagram, $AB = AC$ and $DB = DC$. Explain why $\angle B = \angle C$.

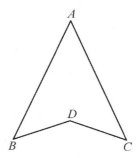

Diagram for question 9

10 The diagram shows $\triangle ABC$. AD bisects $\angle BAC$, EF is the perpendicular bisector of AD (F is on AD and E is on the extension of BC).
Give reasons why $\angle B = \angle CAE$.

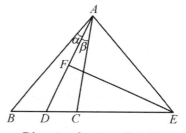

Diagram for question 10

11 In the diagram, AC bisects $\angle BAD$, $CE \perp AB$ with the foot of perpendicular being E, and $\angle D + \angle B = 180°$. Give the reasons why $DC = BC$. (Hint: Take a point F on AB so that $AF = AD$).

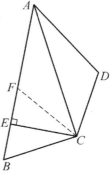

Diagram for question 11

12 (a) In diagram ① below, ∠*EBF* is given. Using the following steps, you can divide it into two equal parts.

(i) Taking *B* as centre and any length as radius, draw an arc (as shown below), crossing *EB* at point *A* and *FB* at point *C*.

(ii) With centres *A* and *C*, respectively, and any fixed length longer than $\frac{1}{2}AC$ as radius, draw two arcs crossing each other at point *M*.

(iii) Draw *BM*. Then *BM* bisects ∠*EBF*.

You can use the congruence of triangles to justify this method. From this, you can see that all geometric construction methods have certain reasons behind them.

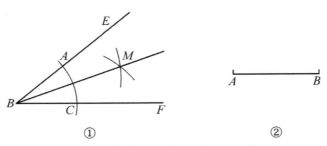

Diagram for question 12

(b) Look at diagram ② and recall the method, using ruler and compasses, for constructing the perpendicular bisector of a line segment. Construct the perpendicular bisector of *AB* and justify your method.

4.14　Properties of isosceles triangles

Learning objective

Identify and use the properties of isosceles triangles

A.　Multiple choice questions

1 Of these statements, the incorrect one is (　　).

A.　A triangle with two sides of equal length is called an isosceles triangle.

B.　An isosceles triangle is a special equilateral triangle.

C.　An equilateral triangle is a special isosceles triangle.

D.　An isosceles triangle can be an acute-angled triangle, a right-angled triangle or an obtuse-angled triangle.

2 In $\triangle ABC$, $AB = AC$ and $\angle A = 60°$. Then $\angle B = ($　　$)$.

A.　60°　　　　　B.　50°　　　　　C.　80°　　　　　D.　70°

3 In $\triangle ABC$, $AB = AC$ and $\angle BAC = 90°$. Then the largest exterior angle of $\triangle ABC$ is

(　　).

A.　160°　　　　B.　140°　　　　C.　135°　　　　D.　145°

4 The base of an isosceles triangle is 6 cm long. A line segment joining a vertex at one end of the base to the midpoint of the opposite side divides the triangle into two parts. If the difference of the perimeters of these two parts is 4 cm, then the length of the two equal sides is (　　).

A.　2 cm　　　　　B.　10 cm　　　　　C.　2 cm or 10 cm　　　D.　uncertain

5 The diagram shows $\triangle ABC$. $AB = AC$, $\angle B = 72°$, CD bisects $\angle ACB$ and intersects AB at point D, and $DE \,/\!/\, AC$ with E being a point on BC. Then there are in total (　　) isosceles triangles.

A.　3

B.　4

C.　5

D.　6

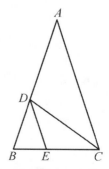

Diagram for question 5

B. Fill in the blanks

6 If an interior angle of an isosceles triangle is 80°, then the other two interior angles are

_____.

7 If the lengths of two sides of an isosceles triangle are 6 cm and 12 cm, then its perimeter

is _____.

8 In an isosceles triangle, if one angle is twice the size of another angle, then the top

vertex angle (the angle opposite the base) is _____°.

9 The height from one of the two equal sides of an isosceles triangle and the other equal

side form an included angle of 35°. The top vertex angle (the angle opposite the base)

is _____.

10 In $\triangle ABC$, $AB = BC$ and D is the midpoint of side AC. If $AD = 2$ and $BD = 6$, then the

area of $\triangle ABC$ is _____.

11 The diagram shows quadrilateral $ABCD$. $AD \parallel BC$, $AD =$
AB and $BC = BD$. If $\angle A = 100°$, then $\angle C =$ _____°.

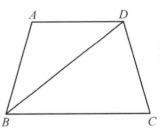

Diagram for question 11

C. Questions that require solutions

12 (a) In the diagram, since $AB = AC$ and $\alpha = \beta$ (given):

_____ $\perp$ _____

(_____)

_____ = _____

(_____).

(b) Since $AB = AC$, $AD \perp BC$ (given):

$\alpha =$ _____

(_____)

_____ = _____

(_____).

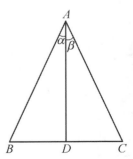

Diagram for question 12

13 In the diagram, $BD = CE$, $AD = AE$, $\angle ADB = \angle AEC$ and H is the midpoint of side BC. Give the reason why $AH \perp BC$.

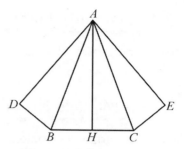

Diagram for question 13

14 In the diagram, D is on the bisector of $\angle BAC$, and $\angle ABD = \angle ACD$.

Determine the relationship between AD and BC.

Give a reason for your conclusion.

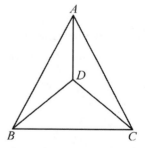

Diagram for question 14

4.15 Identifying isosceles triangles (1)

Learning objective

Use the properties of isosceles triangles to solve problems

A. Multiple choice questions

1 Of the following statements, the incorrect one is (   ).

A. If triangle ABC is an isosceles triangle, then $\angle B = \angle C$.

B. Given $\triangle ABC$ with $\angle B = \angle A$, then $\triangle ABC$ is an isosceles triangle.

C. If two sides of a triangle are equal, then the triangle must be an isosceles triangle.

D. A triangle with two equal angles is an isosceles triangle.

2 In $\triangle ABC$, $\angle A = 70°$ and $\angle B$ is 30° larger than $\angle C$. Then $\triangle ABC$ is (   ).

A. an obtuse-angled triangle   B. an isosceles triangle

C. an isosceles right-angled triangle   D. a right-angled triangle

3 The diagram shows $\triangle ABC$. Point D lies on AC, point E lies on AB, and $AB = AC$, $BC = BD$, $AD = DE = EB$, then $\angle A$ equals (   ).

A. 45°

B. 30°

C. 60°

D. 75°

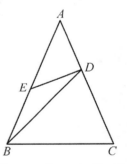

Diagram for question 3

B. Fill in the blanks

4 If an exterior angle of an isosceles triangle is 50°, then the measures of its three interior angles are _____.

5 The diagram shows $\triangle ABC$ with $\angle B = \angle C = 65°$ and $\angle BAD = 25°$. If $AB = 3$, then $AC = $ _____.

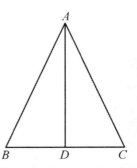

Diagram for question 5

6 In the diagram, $\angle A = 36°$ and $AD = DC = BC$. There are in total _____ isosceles triangles.

7 In the diagram, $AD = DC = BC$. If $\angle ACB = 60°$, then $\angle A =$ _____.

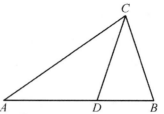

Diagram for questions 6 and 7

8 The diagram shows $\triangle ABC$. $AB = AC$, $\angle DAE = \angle AED = 70°$ and $BD = EC$. $\angle B =$ _____.

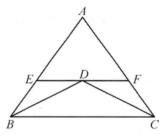

Diagram for question 8

9 The diagram shows $\triangle ABC$ where $\angle ABC = \angle ACB$, and the bisectors of $\angle ABC$ and $\angle ACB$ intersect at point D. EF passes through D and $EF \parallel BC$. EF intersects AB at E and AC at F. There are in total _____ isosceles triangles.

Diagram for question 9

 ## C. Questions that require solutions

10 In the diagram, $\angle BAC = 90°$, $\alpha = \beta$ and $AD \perp BC$, with D being the foot of the perpendicular. Is $\triangle AFE$ an isosceles triangle? Explain how you know.

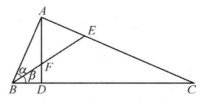

Diagram for question 10

11 In the diagram, $AB = AC$, D lies on AB, $DE \perp BC$, with E being the foot of the perpendicular. The extension of ED intersects the extension of CA at F. Is $\triangle AFD$ an isosceles triangle? Explain how you know.

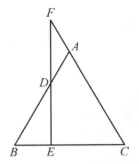

Diagram for question 11

12 The diagram shows $\triangle ABC$. Point E lies on the bisector of $\angle ACB$, $\angle CAE = \angle CBE$, and the extension of CE intersects AB at D. Determine the relationship between CD and AB. Give reasons for your conclusion.

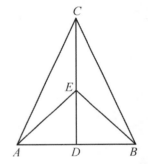

Diagram for question 12

13 The diagram shows $\triangle ABC$ in which the bisectors of $\angle ABC$ and $\angle ACB$ intersect at point D. EF is drawn through D such that $EF \parallel BC$, and EF intersects AB at point E and AC at point F. Determine the relationship between EF and $BE + CF$, giving reasons for your conclusions.

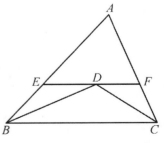

Diagram for question 13

4.16 Identifying isosceles triangles (2)

Learning objective

Use the properties of isosceles triangles to solve problems

A. Multiple choice questions

1. The perimeter of an isosceles triangle is 36 cm, and one of its side is 14 cm. Then the length of the two equal sides is (   ).

   A. 11 cm or 14 cm   B. 11 cm

   C. 12 cm   D. 14 cm

2. The diagram shows $\triangle ABC$. $AD \perp BC$, point D is the midpoint of BC, $DE \perp AB$ with E the foot of the perpendicular, and $DF \perp AC$ with F the foot of the perpendicular. Of the following conclusions, the incorrect one is (   ).

   A. $AB = AC$

   B. $DE = DF$

   C. $BD = \dfrac{1}{2}AD$

   D. $\angle BAD = \angle CAD$

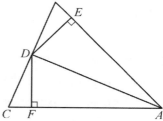

Diagram for question 2

3. The diagram shows $\triangle ABC$, in which $AB = AC$ and $\angle A = 36°$. BD bisects $\angle ABC$ and intersects AC at D. $DE \parallel AB$, with DE intersecting BC at E. $EF \parallel BD$, with EF intersecting CD at F. There are in total (   ) isosceles triangles.

   A. 5

   B. 6

   C. 7

   D. 8

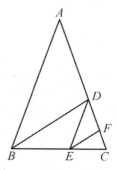

Diagram for question 3

B. Fill in the blanks

4. The lengths of two sides of an isosceles triangle are 4 and 9. The perimeter of the triangle is _____.

5 The diagram shows $\triangle ABC$. Point D lies on AC and $AD = BD = BC$. If $\angle DBC = 24°$, then $\angle A =$ _____, $\angle C =$ _____ and $\angle ABC =$ _____.

6 Given that the perimeter of an isosceles triangle is 8, and the lengths of all the sides are integers, then the length of the two equal sides is _____.

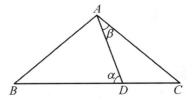

Diagram for question 5

7 In $\triangle ABC$, if D is the midpoint of side AB and $CD = \dfrac{1}{2}AB$, $\angle ACB$ is _____°.

8 In the diagram, D lies on BC and $AB = AC = BD$. If $\alpha = 70°$, then $\beta =$ _____°.

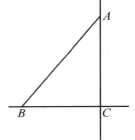

Diagram for question 8

9 The diagram shows $\mathrm{Rt}\triangle ABC$, with $\angle BCA = 90°$ and $\angle BAC = 40°$. If point P is to be taken on either line BC or line AC so that $\triangle PAB$ is an isosceles triangle, then point P can be taken in _____ different positions.
(Hint: Extend the 'axes' and consider two cases, $AB > BC$ and $AC > BC$.

Diagram for question 9

 C. Questions that require solutions

10 The diagram shows $\triangle ABC$. $AB = AC$, $EF \perp BC$, with E being the foot of the perpendicular, and M is the midpoint of DF. Give reasons why $AM \perp FD$.

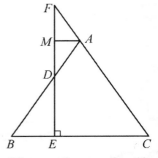

Diagram for question 10

11 The diagram shows $\triangle ABC$ in which $AB = AC = 10$. Point D lies on BC, $DE \parallel AC$ and $DF \parallel AB$. Find the perimeter of quadrilateral $AEDF$.

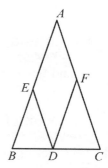

Diagram for question 11

12 In the diagram, $AD = CE$, $\alpha = \beta$, $\angle D = \angle E$ and $AE \parallel BC$. Explain why $\gamma = \theta$.

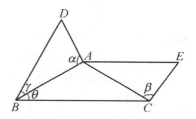

Diagram for question 12

13 In the diagram, AD bisects $\angle BAC$, $\angle B = 2\angle C$, and $AE = AB$ with E being on AC. Explain why $\triangle ECD$ is an isosceles triangle.

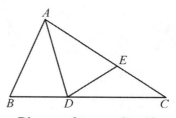

Diagram for question 13

4.17　Equilateral triangles

Learning objective

Identify and use the properties of equilateral triangles to solve problems

A. Multiple choice questions

1 Read these statements. (　　) of them is/are incorrect.

① A triangle with three equal angles is an equilateral triangle.

② A triangle with two of its angles equal to 60° is an equilateral triangle.

③ An isosceles triangle with one angle of 60° is an equilateral triangle.

④ An isosceles triangle in which two angles are equal is an equilateral triangle.

　A. 0　　　　　　B. 1　　　　　　C. 2　　　　　　D. 3

2 In the diagram, points A, B and C are on the same line. $\triangle ABD$ and $\triangle BCE$ are two equilateral triangles. Therefore $\angle AFC$ equals (　　).

　A. 100°　　　　　　　　　　B. 120°

　C. 135°　　　　　　　　　　D. 150°

Diagram for question 2

3 The diagram shows equilateral $\triangle ABC$. $AC = 9$, point O is on AC, and $AO = 3$. Point P moves on AB. OP is the radius of an arc, with O as centre, which intersects BC at point D. $PO = PD$, so the length of AP is (　　).

　A. 5　　　　　　　　　　　B. 8

　C. 7　　　　　　　　　　　D. 6

Diagram for question 3

B. Fill in the blanks

4 A triangle with two interior angles of 60° is _____ triangle. An equilateral triangle has line symmetry, and it has _____ lines of symmetry.

5 In $\triangle ABC$, $AB = AC$. To determine that $\triangle ABC$ is an equilateral triangle it must meet one more condition: _____. (Write one condition only.)

108

6 The diagram shows an equilateral triangle, $\triangle ABC$.
Points P, Q and R are on sides BC, AC and AB, respectively,
$PQ \parallel AB$ and $PR \parallel AC$.
If $AB = 12$, then $PR + PQ =$ _____.

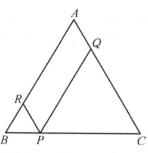

Diagram for question 6

7 In the diagram, $\triangle ABC$ is an equilateral triangle, D is the
midpoint of BC, E lies on AC and $AD = AE$.
$\angle CDE =$ _____$°$.

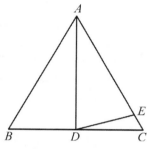

Diagram for question 7

8 The diagram shows an isosceles triangle, $\triangle ABC$,
with $AB = AC$ and points D and E on side BC. If
$\angle BAD = \angle CAE = 30°$ and $\angle BAC = 120°$, then
$\triangle ADE$ is an _____ triangle.

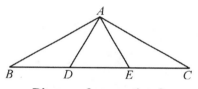

Diagram for question 8

9 The diagram shows triangle ABC with the given side lengths.
Given $AB = AC$ and $\angle B = 60°$, then $x =$ _____,
$y =$ _____.

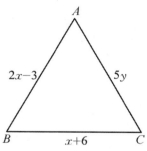

Diagram for question 9

C. Questions that require solutions

10 In the diagram, $\triangle ABC$ is equilateral. Point D lies on side
AC, $\angle ACE = \angle ABD$, and $CE = BD$. Is $\triangle ADE$ an
equilateral triangle? Give reasons for your answer.

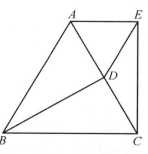

Diagram for question 10

11 * In equilateral $\triangle ABC$, $AD = CE$ and CD intersects BE at point P. Find the size of $\angle BPC$.

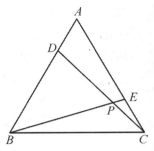

Diagram for question 11

12 * In the diagram, both $\triangle ABC$ and $\triangle CDE$ are equilateral, points A, E and D are on the same line and $\angle EBD = 62°$. Find $\angle AEB$.

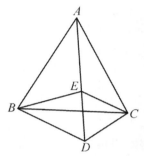

Diagram for question 12

---

* Questions marked with * are more challenging (optional). You are encouraged to discuss them with your friends or ask your teacher for help in solving these problems.

Unit test 4

1 The ratios of the lengths of sets of three line segments are given below. The set that cannot form a triangle is in the ratio of (   ).

A. $1 : 2 : 3$

B. $2 : 3 : 4$

C. $3 : 4 : 5$

D. $4 : 5 : 6$

2 In $\triangle ABC$ and $\triangle A'B'C'$, $AB = A'B'$, $AC = A'C'$ and $\angle C = \angle C'$. The two triangles (   ).

A. are definitely not congruent

B. are not necessarily congruent

C. are definitely congruent

D. definitely have the same area

3 In $\triangle ABC$ and $\triangle A'B'C'$, $\angle A = 50°$, $AB = 4$, $\angle B = 80°$, $\angle A' = 50°$, $\angle B' = 80°$ and $A'B' = 4$. $\triangle ABC$ and $\triangle A'B'C'$ (   ).

A. are definitely not congruent

B. are not necessarily congruent

C. are definitely congruent

D. have the same area

4 If the largest interior angle of a triangle is $60°$, then the triangle is (   ).

A. isosceles

B. equilateral

C. scalene

D. not certain

5 If a line passing through the top vertex (opposite the base, which is neither of the equal sides) of an isosceles triangle, divides the triangle into two isosceles triangles, then the top vertex angle of this isosceles triangle is (   ).

A. $90°$ or $108°$

B. $90°$

C. $60°$

D. $60°$ or $36°$

6 Of the following statements, the incorrect one is (   ).

A. If one side and one acute angle of a right-angled triangle are equal to the corresponding side and angle of another right-angled triangle, then the two triangles must be congruent.

B. If one side of an equilateral triangle is equal to one side of another equilateral triangle, then these two equilateral triangles are congruent.

C. If two sides of a right-angled isosceles triangle are equal to two sides of another right-angled isosceles triangle, then these two isosceles triangles are congruent.

D. If the hypotenuse and one of the shorter sides of a right-angled triangle are equal to the hypotenuse and one of the shorter sides of another right-angled triangle, then the two right-angled triangles are congruent. (Note: the hypotenuse is the side opposite the right angle and the longest side in a right-angled triangle.)

B. Fill in the blanks

7 If in $\triangle ABC$, AD is the height on BC and divides $\angle A$ into two angles of $30°$ and $50°$, then, classifying by sides, $\triangle ABC$ is _____ triangle and classifying by angles, it is _____ triangle.

8 If two sides and the angle opposite one side of a triangle are equal to their corresponding sides and angle of another triangle, the two triangles _____ congruent. (Write 'are definitely', 'are not necessarily' or 'are definitely not'.)

9 In $\triangle ABC$, if $\angle C = \frac{1}{2}\angle B = \frac{1}{3}\angle A$, then $\angle B$ is _____°.

10 The length of the base of an isosceles triangle is 7 cm. A line segment joining the midpoint of one of the two equal sides to the opposite vertex divides the triangle into two parts. If the perimeter of one part is 1 cm longer than that of the other part, then the length of the two equal sides of the isosceles triangle is _____.

11 In an isosceles triangle, if the difference of two angles is $15°$, then the base angle of the isosceles triangle is _____.

12 Given BD is the height on one of the two equal sides of isosceles $\triangle ABC$ and $\angle ABD = 50°$, the three interior angles of $\triangle ABC$ are _____.

⓭ In the diagram, △*ABC* and △*ADE* are both isosceles triangles. If ∠*ADE* = ∠*AED* = 70° and *AD* = *AE* = *BD* = *EC*, then ∠*BAC* = _____.

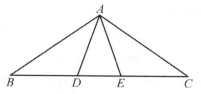

Diagram for question 13

⓮ In the diagram, △*ABD* and △*ACD* are symmetric about line *AD*. If ∠*BAC* = 60° and ∠*BDC* = 150°, then there are in total _____ isosceles triangles, and they are _____ _____.

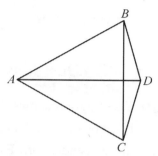

Diagram for question 14

⓯ The diagram shows △*ABC* with *AB* = *AC*. If *BC* = *BD* = *ED* = *EA*, then ∠*A* = _____°.

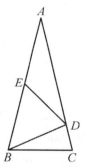

Diagram for question 15

⓰ The diagram shows △*ABC* with *AB* = *AC*, *AD* ⊥ *BC* with perpendicular foot *D* and *CE* ⊥ *AB* with perpendicular foot *E*. If ∠*BAC* = 52°, then ∠*BCE* = _____.

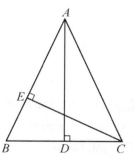

Diagram for question 16

⓱ The diagram shows △*ABC*. If ∠*BAC* = 106°, *EF* and *MN* are the perpendicular bisectors of *AB* and *AC* respectively, then ∠*EAM* equals _____.

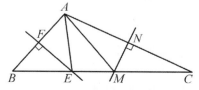

Diagram for question 17

18 The diagram shows two equilateral triangles, $\triangle ABC$ and $\triangle DCE$ with points B, C and E on the same line. BD and AE intersect at F, BD and AC intersect at P and AE and CD intersect at Q. Among the following conclusions:

① $BD = AE$ ② $CP = CQ$ ③ $PD = DE$ ④ $PQ \parallel BE$
⑤ $\angle DFE = 60°$

the correct ones are _____ .

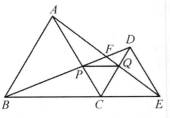

Diagram for question 18

C. Questions that require solutions

19 The diagram shows $\triangle ABC$ with $\angle BAC = 90°$, CE is the bisector of $\angle ACB$ and $AD \perp CE$ with D being the foot of the perpendicular. Explain why $\phi = \gamma + \angle B$.

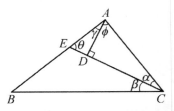

Diagram for question 19

20 The diagram shows quadrilateral $ABCD$ with $AB = BC$, $AB \parallel CD$ and $\angle D = 90°$. $AE \perp BC$ with E the foot of the perpendicular. Give reasons why $CD = CE$.

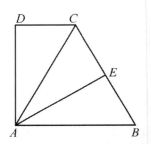

Diagram for question 20

21 The diagram shows $\triangle ABC$. $AD \perp BC$ with D the foot of the perpendicular, point E lies on BD, $EG \parallel AD$, EG intersects AB and the extension of CA at points F and G respectively, and $\angle AFG = \angle G$. Explain why $\triangle ABD \cong \triangle ACD$.

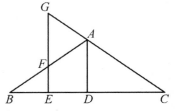

Diagram for question 21

22 The diagram shows $\triangle ABC$ with $\angle C = 90°$. AD bisects $\angle BAC$ and intersects BC at point D. Given $BC = 32$ and $BD : DC = 9 : 7$, find the distance of D from AB.

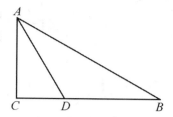

Diagram for question 22

23 The sizes of the three interior angles of $\triangle ABC$ are shown in the diagram. Draw a line MN so that it divides this triangle into two isosceles triangles. Give reasons for your solution.

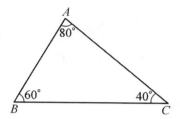

Diagram for question 23

24 The diagram shows an equilateral $\triangle ABC$ with E being on AC extended beyond C. Point D is chosen such that $\triangle CDE$ is an equilateral triangle, M is the midpoint of AD and N is the midpoint of BE. Explain why $\triangle CMN$ is equilateral.

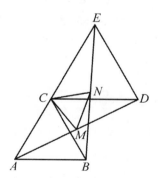

Diagram for question 24

Chapter 5　The co-ordinate plane

5.1　Introduction to the co-ordinate plane (1)

Learning objective

Calculate the distance of points from the axes and that between two points

A.　Multiple choice questions

1 The distance of point $A(-2, 1)$ from the y-axis is (　　).

　　A.　-2　　　　　　B.　2　　　　　　C.　-1　　　　　　D.　1

2 The co-ordinates of point $A(x, y)$ satisify $x = 0$. Point A is (　　).

　　A.　the origin　　　　　　　　　　B.　on the x-axis

　　C.　on the y-axis　　　　　　　　D.　on the x-axis or y-axis

3 If a line passing through $A(-3, 2)$ is parallel to the x-axis, then any point, $P(a, b)$, on the line must satisfy the condition (　　).

　　A.　$a = -3$　　　　　　　　　　B.　$a = 3$ or $a = -3$

　　C.　$b = 2$　　　　　　　　　　D.　$b = 2$ or $b = -2$

B.　Fill in the blanks

4 The distance of point $A(5, -6)$ from the x-axis is _____ and its distance from the y-axis is _____.

5 Given that a and b are both positive, the distance of point $B(-a, b)$ from the x-axis is _____ and its distance from the y-axis is _____.

6 If point $A(2x + y, x - 3)$ is at the origin, then the distance of point $B(x, y)$ from the x-axis is _____.

7 If point $A(a + 3, a - 5)$ is on the y-axis, then $a =$ _____.

8 Given points $A(a+2, a-2)$, $B(4-a, 6-a)$ and AB parallel to the y-axis, then $a =$ _____.

9 In rectangle $ABCD$, given $A(3, 0)$, $B(0, 0)$ and $C(0, -2)$, then point D has co-ordinates _____.

C. Questions that require solutions

10 The diagram shows trapezium $ABCD$ with vertices $A(-1, 0)$, $B(5, 0)$, $C(4, 3)$ and $D(0, 3)$. Work out the area of the trapezium.

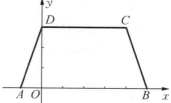

Diagram for question 10

11 (a) If the distance of point P from the x-axis is 5 and its distance from the y-axis is 8, find the co-ordinates of point P.

(b) The distance of point P from the x-axis is a and its distance from the y-axis is b. There are two and only two points satisfying these conditions, find the conditions that a or b should satisfy.

12 Two vertices of a square are $(-1, 0)$ and $(1, 0)$. Draw all the squares that satisfy this given condition and write down the co-ordinates of the other two vertices in each case.

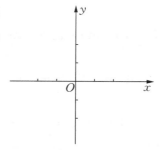

Diagram for question 12

5.2   Introduction to the co-ordinate plane (2)

Learning objective

Identify or calculate the co-ordinates of a point on the co-ordinate plane

A. Multiple choice questions

1 If point $P(a + b, ab)$ is in the second quadrant, then point $Q(a, b)$ is in the (   ).
   A. first quadrant   B. second quadrant
   C. third quadrant   D. fourth quadrant

2 If point $P(a, a + b)$ is in the fourth quadrant, then the distance of point $Q(a, b)$ from the x-axis is (   ).
   A. $-a$ B. $-b$ C. a D. b

3 Three of these points lie on the line that passes through point $P(-2, 5)$ and is perpendicular to the x-axis. The point that does not lie on the line is (   ).
   A. $(2, 5)$ B. $(-2, -5)$ C. $(-2, 0)$ D. $(-2, 6)$

B. Fill in the blanks

4 Point $P(x, y)$ lies in the third quadrant, its distance from the x-axis is 3 and its distance from the y-axis is 4. The co-ordinates of point P are _____ .

5 Point $P(x, y)$ lies in the second quadrant, its distance from the x-axis is a and its distance from the y-axis is b. The co-ordinates of point P are _____ .

6 If point $P(a, b)$ is in the third quadrant, point $Q(b, -a)$ is in the _____ quadrant.

7 If $xy < 0$, then point $P(x, y)$ is in the _____ quadrant.

8 Given $b < a < 0$, then point $P(a + b, a - b)$ is in the _____ quadrant.

9 Given a is an integer and point $P(2a - 7, 3a - 14)$ is in the fourth quadrant, then the co-ordinates of point P are _____ .

10 (a) If the distance of $P(x, y)$ from the x-axis is 2, x or y satisfies the condition _____ .

(b) If the distance of $P(x, y)$ to the y-axis is 3, x or y satisfies _____ .

C. Questions that require solutions

11 Line AB is parallel to the x-axis and line CB is parallel to the y-axis. Given points $A(a + 2, a - 2)$, $C(4 - a, a - 1)$, $B(x, y)$ and that the x-coordinate of point B is 4 less than its y-coordinate, find the co-ordinates of points A, B and C.

12 Given that the distances of point $A(2a + 3, 1 - a)$ to the x-axis and to the y-axis are equal, find the co-ordinates of point A.

13 Point $A(a, b)$ lies on the bisector of the angle formed by the two axes for Quadrants I and III and point $B(c, d)$ lies on the bisector of the angle formed by the two axes for Quadrants II and IV. Given that $a + c = -2$ and $b + d = 4$, find the co-ordinates of points A and B.

14 Point $P(x, y)$ lies in the fourth quadrant and the sum of its distances from the two axes is 8. Given that its distance from the x-axis is 2 greater than its distance from the y-axis, work out the co-ordinates of point P.

5.3 Point movement on the co-ordinate plane (1)

 Learning objective

Find the missing co-ordinates of a shape, including after a rotation

 A. Multiple choice questions

1. Given any two points on a line parallel to the x-axis, then (   ).
   A. their x-coordinates are equal
   B. their y-coordinates are equal
   C. their x-coordinates are zero
   D. their y-coordinates are zero

2. Given points $A(3, 2)$ and $B(3, -2)$, then line AB is (   ).
   A. parallel to the x-axis
   B. parallel to the y-axis
   C. parallel to line $x = 3$
   D. parallel to line $y = 2$ or line $y = -2$

3. Line AB is parallel to the x-axis. Given points $A(3, -5)$, $B(x, y)$, and the distance of point B to the y-axis is 6, the the co-ordinates of point B are (   ).
   A. $(3, 6)$ or $(3, -6)$
   B. $(3, 1)$ or $(3, -1)$
   C. $(6, -5)$ or $(-6, -5)$
   D. $(9, -5)$ or $(-3, -5)$

B. Fill in the blanks

4. Given points $A(a, a)$ and $B(a, b)$, the distance between A and B is _____.

5. Given points $P(5, 3)$ and $Q(5, -3)$, the distance between P and Q is _____.

6. Given points $P(5, 3)$ and $Q(x, 3)$, where $PQ = 6$, then $x =$ _____.

7. Given line segment $PQ = 5$, line PQ is parallel to the x-axis and the co-ordinates of P are $(6, 8)$, then the co-ordinates of Q are _____.

8. Given line segment $PQ = 6$, PQ is perpendicular to the x-axis and the co-ordinates of P are $(6, 8)$, then the co-ordinates of Q are _____.

9 Given line segment $PQ = 5$, line PQ is parallel to line $x = 3$ and the co-ordinates of P are $(6, 8)$, then the co-ordinates of Q are _____.

10 Given line segment $PQ = 6$, line PQ is perpendicular to line $x = 3$ and the co-ordinates of P are $(6, 8)$, then the co-ordinates of Q are _____.

C. Questions that require solutions

11 The diagram shows rectangle $ABCD$, with its four vertices $A(-1, 2)$, $B(b, c)$, $C(a, -3)$ and $D(3, 2)$.

(a) Find the values of a, b and c.

(b) Find the area of rectangle $ABCD$.

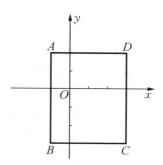

Diagram for question 11

12 The diagram shows the points $A(-1, 0)$, $B(3, 0)$, $C(2, 2)$ and $D(0, 1)$.

Work out the area of quadrilateral $ABCD$.

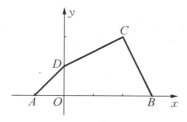

Diagram for question 12

13 In the diagram, given the points $A(2, 0)$, $B(-1, 4)$ and $C(0, -1)$, find the area of $\triangle ABC$.

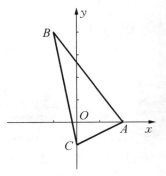

Diagram for question 13

14 The vertices of $\triangle ABC$ are $A(5, 1)$, $B(2, 3)$ and $C(0, 0)$. $\triangle A_1 B_1 C_1$ is obtained by rotating $\triangle ABC$ $90°$ clockwise about the origin.

(a) Find the co-ordinates of A_1, B_1 and C_1.

(b) Find the area of $\triangle A_1 B_1 C_1$.

5.4 Point movement on the co-ordinate plane (2)

Learning objective

Find the missing co-ordinates of a shape after a translation or rotation

A. Multiple choice questions

1. Translating point $A(x, y)$ 1 unit left and then 2 units down gives the point with co-ordinates ( ).

   A. $(x+1, y+2)$　　B. $(x+1, y-2)$　　C. $(x-1, y+2)$　　D. $(x-1, y-2)$

2. Translating point $A(2a+3, a)$ 2 units up gives point B. If B lies on the x-axis, then the co-ordinates of point A are ( ).

   A. $(7, 2)$　　　　B. $(3, 0)$　　　　C. $(7, -2)$　　　　D. $(-1, -2)$

3. Point $A(a, 5)$ lies in the second quadrant. If A is translated 4 units right and the resulting point B lies in the first quadrant, then the range of the possible values of a is ( ).

   A. $a < 0$　　　　B. $-4 < a$　　　　C. $-5 < a < 0$　　　D. $-4 < a < 0$

B. Fill in the blanks

4. If point $A(2, 3)$ is translated 3 units right to point B, the co-ordinates of point B are _____.

5. If point $A(2, 3)$ is translated 3 units down to point B, the co-ordinates of point B are _____.

6. Translating $A(2, 3)$ _____ by _____ units gives point $B(2, -1)$.

7. Translating point $A(-5, -6)$ 6 unit(s) right and 7 units up gives point B with co-ordinates _____.

8. Moving point $A(2, 3)$ to the _____ by _____ units, and then _____ (Write 'up' or 'down') by _____ unit(s) gives point $B(-3, 2)$.

9 In order to translate point $A(-2, 3)$ to the origin, the point can be moved to the _____ (Write 'right' or 'left') by _____ units and then _____ (Write 'up' or 'down') by _____ units.

10 Given points $A(5, 6)$ and $B(4, -2)$, a translation of line AB moves point A to point $A'(0, 3)$ and point B to point B'. The co-ordinates of point B' are _____.

C. Questions that require solutions

11 Two points have co-ordinates $A(-1, 3)$ and $B(2, 5)$. Line segment $A'B'$ is obtained by translating line segement AB 4 units down. Find the co-ordinates of A' and B' and the area covered by the line segment AB in the translation. (This is the area of quadrilateral $AA'B'B$.)

12 Point $A(a, 7)$ is translated 2 units down to point B, and then 4 units right to point $C(6, c)$. Find a, c and the area of $\triangle ABC$.

13 Square $OABC$ has vertices $O(0, 0)$, $A(0, 2)$, $B(-2, 2)$ and $C(-2, 0)$. Its diagonal OB is rotated $90°$ anticlockwise about point O to OD, and $\triangle OBD$ is then translated 1 unit right to $\triangle O_1 B_1 D_1$. Find the co-ordinates of B_1, D_1 and O_1.

14 The diagram shows isosceles triangle ABC, with $\angle C = 90°$ and vertices $A(0, 0)$ and $B(4, 0)$. Point C lies above the x-axis. Translating $\triangle ABC$ 1 unit up gives $\triangle A_1 B_1 C_1$. $A_1 B_1$ intersects AC at point D and BC at point E.
(a) Find the co-ordinates of D and E.
(b) Find the area of $\triangle CDE$.

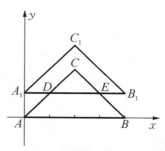

Diagram for question 14

5.5 Point movement on the co-ordinate plane (3)

Learning objective

Find the missing co-ordinates of a shape after a reflection, translation or rotation

A. Multiple choice questions

1 The co-ordinates of a point that is symmetric to point $A(a, b)$ about the x-axis are ( ).

A. $(a, -b)$ B. $(-a, -b)$ C. (a, b) D. $(-a, b)$

2 Point $P(\sqrt{2}, -\sqrt{2} + 1)$ and point $Q(-\sqrt{2}, 1 - \sqrt{2})$ are symmetric to each other about the ( ).

A. x-axis B. y-axis

C. origin D. line $y = -\sqrt{2} + 1$

3 * Given that a is an integer and the point that is symmetric to $P(a+1, 2a-7)$ about the origin lies in the second quadrant, then there are ( ) possible value(s) of a satisfying these conditions.

A. 1 B. 2 C. 3 D. 4

B. Fill in the blanks

4 The point symmetric to point $A(1, -3)$ about the x-axis is in the _____ quadrant and its co-ordinates are _____.

5 The point symmetric to point $A(1, -3)$ about the y-axis is in the _____ quadrant and its co-oridnates are _____.

6 The point symmetric to point $A(3, -5)$ about the origin is in the _____ quadrant and its co-ordinates are _____.

---

* On the co-ordinate plane, point A is symmetric to point B about the origin if both points are at the same distance from the origin but in opposite directions. In general, if point A is at (a, b), then point B is at $(-a, -b)$.

7 If the point symmetric to point $A(a + 3, a - 2)$ about the x-axis is A itself, then $a =$ _____.

8 If point $A(a + 3, b - 1)$ is symmetric to point $B(3, -1)$ about the origin, then $a^b =$ _____.

9 Point $A(a, a + 1)$ is translated 8 units to the right to point B. If points A and B are symmetric to each other about the y-axis, then the cooridnates of point A are _____.

10 Point $A(a, a + 1)$ is translated 7 units down to point B. If points A and B are symmetric to each other about the x-axis, then the co-ordinates of point A are _____.

C. Questions that require solutions

11 Given point $A(3, 4)$ is symmetric to point B about the y-axis and it is also symmetric to point C about the origin, find the length of BC.

12 Isosceles $\triangle ABC$ has one vertex at point $A(-1, 3)$, point C is on the x-axis and the height from one vertex to its base is part of the line $x = 1$. Find the co-ordinates of vertices B and C.

13 Points $A(a-5, -1)$ and $B(1-b, a-1)$ are symmetric about the x-axis, and points $D(a, b)$ and C are symmetric about the origin. Find the co-ordinates of point C and the area of $\triangle ABC$.

14 Two of the vertices of right-angled isosceles $\triangle OAB$ are the points $O(0, 0)$ and $A(2, 0)$. Find the co-ordinates of vertex B.

Unit test 5

1 Point $A(-1, 1)$ is translated first 3 units right and then 6 units up to point B. The co-ordinates of point B are (   ).

A. $(-4, 7)$　　　　B. $(2, 7)$　　　　C. $(2, -7)$　　　　D. $(-4, -7)$

2 a is an integer. The point symmetric to point $P(2a-6, 1-a)$ about the origin lies in the first quadrant. The co-ordinates of P are (   ).

A. $(2, 1)$　　　　B. $(1, 2)$　　　　C. $(-2, -1)$　　　　D. $(-1, -2)$

3 Given that line PQ is parallel to the y-axis, point P is at $(5, -1)$ and the distance of point Q from the x-axis is 3, then the co-ordinates of Q are (   ).

A. $(5, 3)$ or $(5, -3)$　　　　　　B. $(3, -1)$ or $(-3, -1)$

C. $(3, 5)$ or $(-3, 5)$　　　　　　D. $(-1, 3)$ or $(-1, -3)$

4 If point $A(a, b)$ is in the third quadrant, then point $B(-a, 1-b)$ is in the (   ).

A. first quadrant　　　　　　　　B. second quadrant

C. third quadrant　　　　　　　　D. fourth quadrant

B. Fill in the blanks

5 Given $a < 0 < b$, then point $P(a-b, b-a)$ is in the _____ quadrant.

6 If point $P(b-a, a)$ is in the third quadrant, then point $Q(a-b, b)$ must be in the _____ quadrant.

7 Point $A(x, 0)$ is on the _____ -axis, and the co-ordinates of the point that is symmetric to point A about the y-axis are _____.

8 Point $A(3-2a, 2a+3)$ lies in the second quadrant. The range of the possible values of a is _____.

9 Points $A(6, 5)$ and $B(a, a)$ are both on the line $y = 5$. The length of AB is _____.

10 The distance between point $A(\sqrt{5}, -\sqrt{3})$ and point $B(\sqrt{5}, 2\sqrt{3})$ is _____.

11 Line AB is parallel to the y-axis. If $AB = 5$ with A being the point $(3, -2)$, then the co-ordinates of point B are _____.

12 If point $P(1, -2)$ is translated first 2 units right and then 5 units up, then the resulting point has co-ordinates _____.

13 Point $P(1, 2)$ is translated first to the _____ (Write 'right' or 'left') by _____ units and then _____ (Write 'up' or 'down') by _____ units to get to point $Q(-8, 10)$.

14 If point $P(x, -y)$ is translated a units up in the direction of the y-axis, the resulting point has co-ordinates _____.

15 Point Q is symmetric to point $P(x, -y)$ about the x-axis. If Q is translated a units left, then the resulting point has co-ordinates _____.

16 M is symmetric to point $P(x, y)$ about the y-axis, and Q is symmetric to point M about the origin. $PQ = $ _____.

17 The co-ordinates of the point symmetric to $P(3, 4)$ about line $x = 1$ are _____.

18 The co-ordinates of the point symmetric to $P(3, 4)$ about line $y = -2$ are _____.

C. Questions that require solutions

19 Given point $A(2, 10)$, where O is the origin and M is the midpoint of line segment OA, find the co-ordinates of M.

20 Point $P(x, y)$ lies on the bisector of the angle formed by the two axes for quadrants II and IV. The distance of point P from the x-axis is 6. Find the co-ordinates of point P.

21 Using the formula for the distance between points $A(x_1, y_1)$ and $B(x_2, y_2)$ on the co-ordinate plane: $AB = \sqrt{(x_1 - x_2)^2 + (y_1 - y_2)^2}$, find the distance between $A(3, 4)$ and $B(-1, 1)$.

22 Given points $A(1, 3)$, $B(4, 2)$ and the origin O, calculate the area of $\triangle OAB$.

23 Point $A(a, b)$ is translated first 2 units right and then 6 units down. The resulting point B is symmetric to point A about the origin. Find the co-ordinates of point A.

24 The diagram shows point $P(a, b)$ with $a > 0$ and $b > 0$. $OP = OP_1$. PQ and P_1Q_1 are both perpendicular to the x-axis and $OP_1 \perp OP$.

(a) Give the reasons why $\triangle OPQ \cong \triangle OP_1Q_1$.

(b) If P_1 is in the second quadrant, find the co-ordinates of P_1.

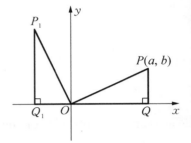

Diagram for question 24

25 The diagram shows two parallelograms $ABCO$ and $OCDE$, which both have the same shape and size. Given points $A(-1, -2)$ and $D(4, 2)$, find the co-ordinates of points B, C and E and the area of parallelogram $ABDE$.

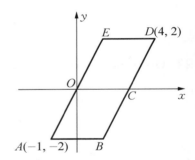

Diagram for question 25

26 In isosceles triangle OAB, with vertices at points $O(0, 0)$ and $A(1, 1)$, OA is one of the two equal sides and point B is on an axis. Find the co-ordinates of B.

Chapter 6　Direct proportion, inverse proportion and their functions

6.1　Variables and functions

Learning objectives

Substitute values into formulae and expressions; rearrange equations to change the subject

A. Multiple choice questions

1 Two places A and B are s km apart. The time t (hours) that a person takes to cover the entire distance, and the average speed v (km/h) at which he travels, satisfy the equation $vt = s$. In this context, of the following, the incorrect statement is (　　).

A. s is a variable　　　　　　　　　　B. t is a variable

C. v is a variable　　　　　　　　　　D. s is a constant

2 The diagram shows squares made from matchsticks. The number of matchsticks, m, varies with the number of squares, n.

In this context, of the following, the incorrect statement is (　　).

A. m and n are both variables.

B. n is an independent variable; m is a dependent variable.

C. m is an independent variable; n is a dependent variable.

D. m varies as n changes.

Diagram for question 2

3 A company made several long-distance calls for business. The table shows the duration and the cost of these phone calls.

Duration (minutes)	1	2	3	4	5	6	7
Amount (£)	0.60	1.20	1.80	2.40	3.00	3.60	4.20

Of the following, the incorrect statement is (　　).

A. The two variables in the table are duration and cost.

B. The independent variable is the duration.

C. The independent variable is the amount.

D. The amount (the cost) increases as the duration increases.

B. Fill in the blanks

4 In the formula for the perimeter of a circle, $C = 2\pi r$, _____ is a constant, _____ and _____ are variables.

5 Given $5y - 3 = 2x + 3$, then $y =$ _____.

6 Given that the market price of beans is £2 per kilogram, then the expression of the function relating the price, y (£), to the weight, x (kg), of the beans is _____.

> The (analytical) expression of a function is usually in the equation form with the left side being y and the right side being an algebraic expression, for example, $y = 2x + 1$.

7 100 kg of flour is put into two bags, A and B. If x kg of flour is put into bag A and y kg of flour is put into bag B, then the expression of the function for y and x is _____ .

8 Given that the area of a triangle has a fixed value S, then the expression of the function for its height, h, and base, a, is $h =$ _____.

C. Questions that require solutions

9 A company has 1500 tonnes of coal. Find the expression of the function for the number, y, of days it will last and the average daily usage, x, of the coal.

10 If the perimeter of an isosceles triangle is 16, find the expression of the function for the length, y, of its base and the length, x, of its two equal sides.

11 Given that $(2x + 1)(y - 3) = 1$, write the expression for y as a function of x.

6.2　Direct proportion and direct proportional functions

Learning objective

Solve algebraic problems involving direct proportion

A. Multiple choice questions

1 Of these quantitative pairs, the two quantities that are in direct proportion are ( ).

> Direct proportion is sometimes simply called 'proportion'.

A. the time taken and the speed of travelling from place A to place B

B. the area of a square and its side length

C. the total cost of a set of identical books and the number of copies of the book that are bought

D. the weight and height of a person

2 Of the following functions, the direct proportion function is ( ).

A. $y = \dfrac{2}{x}$

B. $y = 2x^{-1}$

C. $y = \dfrac{x}{2}$

D. $y = \dfrac{1}{2}x + 1$

3 Of the following statements, the one that is not true is ( ).

A. In the relation $y = 3x - 1$, $y + 1$ and x are directly proportional.

B. In the relation $y = -\dfrac{x}{2}$, y and x are directly proportional.

C. In the relation $y = 2(x + 1)$, y and $x + 1$ are directly proportional.

D. In the relation $y = x + 3$, y and x are directly proportional.

4 If $y = (4 - 2t)x^{t}$ is a direct proportional function, then the value of t is ( ).

A. $t = 0$

B. $t = 1$

C. $t = -1$

D. any number

B. Fill in the blanks

5 Given that $y = kx$ is a direct proportional function, and when the value of the independent variable x is -4 the dependent variable $y = 20$, then the coefficient $k = $ _____.

6 Given that y is directly proportional to $\sqrt{x}$, and when $x = 16$, $y = 16$, then the expression of y as a function of x is _____.

7 If $y = (2m + 6)x^2 + (1 - m)x$ is a direct proportional function, then the value of m is _____.

8 Given $y = (a + 2)x + (a^2 - 4)$, then when $a = $ _____, it is a direct proportional function.

C. Questions that require solutions

9 y is directly proportional to $x - 1$ and when $x = 4$, $y = -12$.
   (a) Write the expression of y as a function of x.
   (b) Find the value of the dependent variable y when $x = -2$.
   (c) Find the value of the independent variable, x, when $y = 20$.

10 Write the expressions of functions between the two variables in the following cases and then say whether they are direct proportional functions.

    (a) In a right-angled triangle, the size of one acute angle is α and the size of the other acute angle is β. Write the expression of β as a function of α.

    (b) Express the circumference, y (cm), of a circle as a function of its radius, x (cm).

11 It may be assumed that a vehicle's mileage is directly proportional to the amount of fuel it consumes. A coach consumes 30 litres of fuel for every 120 km it travels, and a truck consumes 12 litres of fuel for every 50 km. Let the mileage be x km, the fuel consumption of the coach be y_1 litres and that of the truck be y_2 litres. Write expressions for y_1 and y_2 as functions of x. Which vehicle is more fuel-efficient? Give your reason.

12 Given that $y = y_1 - y_2$, y_1 and x^2 are directly proportional, y_2 and $x + 1$ are directly proportional, when $x = -3$, $y = 19$ and when $x = -1$, $y = 2$, write the expression of y as a function of x.

6.3 Graphs of direct proportional functions

Learning objective

Solve graphical problems involving direct proportion

A. Multiple choice questions

1 Of the following functions, only ( ) is a function of direct proportion.

A. $y = \dfrac{8}{x}$
B. $y = x^2$
C. $y = 2(x - 1)$
D. $y = -\dfrac{(\sqrt{2} + 1)x}{3}$

2 Both point $A(5, y_1)$ and point $B(2, y_2)$ are on line $y = -x$. The relation between y_1 and y_2 is ( ).

A. $y_1 \geqslant y_2$
B. $y_1 = y_2$
C. $y_1 < y_2$
D. $y_1 > y_2$

3 Of the following co-ordinate points, ( ) cannot be on the graph of the function of direct proportion $y = \dfrac{1}{k}x \ (k \neq 0)$.

A. $(0, 0)$
B. $(1, k)$
C. $(k, 1)$
D. $\left(1, \dfrac{1}{k}\right)$

4 Of the following functions, only the graph of ( ) is symmetrical to the graph of the function $y = 2x$ about the x-axis.

A. $y = 2x$
B. $y = -2x$
C. $y = \dfrac{1}{2}x$
D. $y = -\dfrac{1}{2}x$

5 Of the following graphs, ( ) represents the function $y = -kx(k < 0)$.

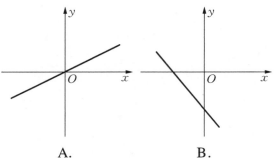

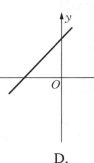

A.
B.
C.
D.

B. Fill in the blanks

6 The graph of the direct proportional function $y = kx(k \neq 0)$ is a straight line passing through points $(0, \underline{\hspace{1.5cm}})$ and $(1, \underline{\hspace{1.5cm}})$; k is called the proportional $\underline{\hspace{1.5cm}}$
$\underline{\hspace{3cm}}$.

7 You can draw the graph of direct proportional function $y = kx$ by $\underline{\hspace{3cm}}$
$\underline{\hspace{1.5cm}}$ and then drawing a line passing through them. Usually you can choose the point
$(\underline{\hspace{1cm}}, \underline{\hspace{1cm}})$ and the point $(\underline{\hspace{1cm}}, \underline{\hspace{1cm}})$.

8 The graph of function $y = -\dfrac{1}{3}x$ passes through quadrants $\underline{\hspace{3cm}}$;
the value of y $\underline{\hspace{4cm}}$ as the value of x increases.

9 If x and y are variables and $y = (k-1)x^{k^2}$ is a direct proportional function, then
$k = \underline{\hspace{1.5cm}}$.

10 Given that y is directly proportional to x and when $x = 2$, $y = -6$, then when $y = 9$,
$x = \underline{\hspace{1.5cm}}$.

11 Given that the graph of the direct proportional function $y = (m-1)x^{m^2-3}$ passes through
Quadrants II and IV, then the expression of the function is $\underline{\hspace{3cm}}$.

C. Questions that require solutions

12 The variables y and x are directly proportional and when $x = 4$, $y = 2$.

(a) Write the expression of y as a function of x.

(b) Find the value of y when $x = 5$.

(c) Find the value of x when $y = 10$.

(d) Draw the graph of the function for
$-2 < x \leqslant 6$.

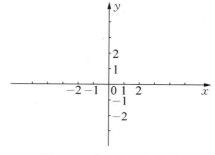

Diagram for question 12

13 Take a point, P, on the graph of the function $y = -3x$. Through P, draw a line PA so that PA is perpendicular to the x-axis, with A being the foot of the perpendicular. Given that the x-coordinate of P is -2, find the area of $\triangle POA$. (O is the origin.)

14 The point $(2, -4)$ is on the graph of the direct proportional function $y = kx$.

(a) Find the value of k.

(b) If point $(-1, m)$ is on the graph of the function $y = kx$, find the value of m.

(c) If points $A(1, y_1)$, $B(2, y_2)$ and $C(-1, y_3)$ are all on the graph of the function, compare the values of y_1, y_2 and y_3.

6.4　Properties of direct proportional functions

Learning objective

Solve problems involving direct proportion

A. Multiple choice questions

1 Of the following pairs of variables, the two variables that are in direct proportion are (　　).

A. the area of a circle and its radius

B. when the width of a rectangle is fixed, the perimeter C of the rectangle and its length b

C. when the distance s is fixed, the speed v of a moving object and the time t it takes from one end to the other end

D. when the speed of a moving object v is fixed, the distance s it covers and the time t it takes

2 Of the following functions, only (　　) shows that y is directly proportional to x.

A. $y = 4x + 1$　　　B. $y = 2x^2$　　　C. $y = -\sqrt{5}x$　　　D. $y = \sqrt{x}$

3 (x_1, y_1) and (x_2, y_2) are the two points on the line $y = -3x$ and $x_1 > x_2$. The relation connecting y_1 and y_2 is (　　).

A. $y_1 > y_2$　　　　　　　　　　　　B. $y_1 < y_2$

C. $y_1 = y_2$　　　　　　　　　　　　D. all of the above are possible

4 For a function, when $x > 0$, its expression is $y = 2x$, when $x \leqslant 0$, its expression is $y = -2x$. Then the sketch of the graph of the function on the co-ordinate plane looks like (　　).

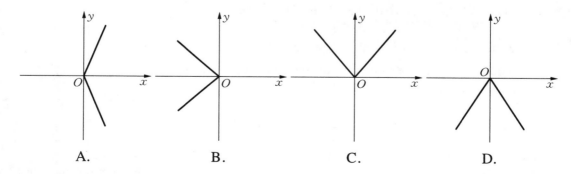

A.　　　　　　　　B.　　　　　　　　C.　　　　　　　　D.

B. Fill in the blanks

5 The graph of a direct proportional function is a straight line that passes through _____ _____. When $k > 0$, the line $y = kx$ passes through quadrants _____ and _____ , and y _____ as x increases. When $k < 0$, the line $y = kx$ passes through quadrants _____ and _____ , and y _____ as x increases.

6 The graph of function $y = -\dfrac{1}{2}x(x > 0)$ is a _____. It passes through quadrants _____ and _____.

7 The graph of the direct proportional function $y = k^2x(k \neq 0)$ must pass through points $(0,$ _____ $)$ and $(1,$ _____ $)$ and it is in quadrants _____ and _____.

8 If the function $y = mx^{m^2-3}$ is a direct proportional function and its graph is in quadrants I and III, then $m =$ _____ and y _____ as x increases.

9 Given that the graph of the function $y = kx(k \neq 0)$ passes through point $P(-3, 7)$, then $k =$ _____ and it is in the _____ and _____ quadrants.

10 $M_1(x_1, y_1)$ and $M_2(x_2, y_2)$ are two points on the graph of the direct proportional function $y = kx(k \neq 0)$. When $x_1 < x_2$, $y_1 < y_2$. Then the set of possible values of k is _____ and the graph is in the _____ and _____ quadrants.

11 The graph of the direct proportional function $y = kx(k \neq 0)$ is in the second and fourth quadrants and it passes through point $P(k + 2, 2k + 1)$. Then $k =$ _____.

C. Questions that require solutions

12 The function $y = (k - 2)x^{k+2}$ is a direct proportional function. Find the expression of the function and then draw the graph.

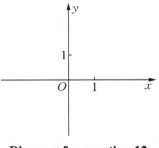

Diagram for question 12

⑬ $y + 3$ and $2x - 1$ are directly proportional and when $x = 2$, $y = 1$.

(a) Write the expression of y as a function of x.

(b) Given that $0 \leqslant x \leqslant 3$, what are the greatest and the least values of y?

⑭ P is a point on the graph of the direct proportional function $y = 3x$. Its x-coordinate is -2. The symmetric points of P about the x-axis and the y-axis are P_1 and P_2 respectively.

(a) Find the co-ordinates of points P, P_1 and P_2.

(b) If the graph of the direct proportional function $y = k_1 x$ passes through point P_1 and the graph of the direct proportional function $y = k_2 x$ passes through point P_2, find the values of k_1 and k_2.

(c) What conclusion can you draw from part (b)? Will the conclusion be true when the condition 'the direct proportional function $y = 3x$' is changed into 'the direct proportional function $y = kx$'?

6.5 Inverse proportion and inverse proportional functions

Learning objective

Solve problems involving inverse proportion

A. Multiple choice questions

1. Of the following pairs of variables, (   ) are in inverse proportion.
   A. when the area of a triangle is fixed, the length of a side of the triangle and its height on the side
   B. when the perimeter of an isosceles triangle is fixed, its base length and the length of its two equal sides
   C. the circumference of a circle and its radius
   D. the area of a circle and its radius

2. When the graph of an inverse proportional function passes through point $(-1, 6)$, it also passes through point (   ).
   A. $(2, 3)$ B. $(3, 2)$ C. $(-3, 2)$ D. $(6, 1)$

3. If y and $-3x$ are inversely proportional and x and $\dfrac{4}{z}$ are directly proportional, y is (   ) of z.
   A. a direct proportional function
   B. an inverse proportional function
   C. neither a direct proportional function nor an inverse proportional function
   D. cannot be determined

B. Fill in the blanks

4. If the product of the values of each pair of two variables is a _____ , then the two variables are in inverse proportion.

5. In the function $y = \dfrac{1}{x-3}$, the condition on the value of the independent variable x is

   _____ .

6 The function $y = \dfrac{1}{2x}$ is _____ function and the coefficient of proportionality is _____.

7 Given that y is an inverse proportional function of x, and when $x = 3$, $y = \dfrac{1}{2}$, then the expression of y as a function of x is _____.

8 Given that the graph of the inverse proportional function $y = \dfrac{k}{x}$ passes through point $(1, -2)$, then $k = $ _____.

9 Given that the function $y = (m - 2)x^{m^2 - 5}$ is an inverse proportional function, then $m = $ _____.

10 If x is directly proportional to $-3y$ and y is directly proportional to $\dfrac{2}{z}$, then x is _____ to z.

11 Given that the graph of the direct proportional function $y = kx$ and that of the inverse proportional function $y = \dfrac{3}{x}$ both pass through point $A(m, 3)$, then $m = $ _____. The expression of the direct proportional function is _____.

C. Questions that require solutions

12 Given that $y = \dfrac{m + 3}{x} + 2m - 1$ is an inverse proportional function, find the value of m and write the expression of the function.

13 Given that y_1 is in direct proportion to x, y_2 is in inverse proportion to x^2, $y = 2y_1 - y_2$, when $x = -1$, $y = -4$, and when $x = 1$, $y = 0$, find the expression of y as a function of x.

14 $y = 2y_1 + y_2$, y_1 is directly proportional to $x - 2$ and y_2 is inversely proportional to $5x$; when $x = 2$, $y = \dfrac{9}{10}$, and when $x = 1$, $y = \dfrac{1}{5}$. Find the expression of y as a function of x, and then the value of y when $x = -1$.

6.6   Graphs of inverse proportional functions

Learning objective

Calculate missing values and solve problems with reciprocal graphs

A. Multiple choice questions

1 Given that the graph of the function $y = \dfrac{2k - 5}{kx}$ is in the second and fourth quadrants, then the set of possible value of k is (   ).

A. $k \neq 0$

B. $k < 0$

C. $0 < k < \dfrac{5}{2}$

D. $k < \dfrac{5}{2}$ and $k \neq 0$

2 On the same co-ordinate plane, the point of intersection of the graphs of the functions $y = -2$ and $y = -\dfrac{1}{2x}$ is in the (   ).

A. first and third quadrants

B. third quadrant

C. fourth quadrant

D. second and fourth quadrants

3 On the same co-ordinate plane, the sketches of the graphs of the direct proportional function $y = (m - 1)x$ and the inverse proportional function $y = \dfrac{4m}{x}$ cannot be like (   ).

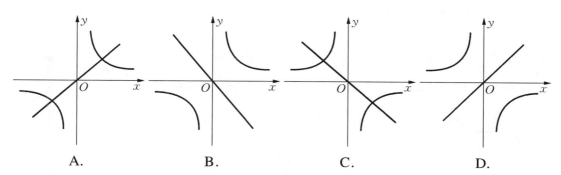

A.   B.   C.   D.

Direct proportion, inverse proportion and their functions

B. Fill in the blanks

4 In the diagram, A is a point on the graph of the inverse proportional function $y = \dfrac{k}{x}$ and AB is perpendicular to the x-axis at point B.

If $S_{\triangle AOB} = 3$, then the value of k is _____.

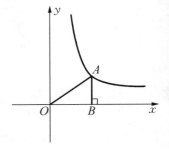

Diagram for question 4

5 If the graph of the inverse proportional function $y = \dfrac{m-1}{x}$ is in quadrants I and III, then the set of the possible value of m is _____.

6 Given that the graph of the function $y = \dfrac{m+2}{x}$ is in two quadrants and in each quadrant the value of y increases as the value of x increases, then the set of possible values of m is _____.

7 If the graphs of the functions $y = -\dfrac{x}{2}$ and $y = \dfrac{k}{x}$ have two intersecting points, then the set of the possible values of k is _____.

8 The co-ordinates of the point of intersection of the graphs of the inverse proportional function $y = \dfrac{2}{x}$ and the direct proportional function $y = 4x$ in the first quadrant are _____.

9 In the diagram, the curve is one part of an inverse proportional function and A is a point on the curve. Then the expression of the function is _____.

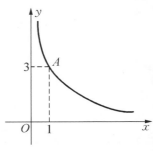

Diagram for question 9

10 Given that A and B are symmetric points about the y-axis, point A is on the graph of $y = \dfrac{4}{x}$ and point B is on the straight line $y = -x$, then the co-ordinates of B are _____ _____.

C. Questions that require solutions

11 In the diagram, the straight line $y = -2x$ passes through point $P(-2, a)$. The symmetric point of P about the y-axis is P', which is on the graph of the inverse proportional function $y = \dfrac{k}{x}(k \neq 0)$.

(a) Find the value of a.

(b) Write down the co-ordinates of point P'.

(c) Find the expression of the inverse proportional function.

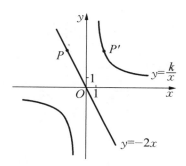

Diagram for question 11

12 The graphs of an inverse proportional function and a proportional function intersect at points A and B. Point A is in quadrant II, it is -3 on the x-axis and $AD \perp x$-axis with D being the foot of the perpendicular. The area of $\triangle AOD$ is 4.

(a) Write the expression of the inverse proportional function.

(b) Find the co-ordinates of point B.

(c) If the co-ordinates of point C are $(6, 0)$, then find the area of $\triangle ABC$.

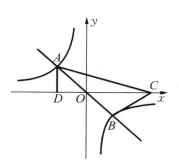

Diagram for question 12

13 A and B are two separate points on the graph of the inverse proportional function $y = \dfrac{8}{x}(x > 0)$. The x-coordinate of point A is 8 and the y-coordinate of point B is 4.

(a) Find the co-ordinates of points A and B.

(b) If both points $C(0, 2)$ and $D(3, 0)$ are also on the same co-ordinate plane, then find the area of the quadrilateral $ABCD$.

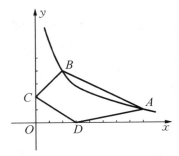

Diagram for question 13

6.7 Properties of inverse proportional functions

Learning objective

Solve problems involving inverse proportion, including graphical and algebraic representations

A. Multiple choice questions

1 Given two points, $A(x_1, y_1)$ and $B(x_2, y_2)$ on the graph of the function $y = -\dfrac{1}{x}$, and $x_1 < x_2$, then the correct statement is ( ).

A. $y_1 < y_2$

B. $y_1 > y_2$

C. $y_1 = y_2$

D. The relation between y_1 and y_2 cannot be identified.

2 If the graph of the inverse proportional function $y = \dfrac{k}{x}$ passes through point $A(-1, -2)$, then when $x > 1$, the set of possible values of y is ( ).

A. $y > 1$

B. $0 < y < 1$

C. $y > 2$

D. $0 < y < 2$

3 In the diagram, line l and the graph of $y = \dfrac{k}{x}(k > 0)$ intersect at points A and B. Point P is on the line segment AB (and does not coincide with A or B). The perpendiculars through points A, B and P meet the x-axis at C, D and E respectively. The lines OA, OB and OP are sides of three triangles. Let the area of $\triangle AOC$ be S_1, the area of $\triangle BOD$ be S_2 and the area of $\triangle POE$ be S_3, then ( ).

A. $S_1 < S_2 < S_3$

B. $S_1 = S_2 > S_3$

C. $S_1 = S_2 < S_3$

D. $S_1 > S_2 > S_3$

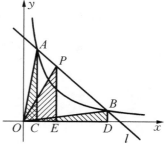

Diagram for question 3

B. Fill in the blanks

4 The graph of the function $y = -\dfrac{3}{x}$ is in the _____ and _____ quadrants, and in each quadrant, y _____ as x increases.

5 If the graph of the function $y = \dfrac{k}{x}$ passes through point $(3, 4)$, then $k =$ _____, and the graph is in the _____ and _____ quadrants. In each quadrant, y _____ _____ as x increases.

6 $A_1(x_1, y_1)$, $A_2(x_2, y_2)$ and $A_3(x_3, y_3)$ are three points on the graph of the function $y = \dfrac{k^2 + 1}{x}$ and $x_1 < x_2 < 0 < x_3$. Then, using $<$ to compare them, the relation between y_1, y_2 and y_3 is _____.

7 In the diagram, point A is on the graph of $y = \dfrac{1}{x}$, point B is on the graph of $y = \dfrac{3}{x}$ and AB is parallel to the x-axis. C and D are points on the x-axis. Given that the quadrilateral $ABCD$ is a rectangle, its area is _____.

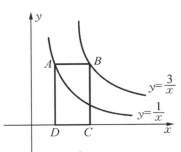

Diagram for question 7

C. Questions that require solutions

8 The function $y = (k - 2)x^{-k+2}$ is an inverse proportional function.
   (a) Find the value of k.
   (b) Which quadrants is the graph of the function in? In each quadrant, does y increase or decrease as x increases?
   (c) Find the set of possible values of the function (the values of y) when $-3 \leqslant x \leqslant -\dfrac{1}{2}$.

9 In the diagram, P is a point on the graph of the inverse proportional function and the area of the triangle is $S_{\triangle PQO} = 10$.

(a) Find the expression of the inverse proportional function.

(b) Given that point $P(m, 5)$ is on the graph, find the value of m and the distance between point P and the x-axis.

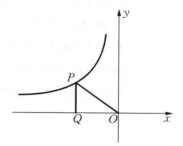

Diagram for question 9

10 The graph of an inverse proportional function is in the second and fourth quadrants, and it passes through points $(2, -a)$ and $(2 - a, 6)$. Find the value of x when $y = \dfrac{1}{2}$.

11 In the diagram, one part of the graph of $y = \dfrac{k}{x}(x > 0)$ is in the first quadrant. A and P are two points on the graph. $AB \perp x$-axis, $AC \perp y$-axis, $PQ \perp x$-axis and $PR \perp AB$, with B, C, Q and R being the feet of the perpendiculars. Both quadrilaterals $ABOC$ and $PQBR$ are squares.

(a) Find the side lengths of the squares $ABOC$ and $PQBR$ when $k = 1$.

(b) Find the side lengths of the squares $ABOC$ and $PQBR$ when $k = 2$.

(c) Find the ratio of the side lengths of squares $ABOC$ and $PQBR$ in parts (a) and (b). What patterns did you find in the ratio? Explore a bit further, can you tell if your conclusion is true for any value of $k(k > 0)$?

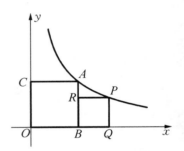

Diagram for question 11

6.8 How to express functions (1)

Learning objective

Solve problems involving distance − time graphs and proportional change

A. Multiple choice questions

1 Given the area of a trapezium is 8, the sum of the two parallel sides is $2x$ and the height is $2y$, then the expression of y as a function of x is (   ).

A. $y = \dfrac{1}{x}$

B. $y = \dfrac{4}{x}$

C. $y = \dfrac{8}{x}$

D. $y = x^2$

2 One evening, Danuta went out for a walk. First, she walked for 20 minutes to a news-stand, which was 900 metres away from her home. After spending 10 minutes reading newspapers at the news-stand, she walked for another 20 minutes from the news-stand to return home. Of the following, graph (   ) shows the relation between the time and the distance that she was away from home.

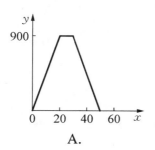

A.

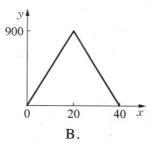

B.

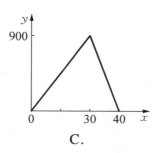

C.

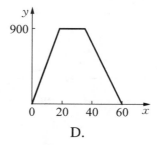

D.

Diagram for question 2

3 Water is running into an empty container at a constant speed. Take the time for which the water runs into the container as t and the height of the water level in the container as h. The diagram shows the relationship between h and t. The possible shape of the container is ( ).

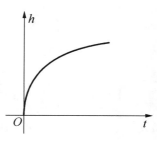

Diagram for question 3

A.   B.   C.   D.

4 Gianni and Tom walked from place A to place B along the same route, both with constant speed. The distance between A and B is 20 km. The diagram shows the graph of the relation between the distance s (km) each of them walked and the time t (h) after Gianni started walking. Based on the information in the graph, statement ( ) is correct.

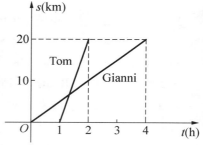

Diagram for question 4

A. Gianni's speed was 4 km/h.

B. Tom's speed was 10 km/h.

C. Tom started 1 hour later than Gianni.

D. Gianni arrived at B 3 hours later than Tom.

5 Jay wrote a computer program. The table shows the inputs and the outputs for the program.

Input	...	1	2	3	4	5	...
Output	...	$\dfrac{1}{2}$	$\dfrac{2}{5}$	$\dfrac{3}{10}$	$\dfrac{4}{17}$	$\dfrac{5}{26}$	...

Based on these figures, if the input is 8, then the output is ( ).

A. $\dfrac{8}{61}$ B. $\dfrac{8}{63}$ C. $\dfrac{8}{65}$ D. $\dfrac{8}{67}$

B. Fill in the blanks

6 _____, _____ and _____ are the three commonly used methods to express functions. (Write 'analytical method', 'graphical method', 'table method' or 'statistical method'.)

7 The method of using an _____ to express the relation between two variables in a function is called the analytical method.

8 The method of using graphs to express the relation between two variables in a function is called the _____.

9 The method of using a table to express the relation between two variables in a function is called the _____.

10 Point $P(x, y)$ is in the fourth quadrant, $x^2 = 1$ and $y^2 = 3$. Then the co-ordinates of point P are _____.

11 Given point $A(a - 1, 3)$ is on the y-axis, then $a = $ _____.

12 Given the perimeter of an isosceles triangle $\triangle ABC$ is 10, the length of base BC is y and the length of side AB is x, then the expression of y as a function of x is _____, the set of possible values of x is _____ and the set of the possible value of y is _____.

C. Questions that require solutions

13 The diagram shows a flowchart for calculation. What is the least positive integer value of input x that makes the value of the output y greater than 100?

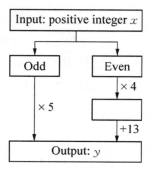

Diagram for question 13

14 Two teams A and B are tasked to dig two equal sections of a small canal at the same time. The diagram shows the part of the graph of the length y (m) of the canal the two teams have dug and time x (h) they took.

(a) It took Team B _____ hours to dig 30 m. After 6 hours, Team A has dug _____ more metres than Team B.

(b) (i) Write an expression for y as a function of x for Team A for the time period $0 \leqslant x \leqslant 6$.

(ii) Write an expression for y as a function of x for Team B for the time period $0 \leqslant x \leqslant 2$.

(c) If Team A's digging speed remains the same but Team B's digging speed increases to 12 m/h after 6 hours of digging, then the two teams will complete the task at the same time. What length of canal will Team A have dug from the start to the completion?

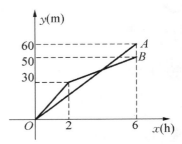

Diagram for question 14

15 Khalid sells some software packages to a company. If the company buys 40 of these software packages, then Khalid can make a profit of £40 from each one sold. In order to increase sales (while making no loss for Khalid) and to reduce the cost for the company, they have negotiated an agreement that if the company buys more than 40 packages, the unit price will be reduced by £1 for each additional one, for example, the unit price will be reduced by £5 if the company buys 45 packages.

(a) If each package is sold at the price reduced by x (pounds) and the profit Khalid makes is y (pounds), write the expression of y as a function of x.

(b) If the price of each package is reduced by £20, then how many should the company buy? In this case, what is the profit for Khalid?

6.9 How to express functions (2)

Learning objective

Solve problems involving distance – time graphs and proportional change

A. Multiple choice questions

1 If two points $A(x_1, y_1)$ and $B(x_2, y_2)$ are on the graph of a direct proportional function, then equation (　　) is incorrect.

A. $x_1 : y_1 = x_2 : y_2$　　　　　　　B. $x_1 y_2 = y_1 x_2$

C. $x_1 : x_2 = y_1 : y_2$　　　　　　　D. $x_1 x_2 = y_1 y_2$

2 Of these diagrams, the one that does not represent y as a function of x is (　　).

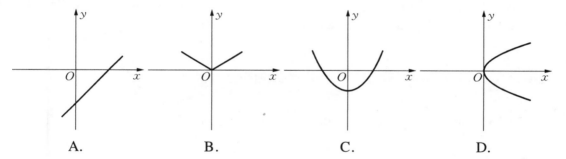

A.　　　　　　　　B.　　　　　　　　C.　　　　　　　　D.

3 If the graphs of the functions $y = kx$ and $y = \dfrac{k}{x}(k \neq 0)$ are on the same co-ordinate plane, but the signs of the x-coordinate and the y-coordinate of the points on the graphs are different, then the graphs are as in figure (　　).

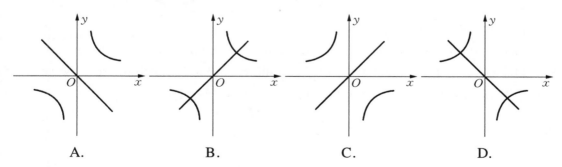

A.　　　　　　　　B.　　　　　　　　C.　　　　　　　　D.

B. Fill in the blanks

4. Given point $A(m, n)$, if $m + n = 0$, then point A is on the line _____.
   If $m - n = 0$, then point A is on the line _____. If $mn = 0$, then point A is on the graph of line _____.

5. If point $P(2, -3)$ is on the graph of the inverse proportional function $y = \dfrac{k - 4}{x}$, then P _____ (Write 'is' or 'is not') on the graph of the direct proportional function $y = \left(k + \dfrac{1}{2}\right)x$.

6. If the perimeter of an isosceles trapezium is 24 cm, the lengths of the upper parallel side and both non-parallel sides are x cm, and the lower base is y cm, then the expression of y as a function of x is _____. Given that the lower base is 9 cm, the lengths of the other three sides of this trapezium are _____.

C. Questions that require solutions

7. Find the intersecting point P of the graphs of the functions $y_1 = 4x$ and $y_2 = \dfrac{4}{x}$, and then construct the graphs.

8. $y = 5x - \sqrt{5 - x}$.
   (a) Find the domain of the possible values of the independent variable x.
   (b) Given that the point $A(4, m)$ is on the graph of the function, find the value of m.
   (c) What is the value of the function y, when $x = -11$?

9 In the diagram, the area of square $OABC$ is 9, point O is the origin, point A is on the x-axis, point C is on the y-axis and point B is on the graph of the function $y = \dfrac{k}{x}$ ($x > 0$, $k > 0$). Point $P(m, n)$ is another point on the graph, to the right of point B. Through point P, construct lines that are perpendicular to the x-axis and the y-axis, with E and F being the feet of the perpendiculars. Let the area of the non-overlapping part of rectangle $OEPF$ and square $OABC$ be S.

(a) Find the co-ordinates of point B and the value of k.

(b) When $S = \dfrac{9}{2}$, find the co-ordinates of point P.

(c) With the condition in (b), find the area of $\triangle BOP$.

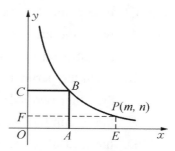

Diagram for question 9

10 In the diagram, A and B are two points on the graph of function $y = \dfrac{k}{x}$ ($k > 0$) in the first quadrant. The lines AC and BD are perpendicular to the x-axis.

Prove that the area of $\triangle AOB$ and the area of trapezium $ABDC$ are equal.

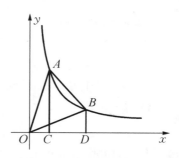

Diagram for question 10

Unit test 6

A. Multiple choice questions

1 Of these pairs of variables, the two variables that are in direct proportion are (   ).

A. when the area of a triangle is fixed, the length of one side of the triangle and its height from that side

B. when the perimeter of an isosceles triangle is fixed, the base length and the length of the other two sides of the triangle

C. the circumference of a circle and its radius

D. the area of a circle and its radius

2 Given that the graphs of two functions $y = k_1 x$ ($k_1 \neq 0$) and $y = \dfrac{k_2}{x}$ ($k_2 \neq 0$) on the same co-ordinate plane have no common point, then k_1 and k_2 (   ).

A. are reciprocals of each other   B. have the same sign

C. add up to zero   D. have opposite signs

3 The diagram shows the graphs of the direct proportional function $y = k_1 x$ ($k_1 \neq 0$) and the inverse proportional function $y = \dfrac{k_2 - 1}{x}$ ($k_2 \neq 1$). The set of the possible value of k_1 and k_2 are (   ).

A. $k_1 > 0$, $k_2 > 1$

B. $k_1 < 0$, $k_2 > 1$

C. $k_1 > 0$, $k_2 < 1$

D. $k_1 < 0$, $k_2 < 1$

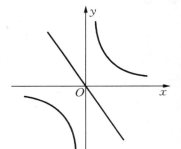

Diagram for question 3

4 The graph of the direct proportional function $y = kx$ ($k > 0$) intersects the graph of the inverse proportional function $y = \dfrac{1}{x}$ at points A and C. A perpendicular line through A intersects the x-axis at point B. Join BC. Given that the area of $\triangle ABC$ is S, then only statement (   ) is true.

A. $S_{\triangle AOB} > S_{\triangle BOC}$ B. $S_{\triangle AOB} < S_{\triangle BOC}$ C. $S = 1$ D. $S = 2$

5 The diagram shows a rectangle $ABCD$, in which $AB = 1$ and $BC = 2$. A point E moves from point C along the route $C \to D \to A$ at a constant speed until it reaches point A. The graph of the function showing the area y of $\triangle BEC$ against the distance x that point E covered is (　　).

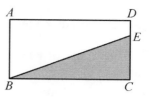

Diagram for question 5

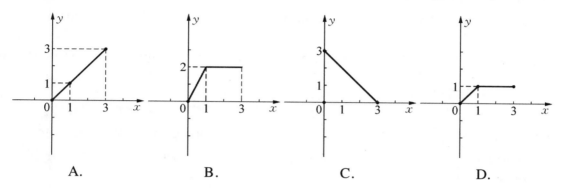

A.   B.   C.   D.

6 Of the four points $A(2, 5)$, $B(1, 1)$, $C(-2, -5)$ and $D(-6, -15)$, the only point that is not on the graph of a given direct proportional function is (　　).
A. point A　　　　B. point B　　　　C. point C　　　　D. point D

B. Fill in the blanks

7 Given that point $A(a, c)$ is in the third quadrant, then point $P(-a, \sqrt{c^2})$ is in the _____ quadrant.

8 Given that the graph of the inverse proportional function $y = (m - 1)x^{3 - m^2}$ is in the second and the fourth quadrants, then the possible value of m is _____.

9 Given $f(x) = -15$ and $g(x) = \dfrac{8}{3x - 11}$, then $f(-1) + g(5) = $ _____.

10 Given that the direct proportional function satisfies $f(3) = 12$, then the expression of this function is _____.

11 If the graph of the function $y = -kx$ is in the second and fourth quadrants, then the graph of the function $y = \dfrac{k}{x}$ does not pass through the _____ and _____ quadrants.

12 Given that y and x are inversely proportional, and $x = 2$ when $y = -1$, then when $y = \dfrac{1}{2}$ the value of x is _____ .

13 If the graph of the direct proportional function $y = k_1 x$ and the graph of the inverse proportional function $y = \dfrac{k_2}{x}$ have an intersecting point P in the first quadrant, and the co-ordinates of point P are $\left(\dfrac{1}{2}, 5\right)$, then the two functions must have the other intersecting point Q (_____ , _____).

14 Given $A(x_1, y_1)$ and $B(x_2, y_2)$ are two points on the graph of the direct proportional function $y = (2m - 1)x$, and when $x_1 < x_2$, $y_1 > y_2$, then the set of the possible value of m is _____ .

15 Given the area of a triangle is a fixed value S, then the relation of the expression of the function between its height h and base a is $h = $ _____ .

16 If y is inversely proportional to x and z is directly proportional to y, then z is _____ to x.

17 If $P(2, m)$ is a point of intersection of the graphs of the direct proportional function $y = 2x$ and the inverse proportional function $y = \dfrac{2k + 1}{x}$, then $m = $ _____ , $k = $ _____ .

18 Let the inverse proportional function be $y = -\dfrac{3}{x}$. Then when $3 \leqslant x \leqslant 6$, the least value of the function is _____ .

C. Questions that require solutions

19 Given that both points $A(2, -1)$ and $B\left(b, \dfrac{1}{2}\right)$ are on the graph of $y = kx$, find the value of b and say whether point $\left(-\dfrac{3}{2}, \dfrac{3}{4}\right)$ is also on the graph of the same function.

20 The graphs of $y = -\dfrac{x}{2}$ and $y = -\dfrac{2}{x}$ intersect at points A and B, AC is parallel to the

y-axis, and BC is parallel to the x-axis. Find:

(a) the co-ordinates of points A and B

(b) the area of $\triangle ABC$.

21 The line $y = 2x - 4 + n$ passes through the origin and intersects the graph of the inverse

proportional function $y = \dfrac{n}{x}$ at points A and B. Find:

(a) the expression of the inverse proportional function

(b) the length of the line segment AB.

22 The diagram shows point $P\left(2, \dfrac{3}{2}\right)$. A line passing through point P, parallel to the

x-axis, intersects the y-axis at point A and the graph of the function $y = \dfrac{k}{x}$ $(x > 0)$ at

point N. PM is perpendicular to AN, intersecting the graph of $y = \dfrac{k}{x}$ $(x > 0)$ at point M.

$PN = 4$.

(a) Find the value of k.

(b) Find the area of $\triangle APM$.

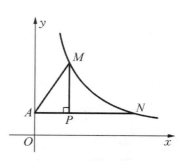

Diagram for question 23

㉓ The diagram shows a rectangle on the co-ordinate plane, in which $OA = 2$, $OC = 3$ and E is the midpoint of AB. The graph of the inverse proportional function passes through point E and intersects BC at point F.

(a) Find the expression of the function representing the line OB and the inverse proportional function.

(b) Find the area of the quadrilateral $OEBF$.

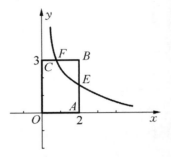

Diagram for question 25

㉔ The point of intersection of the graphs of a direct proportional function and an inverse proportional function is 3 units from the x-axis and 4 units from the y-axis. Find the expressions of the two functions.

Chapter 7　Introduction to proof in geometry

7.1　Statement and proof (1)

 Learning objective

Construct simple proofs and chains of reasoning using deductive reasoning and cause and effect

 A. Multiple choice questions

1　Of the following, (　　) is not a statement.

A. The sum of two odd numbers.

B. The sum of two odd numbers is an even number.

C. The sum of two odd numbers is an odd number.

D. The sum of two odd numbers is zero.

> In the study of logic, a statement is also called a proposition.

2　Deductive proof is a sequence of reasoning by which, starting from the (　　), known facts, properties and rules, a conclusion is deduced to be true. It is a rigorous mathematical proof, or (　　) in short.

A. given conditions　　B. unknown　　C. proof　　D. rigour

3　To prove that a mathematical statement is true, we usually use (　　).

A. a list of a few examples　　　　B. a sequence of deductive reasoning

C. a list of many examples　　　　D. counterexamples

 B. Fill in the blanks

4　Lets try some cause-and-effect reasoning. Fill in the blanks with the reasons (such as 'given', 'known facts', 'properties' and 'rules') for the conclusions deduced. The first one has been done for you.

(a) *One cause with one effect*

　　For example: α and β are vertically opposite angles (given).

　　Therefore $\alpha = \beta$ (Vertically opposite angles are equal.)

　　Another example: α and β are complementary angles (given).

　　Therefore $\alpha + \beta = 90°$ (　　　　　　　　　　　　　　　　)

(b) *One cause with multiple effects*

In the diagram, two parallel lines a and b are intersected by a third line c.

Since $a \mathbin{/\mkern-5mu/} b$ (given):

$\beta = \theta$ (   )

$\alpha = \theta$ (   )

$\gamma + \theta = 180°$ (   )

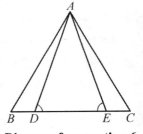

Diagram for question 4b

(c) *Multiple causes with one effect*

In $\triangle ABC$, $\angle A = 60°$ and $\angle B = 80°$ (given)

Therefore, $\angle C = 180° - 60° - 80° = 40°$ (   )

5 The four methods of determining congruent triangles are _____, _____, _____ and _____. (Write 'SSS', 'AAA', 'AAS', 'ASA', 'SAS' or 'ASS'.)

6 In the diagram, points D and E are on BC, $AB = AC$ and $BD = CE$. Prove that $\angle ADE = \angle AED$. (Fill in the blanks to show different ways of proving the equality of the two angles.)

Method 1

First, prove $\triangle ABD \cong$ _____ and get $AD =$ _____.

Therefore $\angle ADE = \angle AED$

Method 2

First, prove $\triangle ABE \cong$ _____ and therefore

$\angle ADE = \angle AED$.

Method 3

Through point A, draw a line AH perpendicular to BC, intersecting BC at point H^{*}.

Since $BH =$ _____, based on the property of equality, we get $DH =$ _____.

Then $\triangle ADH \cong$ _____.

Hence $\angle ADE = \angle AED$

Diagram for question 6

---

* In this method, AH is an **auxiliary line**. In geometric proof, an auxiliary line is an additional line constructed to help complete the proof.

C. Questions that require solutions

7 Write suitable reasons in the brackets.

In the diagram, $AD \parallel BC$ and $DF \parallel EB$.

Prove that $\angle B = \angle D$.

Proof:

Since $AD \parallel BC$ (   )

$\angle D + \angle DCB = 180°$ (   )

Since $DF \parallel EB$ (   )

$\angle B + \angle DCB = 180°$ (   )

Hence $\angle B = \angle D$ (   )

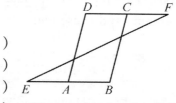

Diagram for question 7

8 The diagram shows $\triangle ABC$ with $\angle B = \angle C$. D, E and F are points on AB, BC and AC, respectively, $BD = CE$ and $\angle DEF = \angle B$.

Prove that $ED = EF$.

Proof:

Since $\angle DEC = \angle B + \angle BDE$ (   )

and $\angle DEF = \angle B$ (given)

$\angle$_____ $= \angle$_____ (property of equality)

In $\triangle EBD$ and $\triangle FCE$:

$\left\{\begin{array}{l} \angle \text{_____} = \angle \text{_____} \ (\text{proved}) \\ \text{_____} = \text{_____} \ (\text{given}) \\ \angle B = \angle C \ (\text{given}) \end{array}\right.$

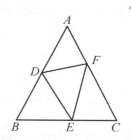

Diagram for question 8

therefore, $\triangle EBD \cong \triangle FCE$ (   )

Hence $ED = EF$ (   )

9 The diagram shows $\triangle ABC$ in which $\angle ACB = 90°$, $CA = CB$ and $CD \perp AB$, with D being the foot of the perpendicular. E is a point on AB and $EF \perp AC$, with F being the foot of the perpendicular. G is a point on BC and $CG = EF$.

Prove that: (a) $DF = DG$ (b) $DF \perp DG$.

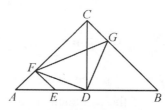

Diagram for question 9

7.2   Statement and proof (2)

Learning objective

Construct simple proofs and chains of reasoning for angles and triangles using deductive reasoning and cause and effect

A. Multiple choice questions

1 Of these statements, the correct one is (   ).

A. Equal angles are vertically opposite angles.

B. When the length of one side of a triangle is half of the length of the other side, the angle opposite to the side is 30°.

C. Two acute angles in a triangle are complementary to each other.

D. To identify that two triangles are congruent, we need to know that at least one pair of corresponding sides are equal.

2 Of these statements, only (   ) is true.

A. If $ab > ac$, then $b > c$.

B. A right-angled triangle cannot be an isosceles triangle.

C. If $x = 0$ or $y = 0$, then $xy = 0$.

D. Two corresponding angles are always equal.

3 The diagram shows a right-angled triangle ABC in which CD is the perpendicular height (or simply the height) on the hypotenuse AB, and E is the midpoint of AB. Then (   ) of the following conclusions are correct.

① $\angle ACD = \angle B$

② $\angle ECB = \angle DCE$

③ $\angle ACD = \angle ECB$

④ $\angle ECB = \angle A - \angle ECD$

A. 1   B. 2   C. 3   D. 4

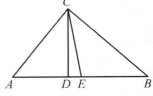

Diagram for question 3

B. Fill in the blanks

4 A sentence expressing an opinion or judgement is a _____.
If the statement is true, it is called a _____. If it is false, it is called a _____.

5 The statement: 'If $ab > 0$, then $a > 0$, $b > 0$' _____ a statement. (Write 'is' or 'is not'.)

6 The statement: 'A quadrilateral in which the diagonals bisect each other is a parallelogram' is a _____ statement. (Write 'true' or 'false'.)

7 In the statement 'the two acute angles of a right-angled triangle are complementary to each other', the given premise (condition) is '_____' and the conclusion is '_____'.

8 In the statement 'If $a \parallel b$ and $b \parallel c$, then $a \parallel c$.' the given is '_____ _____' and the conclusion is '_____'.

9 The statement, 'two lines that are parallel to the same line are parallel', can be rewritten as 'If _____, then _____.'

C. Questions that require solutions

10 Rewrite each statement in 'if ..., then ...' form. The first one has been done for you.

(a) Vertically opposite angles are equal.

    Solution: <u>If two angles are vertically opposite angles, then they are equal.</u>

(b) Two triangles with each pair of corresponding sides being equal are congruent.

_____

(c) The angles opposite to equal sides of an isosceles triangle are equal.

_____

(d) Two angles that are both complementary to the same angle are equal.

_____

11 In the diagram, $DB \parallel EC$ and $\angle C = \angle D$.

Prove that: (a) $\alpha = \beta$ (b) $\angle A = \angle F$.

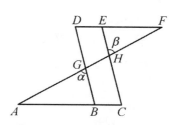

Diagram for question 11

7.3 Practice and exercise in proof (1)

Learning objective

Find missing angles and begin to construct simple proofs using angle facts and congruence

A. Multiple choice questions

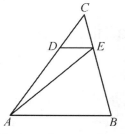

Diagram for question 1

① In the diagram, $DE \parallel AB$, $\angle CAE = \frac{1}{3} \angle CAB$, $\angle CDE = 75°$ and $\angle B = 65°$. Then $\angle AEB$ is (   ).

A. 70°

B. 65°

C. 60°

D. 55°

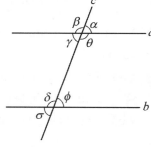

Diagram for question 2

② In the diagram the parallel lines a and b are intersected by line c. Of the following conclusions, the one that cannot be deduced from the given is (   ).

A. $\alpha = \phi$

B. $\alpha = \sigma$

C. $\beta + \sigma = 180°$

D. $\theta = \sigma$

B. Fill in the blanks

③ In the diagram, lines AB and CD are intersected by line EF. $AB \parallel CD$. Prove that $\alpha = \beta$. (Write suitable reasons in the blanks.)

Proof:

Since $AB \parallel CD$ (given)

$\alpha = $ _____ (when two lines are parallel

_____)

Since $\beta = \gamma$ (   )

$\alpha = \beta$ (   )

Diagram for question 3

4 The diagram shows that line AB intersects CD at point E and $DF /\!/ AB$.

If $\angle AEC = 100°$, then $\angle D$ is equal to _____.

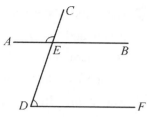

Diagram for question 4

5 In the diagram, given that $l_1 /\!/ l_2$, $\alpha = 120°$ and $\beta = 100°$, then $\gamma =$ _____.

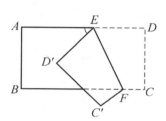

Diagram for question 5

6 The diagram shows a rectangular sheet of paper folded along EF. Points D and C are transformed into points D' and C'. If $\angle EFB = 65°$, then $\angle AED' =$ _____.

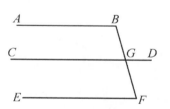

Diagram for question 6

C. Questions that require solutions

7 In the diagram, $AB /\!/ CG /\!/ EF$. Prove that $\angle B + \angle F = 180°$.

Diagram for question 7

8 In the diagram, $AB /\!/ CD$ and $\angle M = \angle N$. Prove that $\alpha = \beta$.

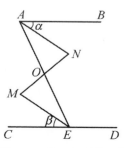

Diagram for question 8

9 Read the statement below. Look at the diagram provided, write down what you are given and what you are required to prove. Then complete the proof to show this statement is true. (Note: A median of a triangle is a line segment joining the midpoint of one side to the vertex opposite that side.)

Statement: In an isosceles triangle, the medians on the two equal sides are equal.

Given:

Prove:

Proof:

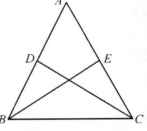

Diagram for question 9

7.4　Practice and exercise in proof (2)

Learning objective

Find missing angles and construct simple proofs using angle facts and congruence

A. Multiple choice questions

1 In the diagram, $\alpha = \beta$ and $BC = EF$. One more condition is needed, to prove $\triangle ABC \cong \triangle DEF$. This is (   ).

A. $AB = DE$

B. $\angle ACE = \angle DFB$

C. $BF = EC$

D. $\angle ABC = \angle DEF$

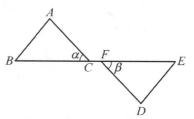

Diagram for question 1

2 Given that one exterior angle of an isosceles triangle is $100°$, then the two interior angles that are not adjacent to the exterior angle are (   ).

A. $40°$ and $40°$

B. $80°$ and $20°$

C. $50°$ and $50°$

D. $50°$ and $50°$ or $80°$ and $20°$

B. Fill in the blanks

3 In the diagram, $\triangle ABC \cong \triangle DEB$, $AB = DE$ and $\angle E = \angle ABC$. Then the angle corresponding to $\angle C$ is _____ and the side corresponding to BD is _____.

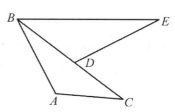

Diagram for question 3

4 In the diagram, $AD = AE$, $\alpha = \beta$ and $BD = CE$. Then $\triangle ABD \cong$ _____, reason: _____, and $\triangle ABE \cong \triangle$ _____.

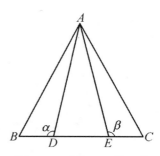

Diagram for question 4

5 In the diagram, $AB /\!/ CD$, line EF intersects AB and CD at points E and F. EG bisects $\angle BEF$ and intersects CD at point G. If $\angle EFG = 50°$, then $\angle EGF = $ _____°.

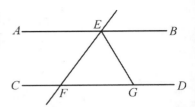

Diagram for question 5

6 In the diagram, $AD \perp BC$, $DE \perp AB$, $DF \perp AC$ with D, E and F being the feet of the perpendiculars and $BD = CD$. Then there are _____ pairs of congruent triangles in the diagram.

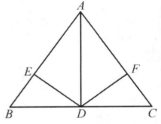

Diagram for question 6

C. Questions that require solutions

7 In the diagram, D is a point on the side AB of $\triangle ABC$. DF intersects AC at point E, $DE = FE$ and $FC /\!/ AB$. Prove that $AD = CF$.

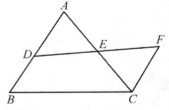

Diagram for question 7

8 In the diagram, three points B, C and E are on the same line, $AC /\!/ DE$, $AC = CE$ and $\angle ACD = \angle B$. Prove that $AB = CD$.

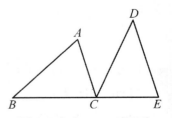

Diagram for question 8

7.5 Practice and exercise in proof (3)

Learning objective

Find missing angles and construct simple proofs using angle facts, lengths and midpoints

A. Multiple choice questions

1 In the diagram, $AB \perp EF$, $CD \perp EF$ and $\angle F = \alpha = 45°$.
There are (   ) angles equal to $\angle FCD$.

A. 1

B. 2

C. 3

D. 4

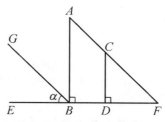

Diagram for question 1

2 The diagram shows $\triangle ABC$, in which $AB = AC$
and $\angle A = 100°$. BD bisects $\angle ABC$ and $BD = BE$.
$\angle DEC = ($ $)$.

A. 120°

B. 100°

C. 80°

D. 160°

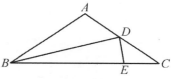

Diagram for question 2

B. Fill in the blanks

3 In the diagram, $AB \parallel CD$.
Therefore, $\beta + \gamma - \alpha - \theta = $ _____.

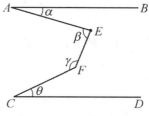

Diagram for question 3

4 The diagram shows $\triangle ABC$ in which $AB = AC$, $BC = BE$ and
$AE = DE = DB$. Then $\angle A = $ _____.

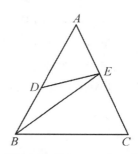

Diagram for question 4

5 In an isosceles triangle, the height from one of the base vertices to the side opposite it forms an angle of 35° at that vertex; the size of its top vertex angle is _____. (Note: In this question, the base vertices refer to the vertices in which the angles are equal.)

6 In the diagram, AD is the bisector of $\angle BAC$, $AE = AC$ and EF is parallel to BC and intersects AC at point F.

$\angle DEC = \angle$ _____ $= \angle$ _____.

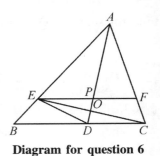

Diagram for question 6

C. Questions that require solutions

7 In the diagram, $AD \parallel BC$, M is the midpoint of BC and $MA = MD$. Prove that $\triangle ABM \cong \triangle DCM$.

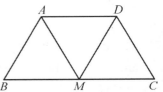

Diagram for question 7

8 In the diagram, $\triangle ABC$ is an equilateral triangle and D is the midpoint of AC. BC is extended beyond C to E so that $CE = CD$. The lines BD and DE are drawn.

(a) Find $\angle E$.

(b) Prove that $DB = DE$.

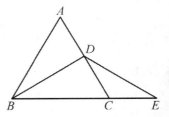

Diagram for question 8

9 As shown in the diagram, $AC = 2AB$ and D is the midpoint of AC. E is the midpoint of AD, point F is on the extension of BE beyond E, and $BE = EF$.

Prove that $BC = 2EF$ and $\angle F = \angle C$.

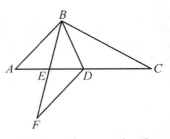

Diagram for question 9

178

7.6   Practice and exercise in proof[*](4)

Learning objective

Find missing angles and construct simple proofs and chains of deductive reasoning using angle facts, lengths and midpoints

A. Multiple choice questions

1 As shown in the diagram, $\angle ABC = 36°$, $DE \parallel BC$ and $DF \perp AB$ at F. Then $\angle D$ is (   ).

A. $36°$

B. $54°$

C. $45°$

D. not fixed

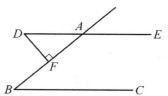

Diagram for question 1

2 In $\triangle ABC$, $AD \perp BC$ at D and $BE \perp AC$ at E. AD intersects BE at F. If $BF = AC$, then $\angle ABC$ equals (   ).

A. $45°$

B. $48°$

C. $50°$

D. $60°$

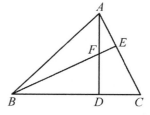

Diagram for question 2

B. Fill in the blanks

3 In the statement, 'two angles supplementary to the same angle are equal', the given is _____ and the conclusion is _____.

4 In the diagram, $AB \parallel EF \parallel CD$, $\angle B = \alpha$ and $\angle D = \beta$. Then $\angle BED$ is _____.

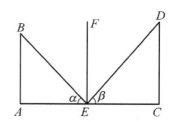

Diagram for question 4

---

* This unit includes several more challenging questions; you are encouraged to discuss them with your friends or ask your teacher for help in solving them.

5 If in an isosceles triangle, the included angle formed between the height on one of its two equal sides and the other equal side is 40°, then three interior angles are

_____ .

6 In the diagram, △ABC is rotated 40° clockwise around point C so its image is △A′B′C, and AC ⊥ A′B′. Then ∠BAC = _____°.

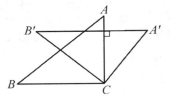

Diagram for question 6

 ## C. Questions that require solutions

7 In the diagram, AB is parallel to MN and intersects EF at C and MN intersects EF at D; the angle bisectors of ∠BCD and ∠CDN intersect at point G. Prove that CG ⊥ DG.

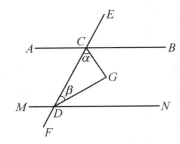

Diagram for question 7

8 In the diagram, AB // CD, α = ∠B and β = ∠D. Prove that BE ⊥ DE.

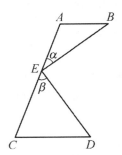

Diagram for question 8

9 In the diagram, $AB = AC$, $\alpha = \beta$ and $BE = CF$. M is the midpoint of EH.
Prove that $FM \perp EH$.

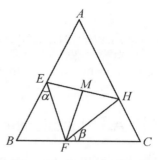

Diagram for question 9

10 In the diagram, BE and CF are the heights of $\triangle ABC$. $BP = AC$ and $CQ = AB$.
Prove that $AP \perp AQ$.

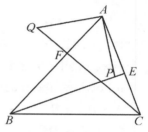

Diagram for question 10

7.7 Perpendicular bisector of a line segment

Construct and solve problems involving perpendicular bisectors

A. Multiple choice questions

1 In the diagram, CD is the perpendicular bisector of the line segment AB and point P is on line CD. Given that the length of segment $PA = 5$, then the length of segment $PB = ($ $)$.

A. 6   B. 5

C. 4   D. 3

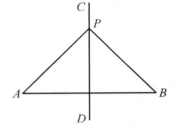

Diagram for question 1

2 In $\triangle ABC$, $\angle C = 90°$ and $\angle B = 30°$. DE is the perpendicular bisector of AB and intersects AB at D and BC at E. Of the following, the incorrect conclusion is ($\quad$).

A. $AE = BE$ B. $AC = BE$

C. $CE = DE$ D. $\angle CAE = \angle B$

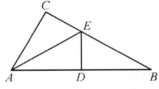

Diagram for question 2

3 The diagram shows an isosceles triangle ABC in which $AB = AC$ and $\angle A = 20°$. The perpendicular bisector of the segment AB intersects AB at D and AC at E. $\angle CBE$ is ($\quad$).

A. 80°

B. 70°

C. 60°

D. 50°

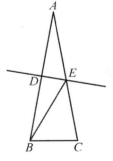

Diagram for question 3

4 In $\triangle ABC$, $AB = AC$ and $\angle A = 36°$. DE is the perpendicular bisector of AB, intersecting AC at D and AB at E. One of the following conclusions is incorrect. The incorrect conclusion is ($\quad$).

A. BD bisects $\angle ABC$.

B. The perimeter of $\triangle BCD$ equals $AB + BC$.

C. $AD = BD = BC$.

D. Point D is the midpoint of line segment AC.

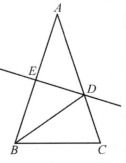

Diagram for question 4

B. Fill in the blanks

5 It is _____ that a point on the perpendicular bisector of a line segment is equidistant from the endpoints of the segment. (Write 'true' or 'false'.)

(Note: The converse of the above statement is also true: a point that is equidistant from the endpoints of a line segment is on the perpendicular bisector of the segment.)

6 The diagram shows $\triangle ABC$ with $\angle C = 90°$. The perpendicular bisector of AB intersects AB at D and AC at E. Given that $\angle CBE = 40°$, then $\angle A = $ _____°.

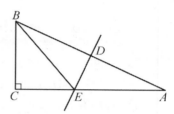

Diagram for question 6

7 The diagram shows isosceles triangle ABC, in which $AB = AC$ and $\angle A = 30°$. The perpendicular bisector of AB intersects AC at D, so $\angle CBD$ is _____°.

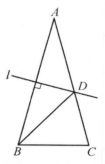

Diagram for question 7

8 The diagram shows $\triangle ABC$, in which DE is the perpendicular bisector of AC, intersecting AB at E, $\angle A = 30°$ and $\angle ACB = 80°$. Then $\angle BCE = $ _____°.

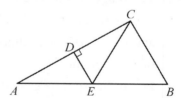

Diagram for question 8

9 In $\triangle ABC$, $AB = 5$ cm and $AC = 3$ cm. The perpendicular bisector of BC intersects AB and BC at D and E. The perimeter of $\triangle ACD = $ _____ cm.

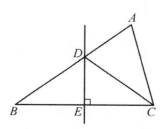

Diagram for question 9

10 In isosceles triangle ABC, $AB = AC$, and MN is the perpendicular bisector of AB, intersecting AC at point D. If $\angle ABD = 40°$, then $\angle ABC = $ _____°. If $AB = 8$ cm and the perimeter of $\triangle BDC$ is 20 cm, then $BC = $ _____ cm.

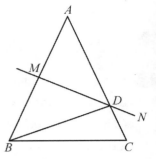

Diagram for question 10

C. Questions that require solutions

11 The diagram shows a right-angled triangle ABC with $\angle C = 90°$. AD is the bisector of $\angle CAB$ and intersects BC at D. If the perpendicular bisector of DE bisects AB, find the size of $\angle B$.

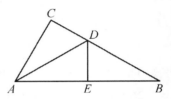

Diagram for question 11

12 The diagram shows a quadrilateral $ABCD$, $AD \mathbin{/\mkern-5mu/} BC$ and E is the midpoint of CD. The line segments AE and BE are drawn, and $BE \perp AE$. AE extended beyond E intersects the extension of BC at point F.
Prove that: (a) $FC = AD$ (b) $AB = BC + AD$.

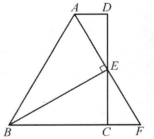

Diagram for question 12

7.8   Angle bisectors (1)

Learning objective

Construct and solve problems involving angle bisectors

A. Multiple choice questions

1 If point P is taken on a line segment CD so that P is equidistant from the sides of $\angle AOB$, then point P is (   ).

A. the midpoint of the segment CD

B. the intersection point of the perpendicular bisectors of OA and OB

C. the intersection point of the perpendicular bisectors of OA and CD

D. the intersection point of the segment CD and the bisector of $\angle AOB$

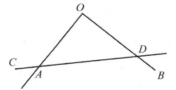

Diagram for question 1

2 In the diagram, P is a point on AD, which is the bisector of $\angle BAC$. $PE \perp AC$ at E and $PE = 3$. The distance from point P to AB is (   ).

A. 3   B. 4   C. 5   D. 6

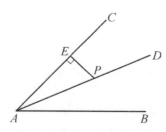

Diagram for question 2

3 In $\triangle ABC$, $AB = AC$. The bisector of $\angle ABC$ and AC intersect at point D. If $\angle BDC = 75°$, then $\angle A = ($ $)$.

A. 20°   B. 30°   C. 40°   D. 50°

Introduction to proof in geometry

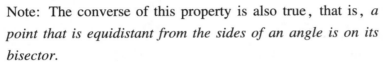

B. Fill in the blanks

4 Look at the diagram, and complete the proof for the property of angle bisectors.

Property: *A point on the bisector of an angle is equidistant from the sides of the angle.*

Proof: Since $\alpha = \beta$, $PE \perp OA$, $PF \perp OB$ and $OP = OP$ (given)

$\triangle OPE \cong \triangle$ _____ (   )

therefore $PE =$ _____ (   )

Note: The converse of this property is also true, that is, *a point that is equidistant from the sides of an angle is on its bisector.*

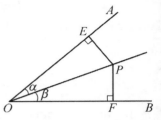

Diagram for question 4

5 In $\triangle ABC$, $\angle C = 90°$. AD is the bisector of $\angle BAC$. $BC = 10$ cm and $BD = 6$ cm. Then the distance from point D to AB is _____ cm.

6 The diagram shows right-angled $\triangle ABC$ with $\angle C = 90°$. BD bisects $\angle ABC$ and $DE \perp AB$ at point E.

(a) If $AE = 4$ cm and $AC = 8$ cm, the perimeter of $\triangle AED$ is _____ cm.

(b) If $AB = 10$ cm and $BC = 6$ cm, then $AE =$ _____ cm.

(c) If $AB = 10$ cm, $BC = 6$ cm and $AC = 8$ cm, the perimeter of $\triangle AED$ is _____ cm.

(d) If $\angle A = 10°$, $\angle ABD =$ _____ °.

(e) If $\angle DBC = 10°$, $\angle A =$ _____ °.

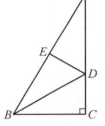

Diagram for Question 6

C. Questions that require solutions

7 In the diagram, AD bisects $\angle BAC$, $DB \perp AB$ at point B and $DC \perp AC$ at point C. Prove that point D is on the line of the perpendicular bisector of BC.

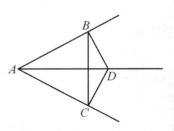

Diagram for question 7

186

8 In the diagram, $BF \perp AC$ at F and $CE \perp AB$ at E. AD is the bisector of $\angle BAC$. Prove that $BD = CD$.

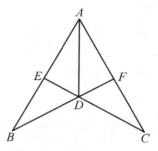

Diagram for question 8

9 In the diagram, BE and CE are the bisectors of the two exterior angles of $\triangle ABC$. $EP \perp AM$ at P and $EQ \perp AN$ at Q. Prove that: (a) $EP = EQ$ (b) Point E is on the bisector of $\angle NAM$.

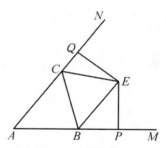

Diagram for question 9

7.9　Angle bisectors (2)

Learning objective

Construct and solve problems involving angle bisectors

A. Multiple choice questions

1 The point that is equidistant from the three vertices of a triangle is (　　).

   A. the point of intersection of the three angle bisectors

   B. the point of intersection of the three medians (Note: A median of a triangle is the line segment connecting a vertex to the midpoint of its opposite side.)

   C. the point of intersection of the three heights

   D. the point of intersection of the perpendicular bisectors of the three sides

2 The point that is equidistant to the three sides of a triangle is (　　).

   A. the point of intersection of the three angle bisectors

   B. the point of intersection of the three medians

   C. the point of intersection of the three heights

   D. the point of intersection of the perpendicular bisectors of three sides

3 The diagram shows $\triangle ABC$, $\angle C = 90°$ and $AC = BC$. AD bisects $\angle CAB$ and intersects BC at point D. $DE \perp AB$ at E and $AB = 6$ cm. The perimeter of $\triangle DEB$ is (　　).

   A.　4 cm

   B.　6 cm

   C.　10 cm

   D.　None of the above

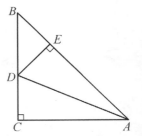

Diagram for question 3

4 In $\triangle ABC$, the lengths of the three sides AB, BC and CA are 20, 30 and 40 respectively. Three angle bisectors intersect at point O, dividing $\triangle ABC$ into three triangles. The ratio of the areas, $S_{\triangle ABO} : S_{\triangle BCO} : S_{\triangle CAO}$, = (　　).

   A. $1 : 1 : 1$ B. $1 : 2 : 3$

   C. $2 : 3 : 4$ D. $3 : 4 : 5$

B. Fill in the blanks

5 The diagram shows $\triangle ABC$ with $\angle C = 90°$. AD bisects $\angle CAB$, $BC = 10$ and $BD = 7$. The distance from point D to AB is _____.

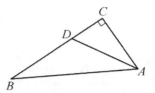

Diagram for question 5

6 In the diagram, AP and BP bisect $\angle DAB$ and $\angle CBA$ respectively. PE and PF are perpendicular to AD and BC, intersecting at E and F. If $AE = 1$ cm, $BF = 3$ cm and $EP = 2$ cm, then $S_{\triangle APB} =$ _____ cm^2.

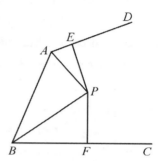

Diagram for question 6

C. Questions that require solutions

7 The diagram shows right-angled $\triangle ABC$ with $\angle ACB = 90°$. AD bisects $\angle BAC$ and $DE \perp AB$ at point E. Point F is on AC and $EF \parallel BC$.

Prove that EC bisects $\angle FED$.

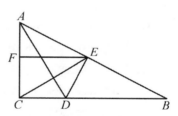

Diagram for question 7

8 In the diagram, OP bisects $\angle MON$. $PA \perp OM$ at point A and $PB \perp ON$ at point B. C is a point on OP. $CE \perp PA$ at E and $CF \perp PB$ at F.

Prove that $CE = CF$.

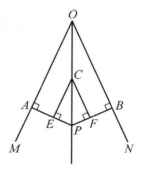

Diagram for question 8

Unit test 7

1 Read these statements. The correct statement is (   ).

A. A quadrilateral must be a square or a rectangle, or a trapezium.

B. A rectangle is also a square.

C. An equilateral triangle is also an isosceles triangle.

D. A right-angled triangle cannot be an isosceles triangle.

2 A point that is equidistant from the three sides of a triangle is (   ).

A. the point of intersection of the three medians

B. the point of intersection of the three angle bisectors

C. the point of intersection of the three heights

D. the point of intersection of the perpendicular bisectors of the three sides

3 Of the following statements, (   ) are true.

① If the two angles in a triangle are equal, then their corresponding sides are equal.

② If two lines are parallel, then their alternate interior angles are equal.

③ Two triangles are congruent if two sides and one angle in one triangle are equal to the corresponding sides and angle in the other triangle.

④ When two lines are crossed by a third line, the interior angles on the same side are supplementary to each other.

A. 1   B. 2   C. 3   D. 4

4 In this obtuse-angled $\triangle ABC$, BA is extended to D, AE is the bisector of $\angle DAC$ and $AE \parallel BC$. Then there are (   ) angles equal to $\angle B$.

A. 1   B. 2   C. 3   D. 4

Diagram for question 4

5 Rewrite the statement, 'Vertically opposite angles are equal,' in the form: 'if . . . , then . . .'. _____

190

6 If an exterior angle of an isosceles triangle is $100°$, the two equal angles of the triangle are each _____.

7 In $\triangle ABC$, $AB = AC$ and $\angle A = 120°$. MN is the perpendicular bisector of AB, with M being the foot of the perpendicular and N the point of intersection of MN and BC. $BN = 3$. Then $AN = $ _____ and $\angle NAC = $ _____.

8 The diagram shows $\triangle ABC$, with $AB = AC = 12$ cm. The bisectors of $\angle ABC$ and $\angle ACB$ intersect at point O. DE passes through point O and $DE \parallel BC$. The perimeter of $\triangle ADE$ is _____ cm.

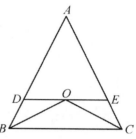

Diagram for question 8

9 The diagram shows $\triangle ABC$ with $AB = AC$.
The perpendicular bisector MN of AB intersects AC at D.
If $BC = 9$ cm and the perimeter of $\triangle BDC$ is 21 cm,
$AB = $ _____ cm.

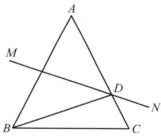

Diagram for question 9

10 In an isosceles triangle, the included angle formed between the height on one of the equal sides and the base is $20°$. Then the third angle (between the equal sides) of the isosceles triangle is _____ $°$.

C. Questions that require solutions

11 Prove that when two parallel lines are crossed by a third line, the bisectors of the two interior angles on the same side are perpendicular to each other.
(Note: Look at the diagram provided, write down what is given and what you are asked to prove, and then complete the proof.)

Given:

Prove:

Proof:

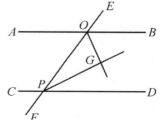

Diagram for question 11

12 In the diagram, $\angle A = \angle D$, $\angle B = \angle E$ and $BF = CE$. Prove that $AC = DF$.

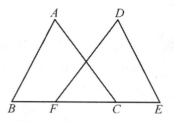

Diagram for question 12

13 In the diagram, $BD = CD$ and $\angle B = \angle C$. Prove that $AC = AB$. (Hint: Join AD.)

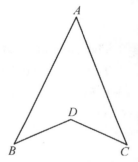

Diagram for question 13

14 The diagram shows $\triangle ABC$ with $\angle C = 120°$. DE is the perpendicular bisector of AC and intersects AC and AB at points D and point E respectively.

(a) Construct DE as the perpendicular bisector of AC.

(b) Given that $AE = BC$, find $\angle A$.

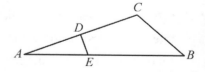

Diagram for question 14

Chapter 8　Right-angled triangles and Pythagoras' theorem

8.1　Congruence testing for right-angled triangles

Learning objective

Know and use the criteria for congruence of triangles

A. Multiple choice questions

1　A right-angled triangle has (　　).

A.　three acute angles

B.　two acute angles and one obtuse angle

C.　one acute angle, one right angle and one obtuse angle

D.　one right angle and two acute angles

2　The following list includes (　　) correct statements.

① Two right-angled triangles are congruent if two pairs of corresponding sides are equal.

② Two right-angled isosceles triangles are congruent if one pair of corresponding non-hypotenuse sides are equal.

③ Two right-angled triangles are congruent if one pair of corresponding acute angles and one pair of corresponding sides are equal.

④ Two right-angled triangles are congruent if two pairs of corresponding acute angles are equal.

A.　1

B.　2

C.　3

D.　4

3　The condition for the congruence of two right-angled triangles is (　　).

A.　One pair of corresponding acute angles are equal.

B.　Two pairs of corresponding acute angles are equal.

C.　Two pairs of corresponding sides are equal.

D.　Two pairs of the non-hypotenuse sides are equal.

4 Of the following, statement (   ) is false.

A. Two right-angled triangles are congruent if the hypotenuses and one pair of corresponding acute angles are equal.

B. Two right-angled isosceles triangles are congruent if one pair of corresponding non-hypotenuse sides are equal.

C. Two triangles must be congruent if two pairs of corresponding sides and one pair of corresponding angles (each opposite to one of the corresponding sides) are equal.

D. Two right-angled isosceles triangles are congruent if the two hypotenuses are equal.

B. Fill in the blanks

5 If the _____ and _____ of one right-angled triangle are equal to the _____ and _____

_____ of another right-angled triangle, then the two right-angled triangles are congruent. (This is abbreviated as _____.)

6 The diagram shows two right-angled triangles, $\triangle ABC$ and $\triangle DEF$, with $\angle C = \angle F = 90°$.

(a) If $\angle A = \angle D$ and $BC = EF$, then $\triangle ABC \cong \triangle DEF$.
   Reason: _____.

(b) If $\angle A = \angle D$ and $AC = DF$, then $\triangle ABC \cong \triangle DEF$.
   Reason: _____

(c) If $AC = DF$ and $AB = DE$, then $\triangle ABC \cong \triangle DEF$.
   Reason: _____

(d) If $AC = DF$ and $CB = FE$, then $\triangle ABC \cong \triangle DEF$.
   Reason: _____.

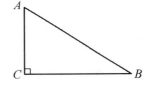

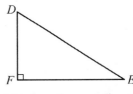

Diagram for question 6

C. Questions that require solutions

7 In the diagram, $AC \perp BC$ and $AD \perp BD$. $AC = AD$. AB intersects CD at E. Prove that $CE = DE$.

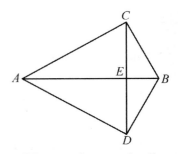

Diagram for question 7

8 In the diagram, $AE \perp BD$ and $CF \perp BD$. $AD = BC$ and $BE = DF$. AC intersects BD at G.

Prove that $AG = CG$.

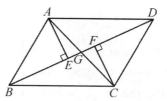

Diagram for question 8

9 The diagram shows $\triangle ABC$, in which the bisector of $\angle ABC$ intersects the perpendicular bisector of AC at N. $ND \perp AB$ at D and $NE \perp BC$ at E.

Prove that $AD = CE$. (Hint: Join AN and CN.)

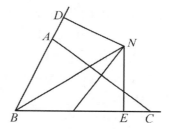

Diagram for question 9

10 (a) In Figure (1), the points A, E, F and C are on a line and $AE = CF$. $DE \perp AC$ and $BF \perp AC$. Given that $AB = CD$, explain why BD bisects EF.

(b) The side EC of $\triangle DEC$ is moved in the direction of AC, to produce Figure (2). Given that the other conditions remain unchanged, is the conclusion from part (a) still true? Give reasons.

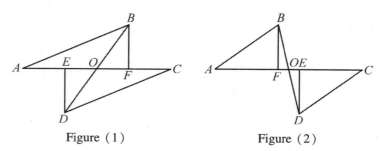

Figure (1)   Figure (2)

Diagram for question 10

8.2 Properties of right-angled triangles (1)

Learning objective

Construct simple chains of deductive reasoning to prove angle facts using medians, midpoints and the properties of right-angled triangles

A. Multiple choice questions

1 Of the following statements, (　　) of them is (are) correct. (Note: A median is the segment joining the midpoint of one side to the vertex opposite that side.)

① The two acute angles in a right-angled triangle are equal.

② The median on one side of a right-angled triangle is half the length of the side.

③ The median on the hypotenuse of a right-angled triangle divides the triangle into two parts of equal area.

④ The perpendicular height (or simply the height) on the hypotenuse of a right-angled triangle equals half the length of the hypotenuse.

A. 1　　　　　　　　　　　　　　　B. 2

C. 3　　　　　　　　　　　　　　　D. 4

2 In the diagram, $\triangle ABC$ is a right-angled triangle and $\angle C = 90°$. CD is the median on AB and CE is the height from C to AB.

Of the following statements, (　　) is incorrect.

A. $\angle B = \gamma$

B. $\alpha = \gamma$

C. $\beta = \gamma$

D. $\angle A + \gamma = 90°$

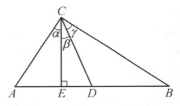

Diagram for question 2

B. Fill in the blanks

3 In Rt $\triangle ABC$, given that $\angle C = 90°$ and $\angle A - \angle B = 40°$, then $\angle A = $ _____° and $\angle B = $ _____°.

4 In a right-angled triangle, the bisectors of two acute angles intersect at a point forming an acute angle. The size of the acute angle is _____°.

5 The area of a right-angled triangle is 6. If the height based on its hypotenuse is 3, then the length of the median on the hypotenuse is _____.

6 The diagram shows $\triangle ABC$ with $\angle C = 90°$ and $CD \perp AB$. Point E is the midpoint of AB and $\angle ACD = 35°$. Then $\angle ECD =$ _____°.

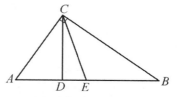

Diagram for question 6

7 The diagram shows $\triangle ABC$, in which $\angle ACB = 90°$, $\angle BAC = 35°$ and $\angle ACD = \angle B$. E is the midpoint of AC. Then $\angle EDB =$ _____°.

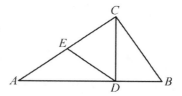

Diagram for question 7

C. Questions that require solutions

8 The diagram shows $\triangle ABC$, in which $CD \perp AB$, $BD = CD$ and $DE = DA$. M and N are the midpoints of BE and AC. Prove that $DM = DN$.

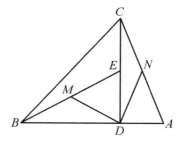

Diagram for question 8

9 The diagram shows $\triangle ABC$, in which AD is the height and CE is the median on the side AB. $DG \perp CE$ at G and $2CD = AB$.

Prove that: (a) G is the midpoint of CE

(b) $\angle B = 2\angle BCE$. (Hint: Join DE.)

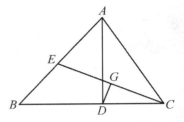

Diagram for question 9

10 In $\triangle ABC$ and $\triangle ADC$, $\angle ABC = \angle ADC = 90°$ and E is the midpoint of AC.

(a) For Figure 1, prove that $\angle DEB = 2\angle DCB$.

(b) Now look at Figure 2. Is the statement in part (a) still true? If it is, provide a proof for it. If it is not, give your reasons.

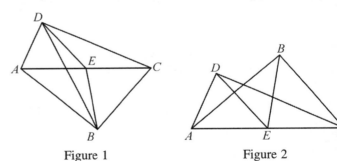

Figure 1   Figure 2

Diagram for question 10

8.3   Properties of right-angled triangles (2)

Learning objectives

Use medians, mid-points and right-angled triangle properties to prove angle facts and find missing angles and side lengths in triangles and compound shapes
Know that the perpendicular distance from a given point to a line is the shortest distance to a line

A. Multiple choice questions

1. If a right-angled triangle has an acute angle of $30°$, then the length of its opposite side is equal to the length of (   ).

A. the hypotenuse

B. the perpendicular height on the hypotenuse

C. the median on the hypotenuse

D. the other non-hypotenuse side

2. The diagram shows $\triangle ABC$, with $\angle A = 60°$ and $\angle C = 90°$. $CD \perp AB$ at D. Of the following conclusions, (   ) is incorrect.

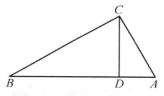

Diagram for question 2

A. $CD = \frac{1}{2}CB$

B. $AC = \frac{1}{2}AB$

C. $AD = \frac{1}{2}AC$

D. $DB = \frac{1}{2}BC$

3. The diagram shows triangle ABC, in which $\angle ACB = 90°$ and $CD \perp AB$. M is the midpoint of AB. Given that $CM = 2CD$, then conclusion (   ) is incorrect.

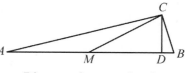

Diagram for question 3

A. $\angle ACM = 15°$

B. $\angle BCD = 15°$

C. $\angle A = 30°$

D. $\angle BCM = 75°$

B. Fill in the blanks

4. In a triangle, the ratio of the sizes of its three angles is $1 : 2 : 3$. Given the length of its longest side is 20, the length of its shortest side is _____.

5 In $\triangle ABC$, $\angle C = 90°$, D is on BC and $AD = 2CD$. $\angle ADB$ is _____°.

6 The diagram shows $\triangle ABC$, in which $\angle C = 90°$ and $\angle B = 15°$. The perpendicular bisector of AB intersects BC at point D and AB at point E. If $DB = 10$ cm, then $AC = $ _____ cm. Given that the perimeter of $\triangle ACD$ is 50 cm, then $AC + BC = $ _____ cm.

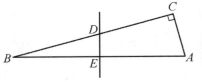

Diagram for question 6

7 The diagram shows equilateral triangle $\triangle ABC$. $AD \parallel BC$ and $CD \perp BC$ at C, intersecting AD at D. If $AD = 10$, the perimeter of $\triangle ABC$ is _____.

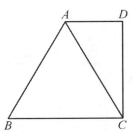

Diagram for question 7

8 In the diagram, OF bisects $\angle AOB$, $FC \parallel OB$ intersecting OA at C, and $FD \perp OB$. Given that $\angle AOB = 30°$ and $FD = 3$, then the length of OC is _____.

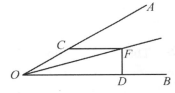

Diagram for question 8

C. Questions that require solutions

9 The diagram shows $\triangle ABC$, in which $\angle CAB = 90°$ and $AD \perp BC$. AE is the median on BC and $4AD = BC$. Find the size of $\angle C$.

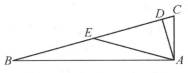

Diagram for question 9

10 In the diagram, $\angle A = 60°$, $BD \perp AC$ and $CE \perp AB$. BD intersects CE at point F. Given that $FD = 2$ cm and $FE = 4$ cm, find the lengths of BD and CE.

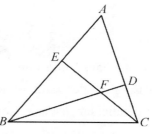

Diagram for question 10

11 In the diagram, AD is the bisector of $\angle BAC$. $\angle C = \frac{1}{2}\angle BAC$ and $AC = 2AB$.

Prove that: (a) $\angle B = 90°$ (b) $AD = 2BD$.

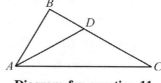

Diagram for question 11

8.4   Properties of right-angled triangles (3)

Learning objectives

Use medians, mid-points and right-angled triangle properties to prove angle facts and find missing angles and side lengths in triangles and compound shapes; know that the perpendicular distance from a given point to a line is the shortest distance to a line

A. Multiple choice questions

1 The number of heights in a right-angled triangle is (   ).

   A. 3   B. 2

   C. 1   D. 0

2 The diagram shows $\triangle ABC$, in which $\angle A = 60°$ and $\angle C = 90°$.

   Given that $CD \perp AB$ at D, then the ratio $AD : BD$ is equivalent to (   ).

   A. $\dfrac{1}{2}$ B. $\dfrac{1}{3}$

   C. $\dfrac{1}{4}$ D. $\dfrac{1}{5}$

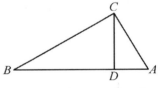

Diagram for question 2

B. Fill in the blanks

3 The diagram shows a set square with an angle of 30° rotated 90° clockwise around vertex C. The images of points A and B are A_1 and B_1 respectively. A line AA_1 is drawn. $\angle A_1AB$ is _____°.

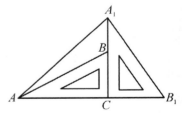

Diagram for question 3

4 The diagram shows $\triangle ABC$, in which $\angle C = 90°$ and $\angle A = 30°$. BD is the angle bisector and $AC = 3$. AD is _____.

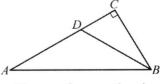

Diagram for question 4

5 The diagram shows $\triangle ABC$, in which $AB = AC$, $AD \perp BC$ at D and $DE \perp AB$ at E. If $AD = \frac{1}{2}AC$ and $AD = 8$, then $BE = $ _____.

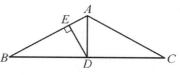

Diagram for question 5

6 The non-equal angle of an isosceles triangle is $30°$. If the length of the two equal sides is 5, then the height on one of the equal sides is _____.

7 If the height on one of the two equal sides in an isosceles triangle is half the length of the side, then the size of the non-equal angle of the isosceles triangle is _____ °.

C. Questions that require solutions

8 The diagram shows $\triangle ABC$, in which $\angle ACB = 90°$. D is a point on AC. $DE \perp AB$ with E being the foot of the perpendicular. M and N are the midpoints of BD and CE respectively.

Prove that $MN \perp CE$. (Hint: Join EM and CM.)

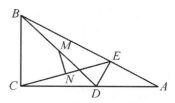

Diagram for question 8

9 The diagram shows $\triangle ABC$, in which $AC = BC$ and $AE \perp BC$ at E. F is the midpoint of AC and $FE = AE$. Find the size of $\angle BAE$.

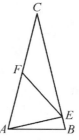

Diagram for question 9

10 The diagram shows $\triangle ABC$, in which $AB = AC$ and $\angle A = 120°$. E is the midpoint of BC and $DE \perp AC$ at D.

Prove that $DC = 3AD$.

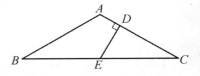

Diagram for question 10

11 In the diagram, $\triangle ABC$ is an equaliteral triangle, $BE = CD$, $EH \perp AD$ at H and $DG \mathbin{/\!/} EH$ intersecting CE at G.

Prove that $EG = 2HD$.

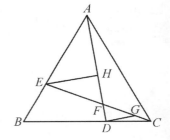

Diagram for question 11

8.5 Pythagoras' theorem

Learning objective

Apply Pythagoras' theorem to find missing lengths in right-angled triangles

A. Multiple choice questions

1 Given that the two non-hypotenuse sides of a right-angled triangle are 6 and 8, then its hypotenuse is (   ).

A. 6   B. 8   C. 10   D. 100

2 The two non-hypotenuse sides of a right-angled triangle are 5 and 12 respectively. Then the length of the median on the hypotenuse is (   ).

A. 6   B. 6.5   C. 10   D. 13

3 The diagram shows $\triangle ABC$, in which $\angle C = 90°$ and $\angle A = 30°$. BD is the median on AC and $BC = 1$. Then conclusion (   ) is incorrect.

A. $AB = 2$

B. $AC = \sqrt{3}$

C. $CD = \dfrac{1}{2}\sqrt{3}$

D. $BD = \sqrt{3}$

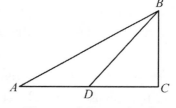

Diagram for question 3

4 The diagram shows $\triangle ABC$ with $\angle C = 90°$, $BC = 3$ and $AC = 4$. CD is the height from C to AB. Of the following, the incorrect conclusion is (   ).

A. $AB = 5$

B. $CD = \dfrac{12}{5}$

C. $AD = \dfrac{9}{5}$

D. $BD = \dfrac{9}{5}$

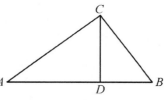

Diagram for question 4

B. Fill in the blanks

5 The diagram shows $\triangle ABC$ with $\angle C = 90°$.

(a) If $a = 12$ and $b = 16$, then $c =$ _____.

(b) If $a = 7$ and $c = 25$, then $b =$ _____.

(c) If $b = 40$ and $c = 41$, then $a =$ _____.

(d) If $a = \sqrt{7}$ and $c = 4$, then $b =$ _____.

(e) If $c = 15$ and $a : b = 3 : 4$, then $a =$ _____, $b =$ _____.

(f) If $\angle A = 30°$ and $BC = 6$, then $AB =$ _____, $AC =$ _____.

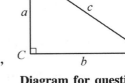

Diagram for question 5

6 In $\triangle ABC$, if $\angle A : \angle B : \angle C = 1 : 1 : 2$, then $BC : AC : AB =$ _____.

7 In $\triangle ABC$, if $\angle A : \angle B : \angle C = 1 : 2 : 3$, then $BC : AC : AB =$ _____.

8 The lengths of the two shorter sides of a right-angled triangle are 3 and 4 respectively. Then the length of the median on the hypotenuse is _____.

9 The perimeter of a right-angled triangle is 24 and the length of the median on the hypotenuse is 5. The area of the triangle is _____.

C. Questions that require solutions

10 The diagram shows $\triangle ABC$, in which $AB = AC$ and AD is the height from A to BC. $AB = 8$ and $BC = 10$. Find the area of $\triangle ABC$.

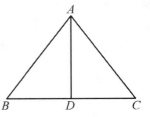

Diagram for question 10

11 In $\triangle ABC$, $\angle C = 90°$, D is a point on BC and $AB = 10$. $\angle B = 60°$ and $BD : DC = 2 : 3$. Find the lengths of AC and AD.

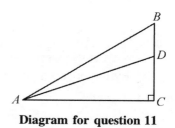

Diagram for question 11

12 The diagram shows $\triangle ABC$ with $\angle C = 90°$ and $AC = BC$. AD bisects $\angle BAC$, $DE \perp AB$ at E and $EF \perp AC$ at F.
Prove that $AC^2 = 2EF^2$.

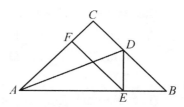

Diagram for question 12

8.6 Applications of Pythagoras' theorem

Learning objective

Apply Pythagoras' theorem to contextual problems to find missing lengths in right-angled triangles

A. Multiple choice questions

1 If the two non-hypotenuse sides of a right-angled triangle are $n^2 - 1$ and $2n\,(n > 1)$, then the length of the hypotenuse is (　　).

A. $2n$　　　　　　B. $n + 1$　　　　　　C. $n^2 - 1$　　　　　　D. $n^2 + 1$

2 The diagram shows a piece of paper in the shape of a right-angled triangle, with two non-hypotenuse sides $AC = 6$ cm and $BC = 8$ cm. It is folded to bring AC along AD, so that the image of AC is AE on the hypotenuse AB. CD is (　　).

A. 2 cm　　　　　　B. 3 cm

C. 4 cm　　　　　　D. 5 cm

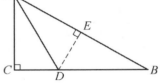

Diagram for question 2

3 The diagram shows $\triangle ABC$, in which $AB = AC$ and $\angle BAC = 120°$. DE is a perpendicular bisector of AC. If $DE = 2$, then conclusion (　　) is incorrect.

A. $BC = 12$　　　　B. $AB = 2\sqrt{3}$

C. $BD = 8$　　　　　D. $AE = 2\sqrt{3}$

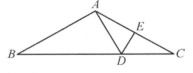

Diagram for question 3

B. Fill in the blanks

4 Given the non-equal angle of an isosceles triangle is 120° and the length of the two equal sides is 10 cm, its base is _____ cm long.

5 Given that an equilateral triangle has a side length of a, its area is _____.

6 Given the median on the hypotenuse of a right-angled triangle is 10 and the difference between the lengths of the two non-hypotenuse sides is 4, then the length of the shorter non-hypotenuse side is _____.

7 The diagram shows $\triangle ABC$, in which $AB = AC = 10$ and $BC = 8\sqrt{5}$. AD is the height from A to the base and CE is the height from C to AB (produced).
Then $AD =$ _____ and $CE =$ _____ .

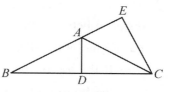

Diagram for question 7

8 In an isosceles triangle, the lengths of two sides are 5 and 6 respectively. Its height on the base is _____ .

C. Questions that require solutions

9 The diagram shows rectangle $ABCD$, in which $AB = 3$ and $AD = 9$. The rectangle is folded along EF, so that point A coincides with point C. Find the length of EC.

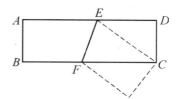

Diagram for question 9

10 The diagram shows quadrilateral $ABCD$, in which $\angle ABC = 90°$ and $\angle BCD = 120°$. $AB = 1$, $BC = \sqrt{3}$ and $CD = 2$. Find the length of AD.

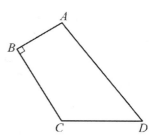

Diagram for question 10

11 The diagram shows a ladder, AB, leaning against a wall. The ladder is 25 m long. The distance between the base, O, of the wall and B, the bottom of the ladder, is 7 m.

(a) What is the distance between the top of the ladder and the ground?

(b) If the top of the ladder slides down the wall by 4 m, to A', how many metres does the bottom of the ladder slide away from the wall, along the ground, to B'?

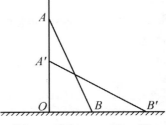

Diagram for question 11

8.7 The converse of Pythagoras' theorem

Learning objectives

Derive Pythagorean triples; rearrange the formula for Pythagoras' theorem to find missing lengths in right-angled triangles

A. Multiple choice questions

1 Of the following groups of numbers, (   ) of them are Pythagorean triples (satisfying $a^2 + b^2 = c^2$).

① 1.5, 2.5, 2 ② $\sqrt{2}$, $\sqrt{2}$, 2 ③ 12, 16, 20 ④ 0, 1.2, 1.3

A. 1   B. 2   C. 3   D. 4

2 Of the following statements, (   ) are correct.

① If a, b and c form a Pythagorean triple, then $2a$, $2b$ and $2c$ also form a Pythagorean triple.

② If the two sides of a right-angled triangle are 3 and 4, then the hypotenuse must be 5.

③ If the three sides of a triangle are 12, 25 and 21, then the triangle must be a right-angled triangle.

④ The three sides of a right-angled isosceles triangle are a, b and c ($a > b$, $b = c$). Then $a^2 : b^2 : c^2 = 2 : 1 : 1$.

A. ① and ②   B. ① and ③

C. ① and ④   D. ② and ④

B. Fill in the blanks

3 In $\triangle ABC$, the lengths of the three sides are $8k$, $15k$ and $17k$ ($k > 0$) respectively. $\triangle ABC$ _____ a right-angled triangle. (Write 'is' or 'is not'.)

4 Given that the three sides of a triangle are $AB = 2$ cm, $BC = 2\sqrt{3}$ cm and $CA = 4$ cm, the area of the triangle is _____.

5 The diagram shows $\triangle ABC$, in which $BC = 7$, $AC = 24$ and $AB = 25$. If CD is the height from C to AB, then $CD =$ _____.

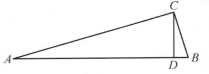

Diagram for question 5

C. Questions that require solutions

6 The diagram shows quadrilateral $ABCD$ with $\angle A = \angle BDC = 90°$, $AD = 8$, $AB = 6$ and $DC = 24$. Find the length of BC.

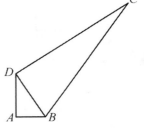

Diagram for question 6

7 The diagram shows a piece of land with $AD = 4$ m and $CD = 3$ m. $AD \perp DC$, $AB = 13$ m and $BC = 12$ cm. Find the area of the piece of land.

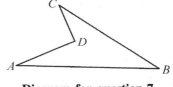

Diagram for question 7

8 * In the diagram, P is a point inside an equaliteral triangle ABC, $AP = 3$, $BP = 4$ and $CP = 5$. Find the size of $\angle BPA$. (Hint: Try to construct an auxiliary figure using the given conditions.)

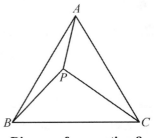

Diagram for question 8

* This is a challenging question. You might discuss it with your friends or your teacher.

8.8 Applications of Pythagoras' theorem and its converse theorem

Learning objective

Rearrange the formula for Pythagoras' theorem to find missing lengths in right-angled triangles in context

A. Multiple choice questions

1. Read these statements. The incorrect statement is (　　).

   A. If the ratio of the sizes of the three angles in a triangle is $2 : 3 : 5$, it is a right-angled triangle.

   B. If the ratio of the sizes of the three angles in a triangle is $3 : 4 : 5$, it is a right-angled triangle.

   C. If the ratio of the lengths of the three sides in a triangle is $3 : 4 : 5$, it is a right-angled triangle.

   D. If the ratio of the lengths of the three sides in a triangle is $1 : \sqrt{5} : 2$, it is a right-angled triangle.

2. The diagram shows $\triangle ABC$, with $\angle B = 90°$ and $\angle C = 30°$. $\triangle ABC$ is rotated $30°$ anticlockwise around point A to its image $\triangle AB'C'$. If $AB = 3$, the area of the overlap of the two triangles is (　　).

   A. $9\sqrt{3}$

   B. $\dfrac{9\sqrt{3}}{2}$

   C. $3\sqrt{3}$

   D. $\dfrac{3\sqrt{3}}{2}$

   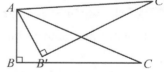

   Diagram for question 2

B. Fill in the blanks

3. A right-angled isosceles triangle has a hypotenuse of length 10 cm. Its area is _____ cm^2.

4. If the lengths of the three sides of a right-angled triangle are three consecutive even numbers, the height on the hypotenuse is _____.

5 If the lengths of the three sides of a right-angled triangle are 5, x and 12, then $x = $ _____ .

6 The diagram shows quadrilateral $ABCD$, $AD = 2\sqrt{2}$, $AB = $ 12, $BC = 13$, $CD = \sqrt{17}$ and $\angle ADC = 90°$. The area of the quadrilateral is _____ .

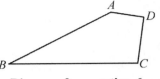

Diagram for question 6

C. Questions that require solutions

7 The diagram shows $\triangle ABC$, in which $CD \perp AB$ at D, $AC = 4$, $BC = 3$ and $BD = \dfrac{9}{5}$.

(a) Find the length of CD.
(b) Find the length of AD.
(c) Find the length of AB.
(d) Determine the shape of triangle $\triangle ABC$. Show your proof.

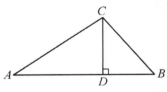

Diagram for Question 7

8 As shown in the diagram, the rectangle $ABCD$ is folded along AE so that point D is transformed onto point F on BC. $AB = 8$ and $AD = 10$. Find the length of EC.

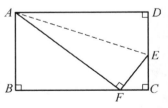

Diagram for question 8

9 * In the diagram, $\triangle ABC$ is a right-angled isosceles triangle and $\angle ACB = 90°$. A $45°$ angle with vertex C is rotated around C so that, when it falls inside $\triangle ABC$, the two sides of the angle intersect AB at E and F respectively. Prove that $EF^2 = AE^2 + BF^2$. (Hint: Try to construct an auxiliary right-angled triangle with side lengths equal to EF, AE and BF, and then apply Pythagoras' theorem)

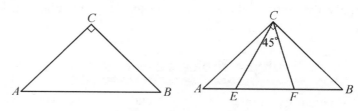

Diagram for question 9

---

* This is a challenging question. You might discuss it with your friends or your teacher.

8.9   The formula for distance between two points

Learning objective

Apply Pythagoras' theorem to find the perpendicular (shortest) distance between two points

A. Multiple choice questions

1 Given two points $A(x_1, y_1)$ and $B(x_2, y_2)$ on a co-ordinate plane, then according to Pythagoras' theorem, the correct formula for finding the distance, denoted as $|AB|$, between the two points is (   ).

A. $|AB| = (x_2 - x_1)^2 + (y_2 - y_1)^2$

B. $|AB| = \sqrt{(x_2 - x_1)^2 + (y_2 - y_1)^2}$

C. $|AB| = \sqrt{(x_2 + x_1)^2 + (y_2 + y_1)^2}$

D. $|AB| = \sqrt{(x_1 - y_1)^2 + (x_2 - y_2)^2}$

2 Given points $A(2, 3)$, $B(-1, -3)$ and $C(-3, -7)$ on a co-ordinate plane, the relation between the positions among the three points is (   ).

A. They are on the same line.

B. They are the vertices of a right-angled triangle.

C. They are the vertices of an equilateral triangle.

D. None of the above.

3 Given the distance between points $(1, 1)$ and $(-3, m)$ is $\sqrt{18}$, then the value of m is (   ).

A. $m = \pm\sqrt{2} - 1$ B. $m = \pm\sqrt{2} + 1$

C. $m = \pm\sqrt{14} + 1$ D. $m = \pm\sqrt{14} - 1$

4 Given the co-ordinates of two points are $A(2, -6)$ and $B(-4, 2)$ and point P is on the y-axis, if $PA = PB$, then the co-ordinates of point P are (   ).

A. $\left(0, -\dfrac{1}{4}\right)$ B. $\left(0, \dfrac{1}{4}\right)$

C. $\left(0, -\dfrac{3}{4}\right)$ D. $\left(0, -\dfrac{5}{4}\right)$

B. Fill in the blanks

5 Given the three vertices of $\triangle ABC$ are $A(-1, 0)$, $B(1, 0)$ and $C\left(\dfrac{1}{2}, \dfrac{\sqrt{3}}{2}\right)$, then $\triangle ABC$

is a _____ triangle.

6 Given the three vertices of $\triangle ABC$ are $A(-6, 8)$, $B(6, -8)$ and $C(8, 6)$, then $\triangle ABC$
is a _____ triangle.

7 Given the co-ordinates of two vertices of an equilateral triangle ABC are $A(-4, 0)$ and
$B(2, 0)$, then the co-ordinates of point C are _____.

8 Given point $A(-2, 3)$, $AB \parallel x$-axis, and the distance between A and B, $|AB|$, is 5.
Then the co-ordinates of point B are _____.

C. Questions that require solutions

9 Find the distance between two points $A(1, 2 + \sqrt{3})$ and $B(-1, -2 + \sqrt{3})$.

10 Given point $A(-1, 0)$, with point B on the graph of function $y = x$ and $|AB| = 5$, find
the co-ordinates of point B.

11 The three vertices of $\triangle ABC$ are $A(1, 4)$, $B(4, a)$ and $C(5, 5)$, and $|AC| = |BC|$. Find the co-ordinates of point B and the area of $\triangle ABC$.

12 Given points $A(2, 2)$ and $B(5, -2)$, and M being a point on the x-axis so that $\angle AMB$ is a right angle, find the co-ordinates of M.

13 Point P is on a co-ordinate plane and equidistant from the two axes. It is also equidistant from points $A(-1, 3)$ and $B(2, 4)$. Find the co-ordinates of point P.

Unit test 8

A. Multiple choice questions

1. The incorrect statement is (   ).

   A. A right-angled triangle must have one and only one right angle.

   B. An equilateral triangle cannot also be a right-angled triangle.

   C. A right-angled triangle can also be an isosceles triangle or a scalene triangle.

   D. If a triangle has three sides a, b and c with c being the longest side, then $c^2 = a^2 + b^2$.

2. If the lengths of two non-hypotenuse sides of a right-angled triangle are 3 cm and 10 cm, then the length of the hypotenuse is (   ).

   A. 13 cm   B. 109 cm   C. 109 cm^2 D. $\sqrt{109}$ cm

3. In $\triangle ABC$, the lengths of the three sides are 3, 3 and $3\sqrt{2}$. $\triangle ABC$ is not (   ).

   A. a right-angled triangle

   B. an isosceles triangle

   C. an equilateral triangle

   D. a right-angled isosceles triangle

4. Given the co-ordinates of two points are $A(0, -6)$ and $B(8, 0)$, then the distance between the two points is (   ).

   A. 6   B. 8   C. 10   D. 14

5. The diagram shows $\triangle ABC$ with $\angle ACB = 90°$. CD, CE and CF are the median, the height and the angle bisector on side AB respectively. Conclusion (   ) is incorrect.

   A. $\angle BCD = \angle ACE$

   B. $\angle DCF = \angle ECF$

   C. $CD = \dfrac{1}{2}AB$

   D. $DF = EF$

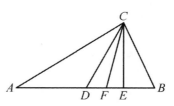

Diagram for question 5

B. Fill in the blanks

6 In right-angled triangle ABC, if the difference between the two acute angles is $10°$, then the smaller acute angle is _____ $°$.

7 In $\triangle ABC$, $\angle C = 90°$, $AB = 18$ and $BC = 9$. Then $\angle B =$ _____ $°$.

8 Given points $O(0, 0)$, $A(1, 2)$ and $B(2, 1)$ on a co-ordinate plane, then the lengths of the three sides of $\triangle OAB$ are _____ , _____ and _____ . It is _____ _____ triangle.

9 The diagram shows $\triangle ABC$ with $\angle ACB = 90°$ and $\angle A = 20°$. CD and CE are the height and median on the hypotenuse AB respectively. $\angle DCE =$ _____ .

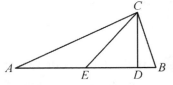

Diagram for question 9

10 In a right-angled isosceles triangle ABC, the length of the hypotenuse BC is 2. $\triangle DBC$ is an equilateral triangle. The distance between points A and D is _____ .

C. Questions that require solutions

11 The diagram shows $\triangle ABC$ with $\angle C = 90°$. AD is the bisector of $\angle CAB$ and intersects BC at D. $BC = 12$ and $BD = 8$. Find the distance from point D to AB.

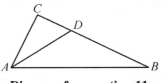

Diagram for question 11

12 The diagram shows two set squares, ADB and CBD, put them together so that $\angle ADB = \angle DCB = 90°$. $BC = CD$ and $\angle ABD = 30°$. E is the midpoint of AB and $AD = 1$.

(a) Find the area of the quadrilateral $BCDE$.

(b) Prove that $CE \perp BD$.

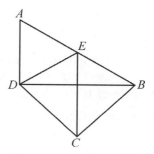

Diagram for question 12

13 The diagram shows quadrilateral $ABCD$, in which $AD /\!/ BC$ and $BD \perp AD$. Points E and F are the midpoints of AB and CD respectively, and $DE = BF$.

Prove that $\angle A = \angle C$.

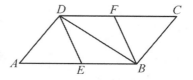

Diagram for Question 13

14 The diagram shows $\triangle ABC$, in which $AD \perp BC$, $BE \perp AC$ and $\angle ABC = 45°$. M is the midpoint of BF and N is the midpoint of AC.

(a) Prove: $\triangle BDF \cong \triangle ADC$.

(b) Identify the relations between the segments DM and DN. (Hint: You may analyse their relations in terms of lengths and positions, respectively.)

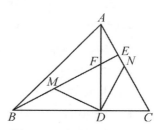

Diagram for question 14

Chapter 9   Statistics (I)

9.1   Organising and presenting data (1)

Learning objectives

Construct tables for categorical data

Interpret pictograms, line graphs and pie charts

A. Multiple choice questions

1. The pictogram shows the types of weather on the days in a winter week in a city. Each symbol stands for one day. Based on the information given, the correct description of the following about the weather in the week is (   ).

Sunny	Rainy	Cloudy

Diagram for question 1

A. It was sunny on most days of the week.

B. It was cloudy on most days of the week.

C. Wednesday was a rainy day.

D. There was no rain on most days of the week.

2. The line graph shows Ann's family's electricity usage from January to May this year. From the graph, the biggest variation of the usage between two consecutive months was from (   ).

A. January to February

B. February to March

C. March to April

D. April to May

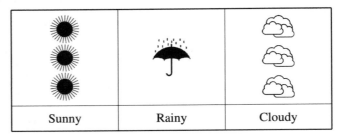

Electricity usage from January to May

Diagram for question 2

3 The pie chart represents the numbers of Class 8 (1) students joining in cross-curricular activities. The percentage of students joining the drama club is (   ) .

A. 10%

B. 20%

C. 30%

D. 50%

Number of Class 8 (1) students in CCAs

Diagram for question 3

B. Fill in the blanks

4 It is not always practical to use a _____ or _____ to present a large set of data. (Write 'pictogram', 'block diagram', 'line graph' or 'pie chart'.)

5 The diagram shows a line graph of the highest and lowest temperatures in a place from 1 June to 7 June. The greatest daily temperature difference was on _____ June.

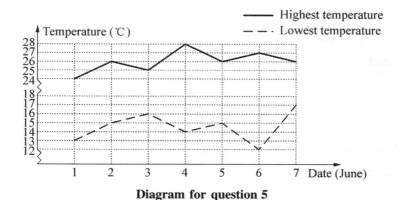

Diagram for question 5

C. Questions that require solutions

6 These two statistical graphs (Figure 1 and Figure 2 on the next page) show information about the cross-curricular activities (CCAs) of the students in schools A and B. Use the information provided in the graphs to answer this question.

(a) Study Figure 1 and write a correct conclusion based on the information it provides.

(b) Study Figure 2 and write a correct conclusion based on the information it provides.

(c) How many students in total, in both schools, took part in the science activities in 2016?

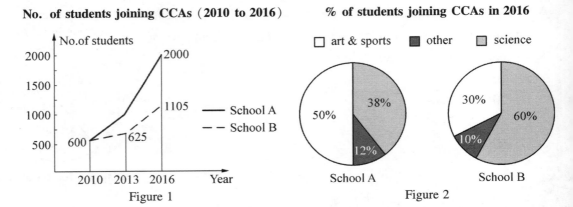

No. of students joining CCAs (2010 to 2016)

% of students joining CCAs in 2016

Figure 1

Figure 2

Diagram for question 6 and question 7

7 (a) Use the data in question 6 to construct a table to present:

(i) the numbers of students joining the CCAs in School A in 2010, 2013, and 2016

(ii) the numbers of students joining the CCAs in School B in 2010, 2013, and 2016

(iii) the total numbers of students joining the CCAs in both School A and School B in 2010, 2013 and 2016.

(b) Is it possible to use just one table to present all the information shown in the above three tables? If it is, draw such a table. Otherwise, explain why it is not possible.

9.2 Organising and presenting data (2)

Learning objective

Compare and interpret pictograms, bar charts, line graphs and pie charts

A. Multiple choice questions

1 Read the pie charts carefully. The correct conclusion is (   ).

A. School *A* has fewer girls than School *B*.

B. School *B* has fewer boys than School *A*.

C. The number of girls in school *B* is smaller than the number of boys in School *A*.

D. It is not clear from the graph which school has more girls.

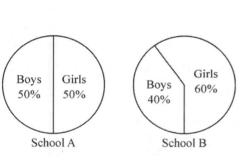

Diagram for question 1

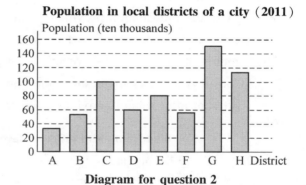

Population in local districts of a city (2011)

Diagram for question 2

2 The vertical bar chart shows demographic information about all the local districts in a city in 2011. Based on the chart, the correct conclusion is (   ).

A. There were three districts with population under 400 000.

B. There is only one district with population over one million.

C. The sum of the populations in District A and District B was more than the population in District C.

D. The population in the city had exceeded 6 million.

B. Fill in the blanks

3 Some commonly used statistical graphs are _____, _____
_____, _____ and _____.
(Write 'pictogram', 'bar chart', 'line graph', 'line segment', 'number line' or 'pie chart' in each space.)

4 To present data of different categories, you could use a _____ . To present data relating to periods of time, you could use a _____ . To present data relating to percentages, you could use a _____ . (Write 'line graph', 'pie chart', or 'bar chart' in each space.)

C. Questions that require solutions

5 A secondary school did a survey about the after-school activities the students took part in. The question asked was:

What is your favourite after-school activity: music appreciation, reading for pleasure, sports activity, or other? (**Choose one only.**)

A number of students were selected to take the survey. The partially completed bar chart below shows some of the data collected. Of all the students surveyed, 12% chose music. Use the information provided to answer this question.

(a) How many students took part in the survey?

(b) Among all the students surveyed, what percentage of the students chose reading?

(c) *Construct a pie chart to show the percentages of students who chose each of the different after-school activities as their favourite.

No. of students with different favourite after-school activities

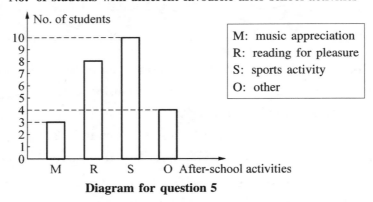

Diagram for question 5

---

* Optional question. Note: There are 360° in a full turn (a circle), which in a pie chart means 100% and half of the circle means 50%, and so on.

6 An environment protection group conducted a survey to collect sales information about bottled drinks bought by the tourists in a park. On one day, the tourists who were leaving the park at Exits A, B and C were invited to take the survey. Afterwards, the environment protection group presented the data collected at Exit A in this chart.

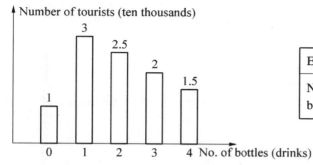

Exit	B	C
Number of bottles (drinks) bought per person	3	2

Diagram for question 6

(a) At Exit A, the tourists surveyed who bought two or more bottled drinks made up _____% of all the tourists surveyed at that exit.

(b) How many bottled drinks, on average, did the tourists surveyed at Exit A buy in the park?

(c) The table shows the numbers of bottled drinks bought per person in the park by the tourists surveyed at Exits B and C. If the number of tourists surveyed at Exit C is 20 thousand more than at Exit B, and the total number of bottled drinks that tourists at both exits bought is 490 thousand in the whole park, then how many tourists were surveyed at Exit B?

9.3 Measuring central tendency of data (1): Mean

Learning objective

Calculate the mean of discrete data

A. Multiple choice questions

1 Lee is an archery athlete. In a practice session, his scores were recorded as follows: 8, 9, 8, 7, 10. The mean of this set of data is (   ).

A. 8   B. 8.4

C. 8.5   D. 9

2 A supermarket purchased a batch of potatoes. The standard bag contains 30 kg potatoes. A sales assistant picked 6 bags of potatoes, weighed them and labelled those that were over this weight as ' + ' and those that were under this weight as ' – '. Here are his results.

+0.5, −0.5, 0, −0.5, −0.5, +1

The mean weight of the six bags of potatoes was (   ).

A. 0   B. 29.5

C. 30   D. 30.5

3 The line graph represents the water usage in a residential area from 1 to 5 June. The mean usage of the water per day over the 5 days is (   ).

A. 30 cubic metres   B. 31 cubic metres

C. 32 cubic metres   D. 33 cubic metres

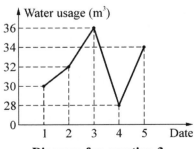

Diagram for question 3

4　A local community launched a water-saving campaign. The water usage of 200 households in the community was reviewed and analysed. The frequency table shows the amount of water saved in March, compared with that in February.

> **A frequency table** records the number of times that each specific data value, usually arranged in ascending order, takes place.

Water saved (cubic metres)	Frequency (number of households)
1	20
1.5	120
2	60

The mean saving of water per household was (　　).

A. 1.5 cubic metres

B. 2 cubic metres

C. 1.8 cubic metres

D. 1.6 cubic metres

B. Fill in the blanks

5　During a city's 'green home' campaign, students from four Year 8 classes: (1), (2), (3) and (4) in a school took part in tree-planting activities. The table shows the number of trees each class planted.

Class	Number of trees planted
1	22
2	25
3	35
4	18

Table for question 5

The mean number of trees planted, per class, was _____.

6　In an art festival, five judges gave Jade's performance these scores: 9 points, 9.3 points, 8.9 points, 8.7 points, 9.1 points. The mean score for her performance was _____ points.

7　If the mean of x_1 and x_2 is 4, then the mean of $x_1 + 1$ and $x_2 + 5$ is _____.

C. Questions that require solutions

8 The numbers of cars owned by residents in a city has steadily increased in recent years. From 2007 to 2011, the numbers of cars owned were 11, 13, 15, 19, x (unit: 10 thousand cars) and the mean of the five numbers was 16.

(a) Find the value of x.

(b) Construct a line graph to present the number of cars the residents owned over the five years.

(c) Do you think it is appropriate to use a bar chart or a pie chart to present the above data? Explain your reasons.

9 A school did a survey of the amount of weekly pocket money students received. 50 students took the survey and the results are shown in the frequency table below, but one value is missing.

Amount of pocket money received (£)	Frequency (number of students)
5	a
10	15
15	20
20	5

Use the information in the table to answer the question.

(a) Find the value of a.

(b) Find the mean amount of weekly pocket money received by the 50 students.

(c) Construct a vertical bar chart to present the data shown in the table.

10 When running for the position of school prefect, Matt needs to go through a debate, where his performance is marked by judges, and an opinion poll, in which each student can vote 'Excellent', 'Good' or 'Fair'. The bar chart shows the scores that 7 judges gave Matt for his performance in the debate, and the pie chart shows the information about votes that 50 students cast in the opinion poll.

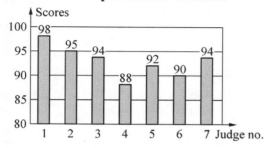

Scores for Matt's performance in debate

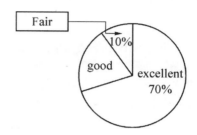

Votes for Matt in opinion poll

Scoring rules

1   The scores from the debate are obtained by ignoring the highest and lowest scores and then calculating the mean of the remaining scores.

2   The scores from votes in the opinion poll: number of 'Excellent' votes $\times 2$ + number of 'Good' votes $\times 1$ + number of 'Fair' $\times 0$.

3   Overall scores = scores from 'debate' $\times 0.4$ + scores from 'opinion poll' $\times 0.6$

Diagram for question 10

(a) Find the mode of the scores that the judges gave Matt in the debate.

(b) What percentage of the students voted 'Good' for Matt in the opinion poll?

(c) Find Matt's overall score in the debate.

(d) In the election, Emmy scored 82 in the opinion poll. If her overall score is not less than Matt's, what is the minimum she could have scored in the debate?

9.4 Measuring central tendency of data (2): Mode and median

Learning objective

Calculate the mode and the median of discrete data

A. Multiple choice questions

1 Nadjah participated in a speaking competition. The scores that six judges gave her are shown in the table.

Judge number	1	2	3	4	5	6
Score	85	90	80	95	90	90

Table for question 1

The mode of Nadjah's scores is (   ).
A. 95   B. 90   C. 85   D. 80

2 In Collis High School, 13 Year 8 students were preparing to take part in a 100 metre race. The six fastest runners would qualify for the final race, based on their results in the preliminary heats. Judy already has her own results and wants to know whether she has qualified for the final. She needs to know the (   ) of the results of all 13 runners.
A. median   B. mode   C. mean   D. none of them

B. Fill in the blanks

3 A primary school had an 'everyone plays an instrument' competition. The results of the 10 participating pupils in Juniper class are shown in the line graph. The median of the results of the 10 pupils is _____ and their mode is _____.

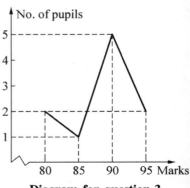

Diagram for question 3

4 Chris did a survey of donations from a local community in an annual charity event. The incomplete bar chart shows some of the data he collected. It is known that 25% of the total participants donated £100. The median value of a donation is _____ pounds.

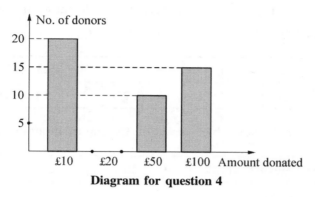

Diagram for question 4

C. Questions that require solutions

5 The table shows the annual incomes of 15 families in a community for the year 2012.

Annual income (£10 000)	2	2.5	3	4	5	9	13
Number of families	1	3	5	2	2	1	1

(a) Find the mean, median and mode of the annual incomes of the 15 families.

(b) Which of the three measures in (a) would be most appropriate to represent the general annual income of the 15 families? Give brief reasons.

6 There are 20 staff members in the household electrical department of a store. To motivate the sales staff, the store adopted the so-called 'target' approach, setting up a monthly sales target for all staff members. Any staff member whose sales volume meets the target will be rewarded with bonus pay. The table shows the sales volumes reached by the 20 staff members in a month (unit: £10 000).

25	26	21	17	28	26	20	25	26	30
20	21	20	26	30	25	21	19	28	26

(a) Complete the frequency table, based on the information above.

Sales volume (£10 000)	17	19	20	21	25	26	28	30
Frequency (number of staff members)	1	1	3	3			2	2

(b) In the data set, the mode is _____, the median is _____ and the mean is _____.

(c) If the mode is set as the monthly target, then is it possible for at least half of the staff members to meet the target? Give a reason.

9.5 Measuring central tendency of data (3): Mode and median

Learning objective

Interpret statistical diagrams and tables and use this information to calculate the mode and the median of discrete data

A. Multiple choice questions

1. These numbers are the results recorded by a group of 10 students in a skipping contest (unit: skips/minute).

   176, 180, 184, 180, 170, 176, 172, 164, 186, 180

   The mode, median and mean of the results for the group are (   ) respectively.

   A. 180, 180, 178

   B. 180, 178, 178

   C. 180, 178, 176.8

   D. 178, 180, 176.8

2. The frequency table shows the numbers of students getting different scores in a test. Given that there are 38 students in the class, the mode of the scores is 50 marks and the median is 60 marks, the values of x and y are (   ) respectively.

Results (marks)	20	30	40	50	60	70	90	100
Number of students	2	3	5	x	6	y	3	4

   Table for question 2

   A. 7 and 8   B. 8 and 7

   C. 50 and 70   D. 70 and 50

B. Fill in the blanks

3. If the mean of a set of figures, 1, 1, 2, 3, x is 3, then the mode of this set of figures is _____.

4 The dual bar chart shows the actual data reported in the media in a city in May 2006. The data came from a commissioned survey on people's degree of satisfaction on safety. To reveal the change, the results of the survey in both 2005 and 2004 were shown (hence a dual bar chart is used).

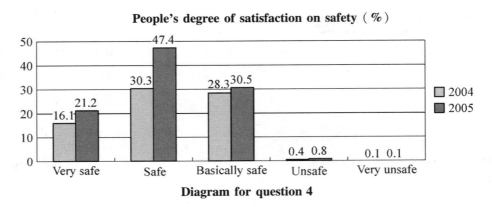

People's degree of satisfaction on safety (%)

Diagram for question 4

The mode of people's degree of satisfaction on safety in 2005 is _____ . In addition, there is a factual error in the chart, that is, _____ .

C. Questions that require solutions

5 A student management team did a survey on the donations during the 'supporting a local charity' campaign, launched by the school's student union. The partially completed bar chart below shows the data collected from a group of students. In the graph, from left to right, the ratio of the heights of the bars is $3:4:5:8:2$. It is known that there are 39 students who donated £15 or £20.

(a) How many students took the survey? What percentage of the donations were £20 or more?

(b) What are the mode and median in this set of data?

(c) If there are 2310 students in the school, estimate how much the students in the whole school have donated in total.

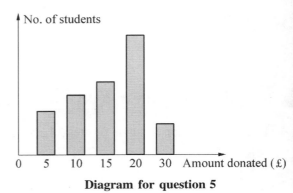

Diagram for question 5

6 A special kind of tree was planted in a park. If a tree's height is within ±2% of the standard height after one year, then it is regarded as a normal height. To find out how many trees have normal heights, the park staff measured 10 trees, one year after they were planted, and recorded their heights in this table (unit: cm).

Tree number	1	2	3	4	5	6	7	8	9	10
Height x (cm)	163	171	173	159	161	174	164	166	169	164

Use the information in the table to answer the questions.

(a) Work out the mean, median and mode of this set of data.

(b) Choose one of the statistics as the standard height and use it to identify which of the 10 trees have normal height.

(c) Given that 280 trees were planted in the park, use the standard height set in (b) to estimate the number of trees with normal height.

Unit test 9

A. Multiple choice questions

1. Of these methods for presenting statistical data, (   ) are commonly used, depending on the purpose and the type of the data.

   A. line graphs

   B. bar charts

   C. pie charts

   D. all of the above

2. A trading company is preparing to export a batch of canned food. The standard weight of a can is 454 grams. After testing 10 cans, it was found that the differences in the actual weight and the standard weight (unit: gram) are: -10, $+5$, 0, $+5$, 0, 0, -5, 0, $+5$, $+10$. The mean and mode of the weights of the 10 cans are (   ).

   A. 454 and 454

   B. 455 and 454

   C. 454 and 459

   D. 455 and 0

3. A secondary school conducted a survey on the theme of 'My favourite job'. A set of data was collected from the students surveyed. The diagrams show a line graph and a pie chart, both incomplete, based on the data collected. Of the following statements, (') is false.

   A. 200 students took the survey.

   B. Among the students surveyed, 40 preferred 'teacher'.

   C. Among the students surveyed, 40% of them preferred other jobs.

   D. Among the students surveyed, 30 preferred 'doctor'.

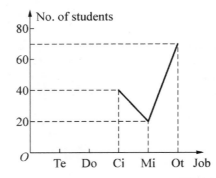

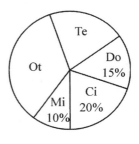

Diagram for question 3

4 A group of Year 8 students in a school were selected to be tested for physical fitness. Their scores were recorded for four levels: 1 point, 2 points, 3 points and 4 points. The partially completed bar chart and the pie chart show the results of the test. Based on the information shown, the mean score was (   ).

A. 2.25   B. 2.5

C. 2.95   D. 3

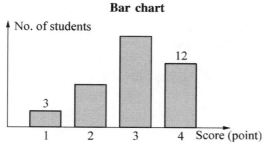

Diagrams for question 4

B. Fill in the blanks

5 The numbers of tickets sold by a cinema in a week, from Monday to Sunday, were: 200, 220, 210, 270, 280, 310, 330. The mean number of the tickets sold per day is _____ and the median is _____.

6 The mean of a set of data 1, 2, a is 2, while the only mode of another set of data -1, a, 1, 2, b is -1. Then the median of the data -1, a, 1, 2, b is _____.

7 The heights of 21 students in a school basketball club are shown in the frequency table.

Height (cm)	180	185	187	190	201
Number of students	4	6	5	4	2

Table for question 7

The median height of the 21 students is (   ) cm.

C. Questions that require solutions

8 The sales of a particular model of TV in a city's electrical store from January to June 2015 are shown in the table.

Month	January	February	March	April	May	June
Number of sets sold	50	51	48	50	52	49

Table for question 8

(a) Find the mean, median and mode of the monthly sales of this TV during the first half of the year.

(b) Construct a line graph to represent the data shown in the table. From the line graph, in which two months did the sales volume decline the most?

(c) The store planned to sell 60 of these TV sets in July. Compared with the average monthly sales volume in the first half of the year, what is the planned percentage increase in the sales volume in July? If the same monthly percentage increase in volume is maintained in August, how many of this model of TV should be sold in August?

9 In a school, there were 320 Year 8 students. They all took tests of the same level before and after a computer training course. The grades given, based on the same marking schemes, were: 'fail', 'pass' and 'distinction'. In order to find out the effects of the computer training course, the test results of 32 students in the pre-and post-tests were selected. These are shown in the graph. Use the information in the graph to answer this question.

(a) The median of the test results of the 32 students before the training course started is _____ level and that for after the training course is _____ level.

Diagram for question 9

(b) Having taken the training course, the percentage of 'fail' for the 32 students was reduced from _____ to _____.

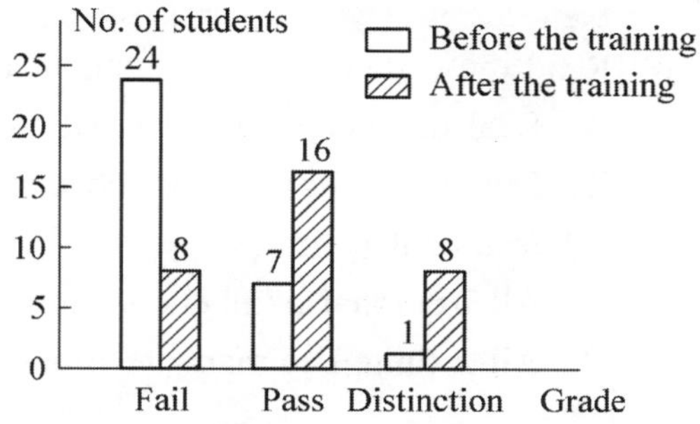

(c) Estimate: there were _____ students in total among all the Year 8 students in the school who had obtained 'pass' or 'distinction' after they had taken the training course.

(d) Do you think the above estimation is reasonable? What are your reasons?
Answer _____. Reasons: _____

End of year test

A. Multiple choice questions (20%)

1 Read these statements. Statement (   ) is incorrect.

A. Real numbers can be classified as rational numbers and irrational numbers.

B. Irrational numbers can be classified into positive irrational numbers and negative irrational numbers.

C. All irrational numbers are infinite decimals.

D. All infinite decimals are irrational numbers.

2 Of these triples of lengths, (   ) cannot be the side lengths of a triangle.

A. 1 cm, 2 cm, 3 cm   B. 3 cm, 4 cm, 5 cm

C. 5 cm, 6 cm, 7 cm   D. 7 cm, 8 cm, 9 cm

3 Of these sets of numbers, (   ) has a median of 5.

A. 1, 3, 3, 5, 6   B. 1, 8, 7, 5, 6

C. 1, 7, 3, 5, 6   D. 1, 0, 3, 5, 8

4 Look at the diagram. Statement (   ) is incorrect.

A. $\angle GBD$ and $\angle HCE$ are corresponding angles.

B. $\angle ABD$ and $\angle ACH$ are corresponding angles.

C. $\angle FBC$ and $\angle ACE$ are alternate angles.

D. $\angle GBC$ and $\angle BCH$ are co-interior angles.

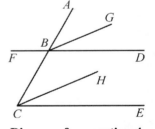

Diagram for question 4

5 The diagram shows $\triangle ABC$ with three given sides and three given angles. Of the three triangles on its right, (   ) triangle(s) is (are) congruent to $\triangle ABC$.

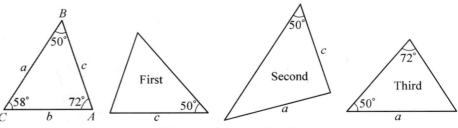

Diagram for question 5

A. The first and second   B. The first and third

C. Only the first   D. Only the third

6 On a co-ordinate plane, point A lies in the fourth quadrant. If the distance from point A to the x-axis is 3 and that to the y-axis is 4, then point A has co-ordinates (   ).

A. $(3, -4)$　　　　　　　　　　B. $(-3, 4)$

C. $(4, -3)$　　　　　　　　　　D. $(-4, 3)$

7 The perimeter of an isosceles trapezium is 48 cm, its area is 96 cm² and its perpendicular height is 8 cm. The length of the lateral sides of this isosceles trapezium is (   ).

A. 24 cm　　　　　　　　　　　B. 12 cm

C. 18 cm　　　　　　　　　　　D. 36 cm

8 The diagram shows a ladder AB leaning against the wall. The distance between the bottom of the ladder A and the foot of the wall O is 2 m and the distance from the top of the ladder B to the ground is 5 m. Now the bottom of the ladder A is moved outwards to A' so that the distance from A' to the foot of the wall O is 3 m. At the same time the top of the ladder B slides down to B'. The distance BB' is then (   ).

A. equal to 1 m

B. less than 1 m

C. more than 1 m

D. None of the above

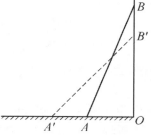

Diagram for Question 8

9 In each of the quadrants where the graph of the inverse proportional function $y = \dfrac{k}{x}$ lies, the value of y decreases as the value of x increases. Then the graph is in the (   ).

A. first and second quadrants　　　　B. first and third quadrants

C. second and third quadrants　　　　D. second and fourth quadrants

10 Jared collected data from the students in his class about how they travelled to school. If he wants to show the percentages of students using different methods of travel, the most suitable statistical diagram for doing so is a (   ).

A. pictogram　　　　　　　　　　B. line graph

C. pie chart　　　　　　　　　　　D. bar chart

B. Fill in the blanks (28%)

11 25 has _____ square root(s) and $\sqrt{25}$ = _____. (Write 'one' or 'two' in the first space.)

12 The shortest distance from the Earth to the Sun is 147 100 000 km. If this number is approximated correct to 3 significant figures, it would be _____ km.

13 In the diagram, $AB \parallel CD$ with point P on line CD. If $\angle APB = 100°$, $\angle A = (2x + 12)°$ and $\angle BPD = (4x + 8)°$, then x = _____.

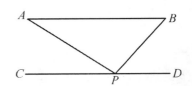

Diagram for question 13

14 In the diagram, $\angle ACB = \angle DBC$. For $\triangle AOB \cong \triangle DOC$, one more condition needs to be met. The condition could be _____.

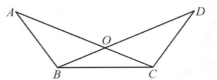

Diagram for question 14

15 In the diagram, boat C is in the direction 35° east of north, viewed from observation station A, and in the direction 20° west of north from observation station B. $\angle ACB$ = _____ degrees.

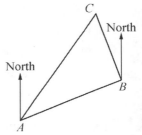

Diagram for question 15

16 The point symmetric to $M(5, -7)$ about the origin has co-ordinates _____.

17 Given a set of data: 11, 12, 11, 13, 15, its mean is _____, its mode is _____ and its median is _____.

18 Given that the vertices of $\triangle ABC$ are $A(5, 0)$, $B(0, 4)$ and $C(3, 4)$ respectively, then the area of this triangle is _____.

19 On an xy-coordinate plane, point A has co-ordinates $(1, 3)$. If point A is rotated 90° anticlockwise around the origin, then the resulting point has co-ordinates _____.

20 In the diagram, given that $\angle A = 30°$, $\angle B = 40°$ and $\angle C = 50°$, then $\angle AOB =$ _____ degrees.

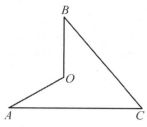

Diagram for question 20

21 The diagram shows $\triangle ABC$, in which $AB = BC$. BO and CO bisect $\angle ABC$ and $\angle ACB$ respectively. $DE \parallel BC$ and DE intersects AB and AC at points D and E respectively. If the perimeter of $\triangle ABC$ is 14 and that of $\triangle ADE$ is 9, then $AC =$ _____.

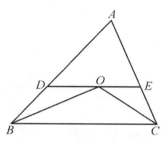

Diagram for question 21

22 The graph of proportional function $y = -2x$ passes through the _____ _____ quadrants.

23 The diagram shows isosceles triangle ABC, in which $AB = AC$ and $\angle A = 40°$. The perpendicular bisector of AB intersects AC at D. $\angle CBD$ is _____°.

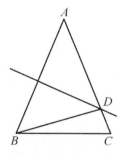

Diagram for question 23

24 The diagram shows a triangular piece of paper ABC, in which $\angle C = 90°$, $\angle A = 30°$ and $AC = 3$. The paper is folded so that point A coincides with point B and the folding line intersects AB and AC at points D and E respectively. The length of DE is _____.

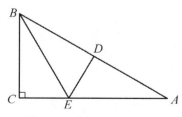

Diagram for question 24

C. Short answer questions

(17% ; 3 marks each for questions 25 – 28 , and 5 marks for question 29)

25 Calculate: If $(a - 6)^3 = -27$, find the value of $\sqrt{a + 6}$.

26 In the diagram, AB and DE intersect at point C, $CF \perp DE$ and $\angle ACD = 25°$. Find $\angle BCE$ and $\angle BCF$.

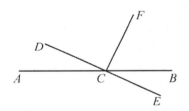

Diagram for question 26

27 In the diagram, points A, B, C and D are on the same line, $AB = DC$, $AE /\!/ DF$ and $AE = DF$. Prove that $EC = FB$.

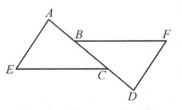

Diagram for question 27

28 In the isosceles $\triangle ABC$, $AB = AC$ and the line of symmetry is the x-axis. The co-ordinates of point A are $(-3, 0)$ and of point B are $(1, 3)$.

(a) Draw $\triangle ABC$.

(b) $\triangle A_1 B_1 C_1$ is symmetric to $\triangle ABC$ about the y-axis.

The co-ordinates of A_1 symmetric to point A are _____.

The co-ordinates of B_1 symmetric to point B are _____.

The co-ordinates of C_1 symmetric to point C are _____.

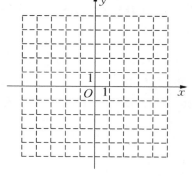

Diagram for question 28

(c) If point D has co-ordinates $(5, -3)$, and $\triangle ABC$ is translated horizontally so that C coincides with point D, then point A is translated to the _____ by _____ units.

29 In the diagram, $AD = BD$, $CD = ED$ and $\alpha = \beta$. Prove that $\gamma = \alpha$. (Complete the proof and fill in the blanks.)

Solution:

Since $\alpha = \beta$ (given)

we get $\alpha + \angle BDE = \beta + \angle BDE$ (property of equality)

So $\angle$ _____ = $\angle$ _____

In $\triangle ADE$ and $\triangle BDC$:

$\begin{cases} AD = BD \text{ (given)} \\ \angle_____ = \angle_____ (\quad) \\ ED = CD \text{ (given)} \end{cases}$

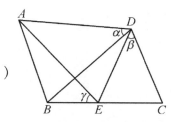

Diagram for question 29

Therefore $\triangle ADE \cong \triangle BDC$. ( )

So $\angle$ _____ = $\angle$ _____ ( )

Since $\angle BED = \beta + \angle C$ ( )

then $\gamma + \angle AED = \beta + \angle C$

So $\gamma = \beta$ ( )

Since $\alpha = \beta$ (given)

$\gamma = \alpha$ ( )

D. Questions that require solutions

(35% ; 3 marks for question 30, 4 marks each for questions 31 – 33, and 5 marks each for questions 34 – 37)

30 The diagram shows a parallelogram $ABCD$. AE divides it into two parts: a triangle ABE and a trapezium $AECD$. If the area of the trapezium is 24 cm² greater than that of the triangle, $BE = 11$ cm and $EC = 4$ cm, what is the area of the parallelogram $ABCD$?

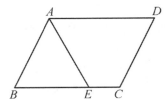

Diagram for question 30

31 The diagram shows equilateral triangle ABC with $AD \perp BC$ and $AD = AC$. CD is extended beyond D so it intersects the extension of AB at point E. Find $\angle E$.

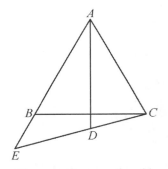

Diagram for question 31

32 Emily did a survey on the numbers of students in her class visiting a local community library in a week. The numbers from Monday to Sunday were: 13, 12, 11, 12, 12, 18, 17.

(a) Complete the frequency table below to present the data Emily collected. What are the mode and median of the numbers of the students on each day of the week visiting the library?

(b) Draw a line graph on the axes provided, to represent the data Emily collected. Then write a conclusion, based on your observations from the graph.

Solution: (a)   (b)

Day	Frequency
Monday	
Tuesday	
Wednesday	
Thursday	
Friday	
Saturday	
Sunday	

The mode is _____ and the median is _____.   Conclusion: _____

33 Figure 1 shows an equilateral triangle ABC with points D and E on the extensions of AB and BC respectively, such that $BD = CE$.

(a) Prove that $\triangle CBD \cong \triangle ACE$.

(b) After $\triangle CBD$ is rotated 60° anticlockwise around point B (see Figure 2), point C coincides with point A and point D reaches point G. The lines AG and EG are joined. What type of triangle is $\triangle AEG$? Give reasons.

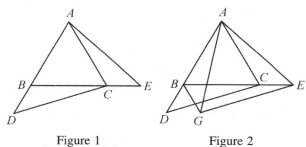

Figure 1   Figure 2

Diagram for question 33

34 The diagram shows the co-ordinate plane, in which point A has co-ordinates $(4, 0)$. Point $B(m, n)$ is in the fourth quadrant. Point B is translated $(3m - 8)$ units left and reaches the position of point $C\left(m > \dfrac{8}{3}\right)$.

(a) Write down the co-ordinates of C (in terms of m and n).

(b) Given that point C lies on line $x = -2$, find the value of m.

(c) Under the same condition as in (b), find the co-ordinates of point P on the line $x = -2$, such that when the lines AP and BP are drawn, $\triangle ABP$ is an isosceles right-angled triangle with AB being one of the two equal sides. (Note: You may use both of the co-ordinate planes given to sketch the triangles.)

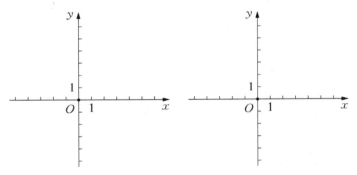

Diagram for question 34

35 In the diagram, P is a point on the graph of the inverse proportion function $y = \dfrac{k}{x}$ ($k > 0$) in the first quadrant. The co-ordinates of point A are $(2, 0)$.

(a) As the x-coordinate of point P increases, what will happen to the area of $\triangle POA$?

(b) Find the equation of the inverse proportional function when $\triangle POA$ is an equilateral triangle.

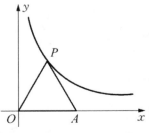

Diagram for question 35

36 Mr Johnson goes to work by bike. First, he cycles along a flat road to point A, then he continues cycling uphill to point B, and finally, he cycles downhill until he reaches his office. The time he spent on the journey and the distance to his office are as shown in the diagram. He takes the same route back home, keeping the same speed as he does on the way to work on the flat road, uphill and downhill. Now answer the questions, based on the information in the diagram.

(a) It takes him _____ minutes to ride from home to his office.

(b) It takes him _____ minutes to ride from his office to home.

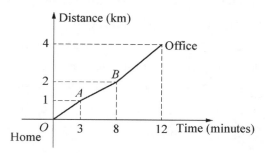

Diagram for question 36

37 The diagram shows $\triangle ABC$, in which point P is the midpoint of BC. Line a is rotated around point A. B and P are on opposite sides of line a, $BM \perp a$ at point M and $CN \perp a$ at point N. The lines PM and PN are constructed and MP is extended beyond P, intersecting CN at point E.

(a) Prove that $\triangle BPM \cong \triangle CPE$.

(b) Prove that $PM = PN$.

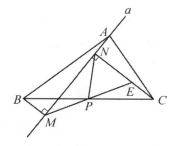

Diagram for question 37

Answers

Chapter 1 Real numbers

1.1 The concepts of real numbers

1 A **2** C **3** B **4** B **5** irrational numbers **6** non-terminating decimals **7** infinitely **8** π, $\sqrt{8}$ **9** 3 **10** Answer may vary (for example, π or $\sqrt{10}$ or $\sqrt{11}$). **11** 2, 3, 5, 6, 7, 8, 10 **12** (a) 5 (b) $\sqrt{5}$ **13** (a) The diagonal with rational length: $AC = 5$. (b) The diagonals with irrational length: $AE = \sqrt{2}$, $AF = \sqrt{5}$, $AG = \sqrt{10}$, $AH = \sqrt{17}$, $AI = \sqrt{20}$ and so on.

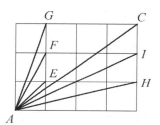

Diagram for question 13

1.2 Square roots: concept and evaluation (1)

1 C **2** B **3** C **4** square **5** $\pm\sqrt{a}$, $\sqrt{a}$, $-\sqrt{a}$ **6** $\pm\dfrac{1}{7}$, $\dfrac{1}{7}$ **7** 5, $\sqrt{5}$ **8** 13, ± 1.3 **9** (a) -0.25 (b) 0.25 (c) ± 0.25 **10** 4 **11** 301.63 **12** (a) ± 6 (b) ± 3 (c) 3 or -7 **13** ± 1 **14** -5 (Hint: from $4 - a = -(2a + 1)$, we can get $a = -5$.)

1.3 Square roots: concept and evaluation (2)

1 C **2** D **3** B **4** 44.8776 **5** 1.4192 **6** ± 19.1050 **7** ± 1.9579 **8** 7 **9** 44 **10** $x \geqslant \dfrac{2}{3}$ **11** $b > a > c$ **12** ± 4.1231 (Hint: $x = 2$, $y = 3$) **13** -24 (Hint: $a = 3$, $b = \sqrt{12} - 3$)

1.4 Cube roots

1 C **2** D **3** B **4** 2, 0, negative **5** (a) 25 (b) -25 (c) 25 **6** (a) 12 (b) 81 **7** (a) -12 (b) 81 **8** (a) 272.0827 (b) -12.6290 **9** -4 **10** $-2a$ **11** 2.88 **12** 6.66 cm **13** $\pm 1\dfrac{1}{2}$ **14** $y = \sqrt[3]{x^2}$

1.5 nth roots

1 C **2** B **3** A **4** 2, 0, no, 1, 0 **5** (a) 2 (b) ± 2 **6** (a) $1\dfrac{1}{2}$ (b) $1\dfrac{1}{2}$ **7** (a) 17.73 (b) -2.51 **8** (a) ± 0.51 (b) 1.58 **9** 3 **10** 0.05 **11** -3 (Hint: from $x - 5 = 0$ and $x + 2y - 1 = 0$, we can get $x = 5$, $y = -2$.) **12** (a) 1 or -3 (b) 1 **13** 1250 (Hint: $\sqrt[5]{80n} = \sqrt[5]{16 \times 5 \times n} = \sqrt[5]{2^4 \times 5 \times n}$; so the least possible integer n is $2 \times 5^4 = 1250$.)

1.6 Representing real numbers on a number line

1 C **2** C **3** D **4** equal **5** points marked correctly ($\approx \pm 1.8$) **6** (a) < (b) > **7** (a) $5 - \sqrt{3}$ (b) -3 **8** $\sqrt{6} - \sqrt{2}$ **9** 1 **10** $-a$ **11** 1 or 5 **12** $\sqrt{2} + \sqrt{3} > \sqrt{5}$ (Hint: $(\sqrt{2} + \sqrt{3})^2 > (\sqrt{5})^2$) **13** 1 (Take care with the value of π, it is not 3.14.)

1.7 Approximation and significant figures

1 A, C, D, B **2** D **3** C **4** B **5** 4, 5 **6** hundred, 3 **7** 1.73, 3 **8** 2.2×10^4, 2 **9** 1.67×10^7 **10** 1.26 **11** 1.260 **12** 0.89 **13** 1.13 **14** $23.445 \leqslant a < 23.455$

Unit test 1

1 C **2** B **3** A **4** $\pm\sqrt{3}$ **5** $\sqrt{5}$ **6** ± 6 **7** ± 2 or $\pm\sqrt[4]{2}$ **8** $-\sqrt{3}$ or $3\sqrt{3}$

⑨ $-2a-2$　⑩ 0.419　⑪ 1.20　⑫ $-\dfrac{4}{5}$

⑬ ≤2　⑭ 8 or −4　⑮ $35\dfrac{7}{12}$　⑯ 33.9 cm³

⑰ (a) 10 (Hint: The area of the large square =

$x^2 = 4 \times \dfrac{1}{2} \times 6 \times 8 + (8-6)^2 = 100$, so $x = 10$.)

(b) $\sqrt{a^2 + b^2}$ (Hint: The area of the large square =

$x^2 = 4 \times \dfrac{1}{2}ab + (a - b)^2 = a^2 + b^2$, so $x =$

$\sqrt{a^2 + b^2}$.)

Chapter 2　Intersecting and parallel lines

2.1　Adjacent, supplementary and vertically opposite angles

① B　② C　③ C　④ C　⑤ (a) γ, β
and θ　(b) 155°, 25°　⑥ 10°　⑦ 35°
⑧ 90°　⑨ 153°　⑩ 45°　⑪ He can
measure the angle outside the wall formed by OB
and the extension of AO beyond O, and then use
the relationship of supplementary angles to find the
angle inside the wall (answer may vary).

⑫ $\angle DOE = \angle COE = \angle AOF = \angle BOF$,
$\angle AOE = \angle COF$, $\angle AOC = \angle BOD$, $\angle AOD =$
$\angle BOC$

2.2　Perpendicular lines (1)

① B　② D　③ C　④ D
⑤ perpendicular, perpendicular
⑥ perpendicular　⑦ 25°, 65°　⑧ 145°
⑨ perpendicular　⑩ 54°　⑪ perpendicular
lines correctly drawn　⑫ 90°　⑬ 55°
⑭ (a) 45°　(b) They are perpendicular to each
other. $\angle COD = 45°$ and OC is the bisector of
$\angle AOD$, therefore $\angle AOD = 2\angle COD = 90°$.

2.3　Perpendicular lines (2)

① A　② D　③ C　④ D　⑤ The
perpendicular line segment is the shortest.
⑥ $CD < AC < AB$　⑦ The larger the angle,
the shorter the line segment.　⑧ 90°, PO
⑨ DF, AC　⑩ 3　⑪ (a), (b) perpendicular
lines correctly drawn (c) $OP = OQ$ or $MP = MQ$

⑫ Passing through the heel of footprint B,
construct $BF \perp CD$ with F being the foot of the
perpendicular. The length of BF is his result for
long jump.　⑬ Passing through point B,
construct a line perpendicular to l, the foot of
perpendicular D is the position of the pumping
station to be built. Link AB, the pipelines should
be laid along the route D—B—A. It is the shortest
route. Diagram correctly drawn.

2.4　Corresponding angles and alternate angles

① C　② B　③ B　④ C　⑤ 2, α and θ,
β and ϕ　⑥ 2, α and γ, γ and ϕ　⑦ 3, β and
γ, γ and θ, β and θ　⑧ $\angle DBC$, $\angle DFE$,
$\angle AFD$; $\angle FDB$, $\angle FBD$, $\angle FBC$, $\angle FDC$
⑨ β, α and θ, α and θ, θ　⑩ There are four
corresponding angles for α: $\angle EBH$, $\angle FCH$,
$\angle GDF$ and $\angle GEF$.　⑪ The alternate angles:
$\angle \alpha$ and $\angle B$, γ and $\angle C$; the co-interior angles:
$\angle C$ and $\angle EAC$, $\angle B$ and $\angle BAF$, β and $\angle B$, β
and $\angle C$, $\angle B$ and $\angle C$　⑫ 3 corresponding
angles for angle α correctly marked

2.5　Properties of parallel lines (1)

① C　② B　③ D　④ A　⑤ 40
⑥ 50　⑦ 63　⑧ 42, 69　⑨ DCG; If two
lines are parallel, the corresponding angles formed
with a third line are equal.　⑩ $A = \angle BEF$, $D =$
$\angle EFC$ (There are others.)
⑪ 98°　⑫ 70°

2.6　Properties of parallel lines (2)

① B　② D　③ C　④ 180°　⑤ 120°
⑥ 135　⑦ 5　⑧ 280　⑨ 30
⑩ Method 1: 180; If two lines are parallel, the
co-interior angles formed with a third line are
supplementary; given; 50; $\beta + \angle C = 180°$; If
two lines are parallel, the co-interior angles
formed with a third line are supplementary; given;
70; α; β; 120　Method 2: As shown in the
diagram, since AB // CD (given), $\angle A + \angle M =$
180° (If two lines are parallel, the co-interior

angles formed with a third line are supplementary.). Since $\angle A = 130°$ (given), $\angle M = 50°$. Since $\angle PCD = 110°$ (given), $\angle MCP = 180° - 110° = 70°$. Since $\angle MPC + \angle M + \angle MPC = 180°$ (The three interior angles in a triangle add up to 180°.), $\angle MPC = 180° - 50° - 70° = 60°$. Since $\angle APC + \angle MPC = 180°$ (The two angles are supplementary.), $\angle APC = 180° - \angle MPC = 180° - 60° = 120°$.

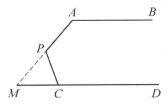

Diagram for question 10

⑪ Since $AB /\!/ CD$, $\alpha + \beta + \gamma + \theta = 180°$. Since AE bisects $\angle DAB$ and DE bisects $\angle ADC$ (given), $\alpha = \beta$, $\gamma = \theta$; therefore $\alpha + \gamma = 90°$, that is, $\angle DEA = 90°$; hence, $DE \perp AE$. ⑫ Since $AD /\!/ BC$, $\angle ADB = \angle CBD$. Again since $\angle ADE = \angle CBF$, $\angle EDB = \angle FBD$, therefore $DE /\!/ BF$, and $\angle E = \angle F$.

2.7 Properties of parallel lines (3)

① D ② B ③ D ④ C ⑤ the length of perpendicular line segment AE, the length of perpendicular line segment DF

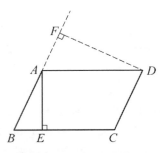

Diagram for question 5

⑥ 5 (Hint: $\triangle CEG$, $\triangle ACG$, $\triangle BHD$, $\triangle BFD$ and $\triangle AEC$.) ⑦ 2 ⑧ 10 ⑨ 24

⑩ $S_{\triangle ECD} = \dfrac{1}{2} S_{\square ABCD} = S_{\triangle FBC}$ ⑪ Since $S_{\triangle ABC} =$

$S_{\triangle DBC}$, $S_{\triangle ABC} - S_{\triangle OBC} = S_{\triangle DBC} - S_{\triangle OBC}$, that is $S_{\triangle ABO} = S_{\triangle DCO}$. ⑫ Link BD. Since $AD /\!/ BC$, we get $S_{\triangle ABE} = S_{\triangle DBE}$, and since $AB /\!/ CD$, $S_{\triangle DBC} = S_{\triangle CDF}$, and $S_{\triangle DBC} - S_{\triangle DEC} = S_{\triangle DFC} - S_{\triangle DEC}$, that is $S_{\triangle DBE} = S_{\triangle CFE}$, therefore $S_{\triangle ABE} = S_{\triangle CEF}$.

2.8 Properties of parallel lines (4)

① C ② C ③ D ④ B ⑤ ϕ; If two lines are parallel, then the alternate angles are equal. ⑥ α; If two lines are parallel, then the corresponding angles are equal. ⑦ 180°; If two lines are parallel, then the co-interior angles are supplementary. ⑧ 120°; If two lines are parallel, then the corresponding angles are equal. ⑨ 45 ⑩ 180 ⑪ $\angle B = 55°$, $\angle C = 70°$ ⑫ 80° ⑬ 65°

2.9 Properties of parallel lines (5)

① C ② B ③ D ④ C ⑤ 110° ⑥ 90° ⑦ 40° ⑧ 25° ⑨ 60° ⑩ 75° ⑪ Since $\alpha = \beta$ (given), $\gamma = \theta$ (Vertically opposite angles are equal). Since $\angle A + \angle C + \theta = \angle F + \angle D + \gamma = 180°$ (The interior angles in a triangle add up to 180°) and $\angle C = \angle D$ (given), $\angle A = \angle F$. ⑫ Extend AB beyond B, intersecting ED at point M. Since $AB /\!/ CD$ (given), $\angle D = \angle AME$ (If two lines are parallel, then the corresponding angles are equal). Since $\angle ABE + \angle EBM = 180°$ (The two angles are supplementary) and $\angle AME + \angle E + \angle EBM = 180°$ (The interior angles in a triangle add up to 180°), $\angle ABE = \angle AME + \angle E$, so $\angle ABE = \angle D + \angle E$. ⑬ $\alpha + \gamma + \phi = \beta + \theta$. As shown in the diagram, through points B, C and D, draw lines BX, CY and DZ parallel to line a, and $a /\!/ b /\!/ BX /\!/ CY /\!/ DZ$ (Two lines parallel to a third line are parallel), therefore, $\alpha = \angle ABX$, $\angle XBC = \angle BCY$, and $\angle YCD = \angle CDZ$, and $\angle ZDE = \phi$ (If two lines are parallel, then the alternate angles are equal). Because $\beta = \angle ABX + \angle XBC$, $\gamma = \angle BCY + \angle YCD$ and $\theta = CDZ + ZDE$, $\beta + \theta = \angle ABX + \angle XBC + \angle CDZ + \angle ZDE =$

$\alpha + \angle BCY + \angle YCD + \phi = \alpha + \gamma + \phi.$

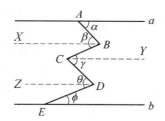

Unit test 2

① C ② B ③ D ④ C ⑤ A ⑥ D
⑦ 3, 3 ⑧ 4 ⑨ 2 ⑩ AE, BD, If two lines are parallel, then the alternate angles are equal. ⑪ ED, AC, If two lines are parallel, then the alternate angles are equal. ⑫ BE, DC, If two lines are parallel, then the corresponding angles are equal. ⑬ $\beta = \phi$, $\alpha = \theta$, $\gamma = \delta$, $\delta = \lambda$, $\gamma = \lambda$ ⑭ 40 ⑮ 90 ⑯ 4 ⑰ 1.8 ⑱ 36 ⑲ $\angle ABC = \angle DEF$. Link BE; from $AB \, // \, EF$ (given), then $\angle ABE = \angle FEB$ (If two lines are parallel, then the alternate angles are equal), and from $BC \, // \, DE$ (given), $\angle CBE = \angle DEB$ (If two lines are parallel, then the alternate angles are equal). Therefore $\angle ABC = \angle ABE - \angle CBE = \angle FEB - \angle DEB = \angle DEF$. ⑳ 25° ㉑ 6 ㉒ (1) $\angle APC + \angle PAB + \angle PCD = 360°$ (2) $\angle APC = \angle PAB + \angle PCD$ (3) $\angle PCD = \angle PAB + \angle APC$ (4) $\angle PAB = \angle PCD + \angle APC$; conclusion selected may vary. ㉓ (a) 120° (b) $\angle CFE = 180° - 3\alpha$

Chapter 3　Trapezia

3.1　What is a trapezium?

① C ② B ③ D ④ C ⑤ one
⑥ right-angled trapezium, an isosceles trapezium ⑦ 180 ⑧ height ⑨ triangle ⑩ 2 ⑪ 4, 5, 2, 6, 5, 3 ⑫ (a) × (b) ✓ (c) ✓ (d) ✓ ⑬ The height of each trapezium correctly drawn. ⑭ 30

3.2　Areas of trapezia (1)

① D ② D ③ 50 ④ 54 ⑤ 3600

⑥ triangle, 18 ⑦ 102 ⑧ (a) 18 cm² (b) 22.1 cm² (c) 96 cm² ⑨ 262.5 m² ⑩ 275 m² ⑪ £82 500

3.3　Areas of trapezia (2)

① C ② D ③ 7.8, 3, 19.5, 2.7 ④ (a) 6 cm (b) 11.5 m ⑤ 2.4 m ⑥ 3.2 cm ⑦ 15 cm², 14 cm² ⑧ 14 cm ⑨ 140 cm² ⑩ 36 cm²

3.4　Areas of composite figures

① C ② C ③ 2 ④ (a) $(5 + 8) \times (6 - 4) \div 2 + 8 \times 4 = 45(\text{cm}^2)$ (b) $(4 + 6) \times (8 - 5) \div 2 + 5 \times 6 = 45(\text{cm}^2)$ (c) $6 \times 8 - (8 - 5) \times (6 - 4) \div 2 = 45(\text{cm}^2)$ (d) $(5 + 8) \times 6 \div 2 + 4 \times (8 - 5) \div 2 = 45(\text{cm}^2)$ (e) $(6 + 4) \times 8 \div 2 + 5 \times (6 - 4) \div 2 = 45(\text{cm}^2)$ ⑤ 132 cm² ⑥ (a) 67 cm² (b) 39 cm² (c) 58 cm² ⑦ (a) 22 cm² (b) 32 cm²

Unit test 3

① C ② D ③ B ④ C ⑤ 17 cm² ⑥ 3.6 ⑦ 7.1 cm² ⑧ 6 cm ⑨ (a) 8 cm (b) 25 cm² ⑩ (a) 79.5 cm² (b) 35.95 cm² ⑪ (a) 18 cm² (b) 63 cm² ⑫ £12 ⑬ 120 m²

Chapter 4　Triangles

4.1　Concepts of triangles (1)

① A ② B ③ A ④ 14 or 16 ⑤ 2 ⑥ 6, △ABH, △ADH, △ACH, △ACD, △ABD, △ABC ⑦ DC, BC ⑧ DAE, $\angle BAD$ ⑨ 45 ⑩ $1 < c < 7$; when $c = 2$, the perimeter is 9 cm; when $c = 4$, the perimeter is 11 cm; when $c = 6$, the perimeter is 13 cm. ⑪ (a) No. The endpoint D should be on side AB. (b) No. The height should be perpendicular to side BC with one endpoint being A and the other endpoint on BC. ⑫ $a = 3$ cm, $b = 4$ cm, $c = 5$ cm ⑬ Yes. There are 12 such triangles and they are (in the order of c, b, a): (6, 6, 6), (6, 6, 5), (6, 6, 4), (6, 6, 3), (6, 6, 2), (6, 6, 1), (6, 5, 5), (6, 5, 4), (6, 5, 3), (6, 5,

2), (6, 4, 4), (6, 4, 3).

4.2 Concepts of triangles (2)

❶ A ❷ D ❸ C ❹ B ❺ 9 ❻ 18 or 21 ❼ 3 ❽ 2 ❾ 6 ❿ 6 or 14

⓫ (a) $1 < x < 7$ (b) $\dfrac{7}{4}$ or $\dfrac{7}{3}$ ⓬ 12

⓭ 12, diagram correctly drawn

4.3 Sum of the interior angles of a triangle (1)

❶ D ❷ B ❸ D ❹ A ❺ 90°

❻ 15° ❼ 20° or 80° ❽ 20° ❾ 43°, 43° ❿ 70°, 70° or 40°, 100° ⓫ 115°

⓬ 108° ⓭ $(2n - 180)$°

4.4 Sum of the interior angles of a triangle (2)

❶ B ❷ C ❸ C ❹ B ❺ 90°

❻ 108 ❼ 2 ❽ 1 ❾ an obtuse-angled ❿ 25° ⓫ $\angle A = 40°$, $\angle B = 80°$ ⓬ 90°

⓭ 24° ⓮ (a) 20° (b) $\angle D = \dfrac{1}{2} \angle A$

4.5 Sum of the interior angles of a triangle (3)

❶ D ❷ C ❸ C ❹ C ❺ 85

❻ 100 ❼ 100 ❽ 40° ❾ an obtuse-angled or a right-angled ❿ 10° ⓫ 48° (Hint: Let $\angle ABE = \angle CBE = \alpha$, then $\angle ACD = 96° + 2\alpha$, $\angle ACE = 48° + \alpha$. Let the intersecting point of AC and BE be O, and in $\triangle AOB$ and $\triangle COE$, $\angle AOB = \angle COE$, then $\angle A + \angle ABO = \angle E + \angle ECO$, that is: $96° + \alpha = \angle E + (48° + \alpha)$, so $\angle E = 48°$.) ⓬ $\angle ABC + \angle ACB = 138°$, $\angle E = 180° - \dfrac{1}{3} \times 138° = 134°$, $\angle D = 180° - \dfrac{2}{3} \times 138° = 88°$

4.6 Congruent triangles: concepts and properties (1)

❶ C ❷ C ❸ B ❹ $\angle A$, $\angle BDC$, $\angle BEC$, BD, EC ❺ AB, AD, AC, AE, BC, ED, $\angle A$, $\angle A$, $\angle B$, $\angle D$, $\angle AED$, $\angle ACB$

❻ 7 ❼ $\triangle ABC$, $\triangle EBD$ ❽ 47°, 20

❾ $2 < CD < 10$ ❿ $EF = BC = 3$, $\angle D = 50°$, $\angle F = 60°$ ⓫ (a) $\triangle AFO \cong \triangle AEO$, $\triangle ABO \cong \triangle ACO$, $\triangle ABD \cong \triangle ACD$, $\triangle FOB \cong \triangle EOC$, $\triangle AEB \cong \triangle AFC$, $\triangle BOD \cong \triangle COD$, $\triangle BEC \cong \triangle CFB$ (b) Answers may vary, depending on triangles chosen. ⓬ $AB = 2$

4.7 Congruent triangles: concepts and properties (2)

❶ A ❷ C ❸ C ❹ can ❺ can

❻ 90° ❼ 180° (Hint: as shown in the diagram, since $\triangle ABF \cong \triangle DCE$, we get $\alpha = \beta$, and since $\alpha + \gamma = 180°$, then $\beta + \gamma = 180°$, that is: $\angle AFB + \angle BED = 180°$.) ❽ 135° (Hint: as shown in the diagram, since BF and AF bisect $\angle B$ and $\angle A$, we get $\alpha + \beta = \dfrac{1}{2} \times 90° = 45°$, then $\angle AFB = 180° - 45° = 135°$.)

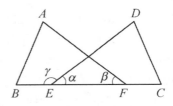

Diagram for question 7

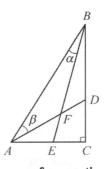

Diagram for question 8

❾ 4 ❿ (a) ① BC ② PBC ③ BP, BA ④ AC (b) ① $\angle DAE$ ② AD, AB ③ point B, AB, ABF, BF, AE, C (c) ① a ② B, c, C, b, A ③ AB, AC ⓫ diagram correctly drawn ⓬ diagram correctly drawn ⓭ diagram correctly drawn ⓮ 2 (as shown in the diagram)

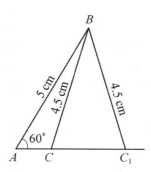

Diagram for question 14

4.8 Testing for congruent triangles (1)

1 C **2** A **3** D **4** SAS **5** $\angle DAC =$ $\angle BCA$ (or $AD /\!/ BC$) **6** $\triangle FED$ SAS

7 definitely **8** Since $AE = DB$, $AE + EB =$ $DB + EB$, that is: $AB = ED$, and since $BC /\!/ EF$, $\angle CBA = \angle FED$. In $\triangle ABC$ and $\triangle DEF$, $\begin{cases} AB = ED \\ \angle CBA = \angle FED \\ BC = EF \end{cases}$, therefore $\triangle ABC \cong \triangle DEF$ (SAS). **9** Meaning of median, shown in the diagram. Vertically opposite angles are equal. SAS. The corresponding sides of congruent triangles are equal. **10** Since points M and N are midpoints of CE and CD, then $CE = 2CM$ and $CD = 2CN$; since $CM = CN$, $CE = CD$; since $\angle 1 = \angle 2$, $\angle 1 + \angle ECD = \angle 2 + \angle ECD$, that is: $\angle ACD = \angle BCE$; since point C is the midpoint of AB, then $CA = CB$. In $\triangle ACD$ and $\triangle BCE$, $\begin{cases} CA = CB \\ \angle ACD = \angle BCE \\ CD = CE \end{cases}$, so $\triangle ACD \cong \triangle BCE$ (SAS); therefore $AD = BE$. **11** (a) Since quadrilaterals $ABDE$ and $BCGF$ are squares, $AB = DB$, $BF = BC$ and $\angle ABD = \angle DBC = 90°$. In $\triangle ABF$ and $\triangle DBC$, $\begin{cases} AB = DB \\ \angle ABF = \angle DBC \\ BF = BC \end{cases}$, so $\triangle ABF \cong \triangle DBC$ (SAS).

(b) Since $\triangle ABF \cong \triangle DBC$, $AF = DC$.

4.9 Testing for congruent triangles (2)

1 D **2** D **3** C **4** $\angle ADC = \angle ABC$

5 $AD = AB$ **6** $\angle A = \angle EDF$ (or $\angle BCA = \angle EFD$ or $AB = DE$ or $BC = EF$) **7** ③

8 Since $BC /\!/ DF$, $\angle ACB = \angle FDE$; since $AD = CE$, $AD + DC = CE + CD$, that is: $AC = DE$. In $\triangle ABC$ and $\triangle EFD$, $\begin{cases} \angle A = \angle E \\ AC = ED \\ \angle ACB = \angle FDE \end{cases}$, so $\triangle ABC \cong \triangle EFD$ (ASA), therefore $AB = EF$.

9 Since $AE \perp AB$ and $AD \perp AC$, $\angle CAD = \angle BAE = 90°$ and $\angle CAD + \angle DAE = \angle BAE + \angle DAE$, that is: $\angle CAE = \angle BAD$. In $\triangle CAE$ and $\triangle BAD$, $\begin{cases} \angle C = \angle B \\ AC = AB \\ \angle CAE = \angle BAD \end{cases}$, so $\triangle CAE \cong \triangle BAD$ (ASA); therefore $BD = CE$. **10** Since $DF \perp AC$, $\angle DFC = 90°$; and since $BE \perp AC$, $\angle BEA = 90°$ so $\angle DFC = \angle BEA = 90°$. In $\triangle ABE$ and $\triangle CDF$, $\begin{cases} \angle B = \angle D \\ BE = DF \\ \angle BEA = \angle DFC \end{cases}$, so $\triangle ABE \cong \triangle CDF$ (ASA), $AB = CD$. **11** In $\triangle BCM$ and $\triangle BDM$, $\begin{cases} \angle \alpha = \angle \beta \\ BM = BM \\ \gamma = \theta \end{cases}$, then $\triangle BCM \cong \triangle BDM$ (ASA), and $BC = BD$. In $\triangle ABC$ and $\triangle ABD$, $\begin{cases} BC = BD \\ \alpha = \beta \\ BA = BA \end{cases}$, so $\triangle ABC \cong \triangle ABD$ (SAS), and $AC = AD$.

4.10 Testing for congruent triangles (3)

1 C **2** D **3** A **4** 60° **5** 40°
6 $AC = CD$, $\angle ABC = \angle DBC$ **7** SSS, 90°
8 58° **9** Answer may vary, e.g., $AB = CD$ or $\angle AFB = \angle DEC$. **10** In $\triangle ABC$ and $\triangle BAE$, $\begin{cases} AC = BE \\ BC = AE \\ AB = BA \end{cases}$, so $\triangle ABC \cong \triangle BAE$ (SSS), and $\angle EAB = \angle CBA$; since $\angle CBA = 35°$, then $\angle EAB = 35°$. **11** Link AC and BD. In $\triangle ABD$

and $\triangle DCA$, $\begin{cases} AB = DC \\ \angle BAD = \angle CDA \\ AD = DA \end{cases}$, so $\triangle ABD \cong$

$\triangle DCA$ (SAS), and $AC = BD$. In $\triangle ABC$ and

$\triangle DCB$, $\begin{cases} AB = DC \\ BC = CB \\ AC = BD \end{cases}$, so $\triangle ABC \cong \triangle DCB$ (SSS),

therefore $\angle ABC = \angle DCB$.

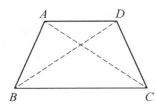

Diagram for question 11

⑫ In the diagram, (a) since quadrilateral $ABCD$ is a square, $AB = BC$ and $\angle ABC = 90°$. In $\triangle ABE$

and $\triangle CBP$, $\begin{cases} BE = BP \\ AE = CP \\ AB = CB \end{cases}$, so $\triangle ABE \cong \triangle CBP$

(SSS). (b) Since $\triangle ABE \cong \triangle CBP$, $\alpha = \beta$. Since $\beta + \gamma = 90°$, $\alpha + \gamma = 90°$, therefore $\angle PBE$ is a right angle.

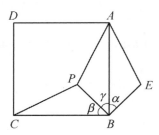

Diagram for question 12

4.11　Testing for congruent triangles (4)

❶ B　❷ D　❸ (a) $BD = BE$, SAS
(b) $\angle A = \angle C$, ASA　(c) $\angle D = \angle E$, AAS
❹ ABC, DEC, SAS　❺ ACD, AEB, SAS
❻ 65°　❼ 30　❽ Link CD. In $\triangle ACD$ and

$\triangle CBD$, $\begin{cases} AC = BC \\ AD = BD \\ CD = CD \end{cases}$, so $\triangle ACD \cong \triangle BCD$ (SSS),

and $\angle A = \angle B$. Since M is the midpoint on AC,

$AM = \dfrac{1}{2}AC$, and similarly $BN = \dfrac{1}{2}BC$. Since $AC = BC$, $AM = BN$. In $\triangle ADM$ and $\triangle BDN$,

$\begin{cases} AM = BN \\ \angle A = \angle B \\ AD = BD \end{cases}$, so $\triangle DAM \cong \triangle DBN$ (SAS),

therefore $DM = DN$.　❾ 16 (Note: from the given, $\triangle ABD \cong \triangle ACE$, and therefore $CE = BD = 16$.)　❿ (a) Yes (Note: first draw $EF \perp AD$ with F as the foot of the perpendicular. From the given, $\triangle DCE \cong \triangle DFE$, so $EF = EC$, and similarly $\triangle ABE \cong \triangle AFE$, and $EF = BE$; therefore $EC = EB$.)　(b) From $\triangle DCE \cong \triangle DFE$, $\angle CED = \angle FED$, and similarly $\angle BEA = \angle FEA$; since $\angle CED + \angle FED + \angle FEA + \angle BEA = 180°$, $\angle FED + \angle FEA = 90°$; therefore $DE \perp AE$.

4.12　Testing for congruent triangles (5)

❶ B　❷ C　❸ B　❹ (a) $BC = EF$ (or $BE = CF$)　(b) $\angle A = \angle D$　(c) $\angle ACB = \angle F$　❺ 70°　❻ 10　❼ 46°　❽ (a) From the question, $\angle DBH + \angle C = 90°$, $\angle DAC + \angle C = 90°$, therefore $\angle DBH = \angle DAC$.　(b) Since $\angle DBH = \angle DAC$, $\angle BDH = \angle ADC = 90°$ and $AD = BD$, then it proves that $\triangle BDH \cong \triangle ADC$.
❾ By proving $\triangle BED \cong \triangle DFC$, we get $DE = DF$, so $AE + AF = AF + FD + DE + AF = 2AF + 2DF = 2AD$ or $AE + AF = AD + DE + AD - DF = 2AD$.　❿ First by proving $\triangle ABD \cong \triangle CBD$, $AB = CB$; and by proving $\triangle AED \cong \triangle CFD$, $AE = FC$, therefore $AB = BC = BF + FC = BF + AE$.

4.13　Testing for congruent triangles (6)

❶ D　❷ D　❸ C　❹ 10　❺ 100°
❻ $\angle CAB = \angle DAB$, $\angle ABC = \angle ABD$
❼ 1.5
❽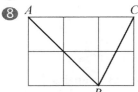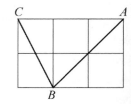

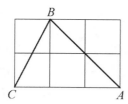

Diagram for question 8

9 Link AD to prove $\triangle ABD \cong \triangle ACD$, then $\angle B = \angle C$ **10** In $\triangle AEF$ and $\triangle DEF$,

$$\begin{cases} AF = DF \\ \angle AFE = \angle DFE = 90° \\ EF = EF \end{cases}$$ so $\triangle AEF \cong \triangle DEF$

(SAS), $\angle EAF = \angle EDF$. Since $\angle ADE = \angle B + \angle \alpha$, $\angle DAE = \angle \beta + \angle CAE$, and AD bisects $\angle BAC$, $\angle \alpha = \angle \beta$, then $\angle B = \angle CAE$.

11 First proving $\triangle ADC \cong \triangle AFC$ leads to $CF = CD$ and $\angle AFC = \angle D$. From $\angle AFC + \angle EFC = 180°$, $\angle D + \angle B = 180°$, then $\angle EFC = \angle B$; again, proving $\triangle BCE \cong \triangle FCE$ leads to $BC = CF$, therefore $DC = BC$. **12** (a) In the diagram, link AC, AD, BC and BD. In $\triangle CAD$ and $\triangle CBD$,

$$\begin{cases} CA = CB \\ DA = DB, \\ CD = CD \end{cases}$$ so $\triangle ACD \cong \triangle BCD$ (SSS),

therefore $\alpha = \beta$. (b) In $\triangle ACO$ and $\triangle BCO$,

$$\begin{cases} AC = BC \\ \angle \alpha = \angle \beta, \\ CO = CO \end{cases}$$ so $\triangle AOC \cong \triangle BOC$ (SAS),

therefore $AO = BO$, $\angle COA = \angle COB$; since $\angle AOC + \angle BOC = 180°$, $\angle AOC = \angle BOC = 90°$, that is: $CD \perp AB$, therefore CD is the perpendicular bisector of AB.

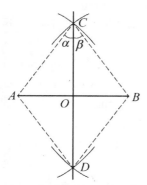

Diagram for question 12

4.14 Properties of isosceles triangles

1 B **2** A **3** C **4** B **5** C
6 80°, 20° or 50°, 50° **7** 30 cm **8** 36 or 90 **9** 55° or 125° **10** 12 **11** 70
12 (a) AD, BC. The bisector of the vertex angle in the isosceles triangle is perpendicular to the base. BD, DC. The bisector of the vertex angle in the isosceles triangle bisects the base. (b) β. The foot of the height on the base of the isosceles triangle coincides with the bisector of the vertex angle. BD, DC. The foot of the height on the base of the isosceles triangle bisects the base.
13 First by proving $\triangle ABD \cong \triangle ACE$, $AB = AC$. Since AH is the bisector of side BC, then $AH \perp BC$. **14** AD is perpendicular to BC, the reason: first, proving $\triangle ABD \cong \triangle ACD$ leads to $AB = AC$; as point D is a point on the bisector of $\angle BAC$, therefore $AD \perp BC$.

4.15 Identifying isosceles triangles (1)

1 A **2** B **3** A **4** 130°, 25°, 25°
5 3 **6** 3 **7** 40° **8** 40° **9** 5
10 Yes. From $\angle BAC = 90°$, $\alpha + \angle AEF = 90°$; from $AD \perp BC$, $\beta + \angle BFD = 90°$, so $\angle AEF = \angle BFD$; from $\angle BFD = \angle AFE$, $\angle AFE = \angle AEF$, therefore $\triangle AFE$ is an isosceles triangle.
11 Yes. From $AB = AC$, $\angle B = \angle C$; from $DE \perp BC$, $\angle BDE + \angle B = 90°$, $\angle F + \angle C = 90°$, so $\angle F = \angle BDE$. Since vertically opposite angles are equal, $\angle BDE = \angle FDA$, therefore $\angle F = \angle FDA$, and $\triangle AFD$ is an isosceles triangle. **12** As shown in the diagram, CE bisects $\angle ACB$, so $\alpha = \beta$; since $\gamma = \theta$ and $CE = CE$, $\triangle ACE \cong \triangle BCE$ (AAS), and $AC = BC$; since $\alpha = \beta$, then CD is perpendicular to AB.

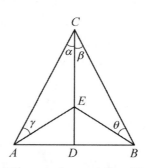

Diagram for question 12

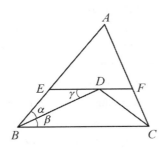

Diagram for question 13

⑬ As shown in the diagram, BD bisects $\angle ABC$, so $\alpha = \beta$; from $EF \parallel BC$, $\beta = \gamma$, so $\alpha = \gamma$ and $ED = EB$; similarly, $FD = FC$, therefore $EB + FC = EF$.

4.16 Identifying isosceles triangles (2)

❶ A　❷ C　❸ C　❹ 22　❺ 39°, 78°, 63°　❻ 3　❼ 90　❽ 30　❾ 8　❿ From $EF \perp BC$, $\angle F + \angle C = 90°$, so $\angle BDE + \angle B = 90°$; from $AB = AC$, $\angle B = \angle C$, so $\angle F = \angle BDE$; from $\angle BDE = \angle FDA$, $\angle FDA = \angle F$, so $AF = AD$; since M is the midpoint of DF, then $AM \perp FD$.　⓫ From $DE \parallel AC$, $\angle EDB = \angle C$; from $AB = AC$, $\angle B = \angle C$, so $\angle B = \angle EDB$ and $BE = DE$; similarly, $FD = FC$, therefore the perimeter $C_{AEDF} = AE + DE + DF + AF = AE + EB + AF + FC = AB + AC$. Since $AB = AC = 10$, the perimeter of the quadrilateral $AEDF$ is 20.　⓬ From proving $\triangle ABD \cong \triangle CEA$, $AB = AC$, $\gamma = \angle EAC$, so $\theta = \angle ACB$; from $AE \parallel BC$, $\angle ACB = \angle EAC$, therefore $\gamma = \theta$.　⓭ From proving $\triangle ABD \cong \triangle AED$, $\angle B = \angle AED$; since $\angle B = 2\angle C$, $\angle AED = 2\angle C$; from $\angle AED = \angle C + \angle EDC$, then $\angle C = \angle EDC$, therefore $\triangle ECD$ is an isosceles triangle.

4.17 Equilateral triangles

❶ B　❷ B　❸ D　❹ an equilateral, 3　❺ $\angle A = 60°$ (or $\angle B = 60°$ or $\angle C = 60°$ or $AB = BC$ or $BC = AC$)　❻ 12　❼ 15　❽ equilateral　❾ 9, 3　❿ First, proving $\triangle ABD \cong \triangle ACE$ leads to $AD = AE$ and $\angle CAE = \angle BAD = 60°$, therefore $\triangle ADE$ is an equilateral triangle.　⓫ Proving $\triangle ADC \cong \triangle CEB$ leads to $\angle ACD = \angle CBE$, so $\angle EPC = \angle CBE + \angle BCP = \angle ACD + \angle BCP = \angle BCA = 60°$; therefore $\angle BPC = 120°$.　⓬ Proving $\triangle AEC \cong \triangle BDC$ leads to $\angle EAC = \angle DBC$; since $\angle EBD = \angle DBC + \angle CBE = 62°$, $\angle EAC + \angle CBE = 62°$; since $\angle BAC = \angle CBA = 60°$, $\angle BAC + \angle CBA = 120°$, that is $\angle BAE + \angle EAC + \angle ABE + \angle CBE = 120°$; therefore $\angle BAE + \angle ABE = 120° - 62° = 58°$, and $\angle AEB = 180° - \angle BAE - \angle ABE = 180° - 58° = 122°$.

Unit Test 4

❶ A　❷ B　❸ D　❹ B　❺ B　❻ A　❼ a scalene, an acute-angled triangle　❽ are not necessarily　❾ 60　❿ 8 cm or 6 cm　⓫ 55° or 65°　⓬ 140°, 20°, 20°　⓭ 110°　⓮ 4, $\triangle ABC$, $\triangle DBC$, $\triangle ABD$, $\triangle ACD$　⓯ $\dfrac{180}{7}$　⓰ 26°　⓱ 32°　⓲ ①②④⑤

⓳ By proving $\alpha + \theta = 90°$, $\alpha + \phi = 90°$ and $\angle \gamma + \phi = 90°$, $\phi = \theta$, $\gamma = \alpha$; since $\theta = \beta + B$ and $\alpha = \beta$, then $\phi = \alpha + \angle B = \gamma + \angle B$.

⓴ From $AB = BC$, $\angle CAB = \angle ACB$, and from $AB \parallel CD$, $\angle DCA = \angle CAB$, so $\angle DCA = \angle ACB$. By proving $\triangle DAC \cong \triangle EAC$, therefore $CD = CE$.

㉑ From $AD \perp BC$ and $EG \parallel AD$, $EG \perp BC$; and $\angle C + \angle G = 90°$ and $\angle B + \angle BFE = 90°$; since $\angle AFG = \angle G$ and $\angle AFG = \angle BFE$, then $\angle G = \angle BFE$ and $\angle B = \angle C$, therefore $\triangle ABD \cong \triangle ACD$.　㉒ Passing through point D, construct $DE \perp AB$ with E being the foot of the perpendicular; and from $BD : DC = 9 : 7$ and $BC = 32$, $CD = 14$ and $BD = 18$. By proving $\triangle ACD \cong \triangle AED$, $DE = CD = 14$, that is the distance from D to AB is 14.　㉓ Passing through point B, construct line MN intersecting AC at point D so that $\angle CBD = 40°$; since $\angle C = \angle CBD = 40°$, $\triangle BCD$ is an isosceles triangle; then, proving $\angle A = \angle ADB = 80°$ leads to $\triangle ABD$ being an isosceles triangle.　㉔ From $\triangle ABC$ and $\triangle CDE$ being equilateral triangles, $CA = CB$, $CE = CD$ and

$\angle ACB = \angle ECD = 60°$; from $\angle ACB + \angle BCD + \angle ECD = 180°$, $\angle BCD = 60°$, so $\angle ACD = \angle BCE = 120°$; by proving $\triangle ACD \cong \triangle BCE$, $AD = BE$ and $\alpha = \beta$; from M being the midpoint of AD and N being the midpoint of BE, $MD = NE$; proving $\triangle CMD \cong \triangle CNE$ leads to $CM = CN$ and $\gamma = \theta$; from $\gamma + \phi = 60°$, we get $\theta + \phi = 60°$, that is $\angle MCN = 60°$, therefore $\triangle CMN$ is an equilateral triangle.

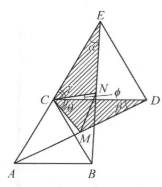

Diagram for question 24

Chapter 5   The co-ordinate plane

5.1   Introduction to the co-ordinate plane (1)

① B ② C ③ C ④ 6, 5 ⑤ b, a
⑥ 6 ⑦ -3 ⑧ 1 ⑨ $(3, -2)$ ⑩ 15
⑪ (a) $(8, 5)$ or $(8, -5)$ or $(-8, 5)$ or $(-8, -5)$ (b) $a = 0$ or $b = 0$, but both a and b cannot be 0 at the same time. ⑫ There are 3 squares satisfying the condition and the other two vertices are $(-1, 2)$, $(1, 2)$ or $(-1, -2)$, $(1, -2)$ or $(0, 1)$, $(0, -1)$.

5.2   Introduction to the co-ordinate plane (2)

① C ② B ③ A ④ $(-4, -3)$
⑤ $(-b, a)$ ⑥ second ⑦ second or fourth
⑧ second ⑨ $(1, -2)$ ⑩ (a) $y = 2$ or $y = -2$ (b) $x = 3$ or $x = -3$ ⑪ $A(7, 3)$, $B(-1, 3)$, $C(-1, 4)$ ⑫ $\left(\dfrac{5}{3}, \dfrac{5}{3}\right)$ or $(-5, 5)$ ⑬ $A(1, 1)$ $B(-3, 3)$ ⑭ $(3, -5)$

5.3   Point movement on the co-ordinate plane (1)

① B ② B ③ C ④ $b - a$ when $b > a$,

and $a - b$ when $a > b$ ⑤ 6 ⑥ -1 or 11
⑦ $(1, 8)$ or $(11, 8)$ ⑧ $(6, 2)$ or $(6, 14)$
⑨ $(6, 3)$ or $(6, 13)$ ⑩ $(0, 8)$ or $(12, 8)$
⑪ (a) $a = 3$, $b = -1$, $c = -3$ (b) 20
⑫ 4.5 ⑬ 5.5 ⑭ (a) $A_1(1, -5)$, $B_1(3, -2)$, $C_1(0, 0)$ (b) 6.5

5.4   Point movement on the co-ordinate plane (2)

① D ② D ③ D ④ $(5, 3)$ ⑤ $(2, 0)$ ⑥ down 4 ⑦ $(1, 1)$ ⑧ left 5, down 1 ⑨ right 2, down 3 ⑩ $(-1, -5)$
⑪ $A'(-1, -1)$, $B'(2, 1)$, the area: 12
⑫ $a = 2$, $c = 5$ the area: 4 ⑬ $B_1(-1, 2)$, $D_1(-1, -2)$, $O_1(1, 0)$ ⑭ (a) $D(1, 1)$, $E(3, 1)$ (b) 1

5.5   Point movement on the co-ordinate plane (3)

① A ② B ③ D ④ first, $(1, 3)$
⑤ third, $(-1, -3)$ ⑥ second, $(-3, 5)$
⑦ 2 ⑧ 36 ⑨ $(-4, -3)$ ⑩ $\left(\dfrac{5}{2}, \dfrac{7}{2}\right)$ ⑪ 8 ⑫ $B(3, 3)$, $C(1, 0)$
⑬ $C(-2, -4)$, 1 (Hint: from the given conditions, $a = 2$, $b = 4$, $A(-3, -1)$, $B(-3, 1)$, $D(2, 4)$ and $C(-2, -4)$.) ⑭ If OA is one of the two equal sides of the right-angled isosceles triangle, then there are four possible co-ordinates for point B: $(0, 2)$ or $(0, -2)$ or $(2, 2)$ or $(2, -2)$; if OA is the hypotenuse of the triangle, then there are two possible co-ordinates for point B: $(1, 1)$ or $(1, -1)$.

Unit test 5

① B ② C ③ A ④ A ⑤ second
⑥ fourth ⑦ $x(-x, 0)$ ⑧ $a > \dfrac{3}{2}$
⑨ 1 ⑩ $3\sqrt{3}$ ⑪ $(3, 3)$ or $(3, -7)$
⑫ $(3, 3)$ ⑬ left 9, up 8 ⑭ $(x, -y + a)$
⑮ $(x - a, y)$ ⑯ $2y$ when $y > 0$ or $-2y$ when $y < 0$ ⑰ $(-1, 4)$ ⑱ $(3, -8)$ ⑲ $(1, 5)$

㉑ $(-6, 6)$ or $(6, -6)$ ㉑ 5 ㉒ 5

㉓ $A(-1, 3)$ ㉔ (a) In the right-angled triangles $\triangle OPQ$ and $\triangle OP_1Q_1$, $OP = OP_1$, $\angle POQ = 180° - 90° - \angle Q_1OP_1 = 90° - \angle Q_1OP_1 = \angle OP_1Q_1$, so $\triangle OPQ \cong \triangle OP_1Q_1$ (AAS) (b) $P_1Q_1 = OQ = a$, $OQ_1 = PQ = b$, therefore $P_1(-b, a)$. ㉕ $B(2, -2)$ $C(3, 0)$ $E(1, 2)$ Area: 12 ㉖ Taking A as the ' top ' (unequal) vertex of the isosceles triangle OAB, the co-ordinates of point B are $(2, 0)$ or $(0, 2)$; taking O as the ' top ' (unequal) vertex, the co-ordinates of point B are $(\sqrt{2}, 0)$ or $(-\sqrt{2}, 0)$ or $(0, \sqrt{2})$ or $(0, -\sqrt{2})$.

Chapter 6   Direct proportion, inverse proportion and their functions

6.1   Variables and functions

① A ② C ③ C ④ 2π, r, C

⑤ $y = \dfrac{2x + 6}{5}$ ⑥ $y = 2x$ ⑦ $y = 100 - x$

⑧ $\dfrac{2s}{a}$ ⑨ $y = \dfrac{1500}{x}$ ⑩ $y = 16 - 2x$

⑪ $y = \dfrac{1}{2x + 1} + 3$

6.2   Direct proportion and direct proportional functions

① C ② C ③ D ④ B ⑤ -5

⑥ $y = 4\sqrt{x}$, $x \geqslant 0$ ⑦ -3 ⑧ 2

⑨ (a) $y = -4(x - 1)$ (b) $y = 12$ (c) $x = -4$ ⑩ (a) $\beta = 90 - \alpha$. It is not a direct proportion function. (b) $y = 2\pi x$. It is a direct proportion function. ⑪ $y_1 = \dfrac{15)}{4}x$, $y_2 = \dfrac{6}{25}x$. The truck is more fuel-efficient. ⑫ $y = 2x^2 - \dfrac{1}{2}(x + 1)$

6.3   Graphs of direct proportional functions

① D ② C ③ B ④ B ⑤ A

⑥ 0, k, coefficient ⑦ plotting two points, $(0, 0)$, $(1, k)$ ⑧ II, IV, decreases

⑨ -1 ⑩ -3 ⑪ $y = -3x$ ⑫ (a) $y =$

$\dfrac{1}{2}x$ (b) $y = \dfrac{5}{2}$ (c) $x = 20$ (d) graph drawn as described, $-1 < y \leqslant 3$ ⑬ $S_{\triangle POA} = 6$ ⑭ (a) $k = -2$ (b) $m = 2$ (c) $y_3 > y_1 > y_2$

6.4   Properties of direct proportional functions

① D ② C ③ B ④ C ⑤ the origin, I, III, increases, II, IV, decreases ⑥ straight line, II, IV ⑦ 0, k^2, I, III ⑧ 2, increases

⑨ $-\dfrac{7}{3}$, II, IV ⑩ $k > 0$, I, III ⑪ -1

⑫ $k = -1$, $y = -3x$, graph drawn as described

⑬ (a) $y = \dfrac{8}{3}x - \dfrac{13}{3}$ (b) The greatest value of y is $\dfrac{11}{3}$ and the least value of y is $-\dfrac{13}{3}$.

⑭ (a) $P(-2, -6)$, $P_1(-2, 6)$, $P_2(2, -6)$ (b) $k_1 = -3$, $k_2 = -3$ (c) Both symmetric points on the graph of the direct proportional function $y = 3x$ about the x-axis and the y-axis are on the direct proportional function $y = -3x$, so the conclusion will be still true when the condition ' the direct proportional function $y = 3x$ ' is changed into ' the direct proportional function $y = kx$ '.

6.5   Inverse proportion and inverse proportional functions

① A ② C ③ A ④ non-zero constant or fixed value ⑤ $x \neq 3$ ⑥ an inversely proportional, $\dfrac{1}{2}$ ⑦ $y = \dfrac{3}{2x}$ ⑧ -2

⑨ -2 ⑩ inversely proportional ⑪ 1, $y = 3x$ ⑫ $m = \dfrac{1}{2}$, $y = \dfrac{7}{2x}$ ⑬ Let the function be $y = 2k_1x - \dfrac{k_2}{x^2}$. Then $k_1 = 1$, $k_2 = 2$, giving $y = 2x - \dfrac{2}{x^2}$. ⑭ Let the function be $y = 2k_1(x - 2) + \dfrac{k_2}{5x}$. Then $k_1 = \dfrac{4}{5}$, $k_2 = 9$, giving $y = \dfrac{8}{5}(x - 2) + \dfrac{9}{5x}$. When $x = -1$, $y = -\dfrac{33}{5}$.

6.6 Graphs of inverse proportional functions

① C **②** C **③** D **④** 6 **⑤** $m > 1$

⑥ $m < -2$ **⑦** $k < 0$ **⑧** $\left(\dfrac{\sqrt{2}}{2}, 2\sqrt{2}\right)$

⑨ $y = \dfrac{3}{x}$ **⑩** $(-2, 2)$ or $(2, -2)$

⑪ (a) $a = 4$ (b) $P'(2, 4)$ (c) $y = \dfrac{8}{x}$

⑫ (a) $y = -\dfrac{8}{x}$ (b) $B\left(3, -\dfrac{8}{3}\right)$ (c) $S_{\triangle ABC} = 16$

⑬ (a) $A(8, 1)$, $B(2, 4)$ (b) $15\dfrac{1}{2}$

6.7 Properties of inverse proportional functions

① D **②** D **③** C **④** second, fourth, increases **⑤** 12, first, third, decreases

⑥ $y_2 < y_1 < y_3$ **⑦** 2 **⑧** (a) $k = 3$
(b) The graph is in the first and third quadrants. y decreases with the increase of x in each quadrant.

(c) $-2 \leqslant y \leqslant -\dfrac{1}{3}$ **⑨** (a) $y = -\dfrac{20}{x}$

(b) $m = -4$. The distance between point P and the x-axis is 5. **⑩** From the given, $\dfrac{k}{2} = -a$,

$\dfrac{k}{2-a} = 6$, so $a = 3$, $k = -6$. The expression of the inverse proportional function is $y = -\dfrac{6}{x}$.

When $y = \dfrac{1}{2}$, $x = -12$. **⑪** (a) 1, $\dfrac{\sqrt{5}-1}{2}$

(b) $\sqrt{2}$, $\dfrac{\sqrt{10}-\sqrt{2}}{2}$ (c) The ratio of the side

lengths is $1 : \dfrac{\sqrt{5}-1}{2}$. The ratio is true for any

value of $k(k > 0)$.

6.8 How to express functions (1)

① B **②** A **③** B **④** C **⑤** C

⑥ analytical method, table method, graphical method **⑦** algebraic expression **⑧** graphical method **⑨** table method **⑩** $(1, -\sqrt{3})$

⑪ 1 **⑫** $y = 10 - 2x$, $\dfrac{5}{2} < x < 5$, $5 < y < 10$

⑬ 21 **⑭** (a) 2, 10 (b) (i) $y = 10x$
(ii) $y = 15x$ (c) 110 m **⑮** (a) $y = (40 + x)(40 - x) = 1600 - x^2$ (b) The company should buy 60 pieces. The profit for Khalid will be £1200.

6.9 How to express functions (2)

① D **②** D **③** D **④** $y = -x$, $y = x$, $y = 0$ or $x = 0$ **⑤** is **⑥** $y = 24 - 3x$, 5 cm

⑦ $(1, 4)$, $(-1, -4)$ graph drawn as described

⑧ (a) $x \leqslant 5$ (b) $m = 19$ (c) $y = -59$

⑨ (a) $B(3, 3)$, $k = 9$ (b) $P\left(6, \dfrac{3}{2}\right)$

(c) $S_{\triangle BOP} = \dfrac{27}{4}$ **⑩** Since $S_{\triangle AOC} = S_{\triangle BOD}$,

$S_{\text{quadrilateral } AODB} - S_{\triangle AOC} = S_{\text{quadrilateral } AODB} - S_{\triangle BOD}$;
therefore $S_{\triangle AOB} = S_{\text{trapezium } ABDC}$.

Unit test 6

① C **②** D **③** B **④** C **⑤** D **⑥** B

⑦ first **⑧** -2 **⑨** -13 **⑩** $y = 4x$

⑪ second, fourth **⑫** -4 **⑬** $\left(-\dfrac{1}{2}, -5\right)$

⑭ $m < \dfrac{1}{2}$ **⑮** $\dfrac{2s}{a}$ **⑯** inversely proportional

⑰ $4\dfrac{7}{2}$ **⑱** -1 **⑲** $b = -1$ Yes

⑳ (a) $A(2, -1)$, $B(-2, 1)$ or $A(-2, 1)$, $B(2, -1)$ (b) 4 **㉑** (a) $y = \dfrac{4}{x}$ (b) $AB =$

$2\sqrt{10}$ **㉒** (a) $k = 9$ (b) 3 **㉓** (a) The expression of the function representing the line OB

is $y = \dfrac{3}{2}x$, and the expression of the inverse

proportional function is $y = \dfrac{3}{x}$ (b) 3 **㉔** $y =$

$\dfrac{3}{4}x$, $y = \dfrac{12}{x}$ or $y = -\dfrac{3}{4}x$, $y = -\dfrac{12}{x}$

Chapter 7 Introduction to proof in geometry

7.1 Statement and proof (1)

① A **②** A, C **③** B **④** (a) definition of complementary angles (b) When two lines are parallel, the corresponding angles are equal. When two lines are parallel, the alternate angles are equal. When two lines are parallel, the interior angles on the same side are supplementary. (c) The angles in a triangle add up to 180°.

5 SAS, ASA, AAS, SSS **6** $\triangle ACE$, AE, $\triangle ACD$, CH, EH, $\triangle AEH$ **7** Given: When the two lines are parallel, the interior angles on the same side are supplementary. Given: When the two lines are parallel, the interior angles on the same side are supplementary, property of equality. **8** An exterior angle of a triangle is equal to the sum of the two non-adjacent interior angles. BDE, FEC, BDE, FEC, BD, CE, ASA. In congruent triangles the corresponding pairs of sides are equal. **9** (a) Since $CA = CB$ and $CD \perp AB$, $\angle ACD = \angle BCD$. Since $\angle ACB = 90°$, $\angle A = \angle ACD = \angle BCD = 45°$, then $AD = CD$. Since $EF \perp AC$, $\angle A = \angle FEA = 45°$, then $EF = AF = CG$; therefore $\triangle AFD \cong \triangle CGD$. Hence $DF = DG$. (b) Since $\triangle AFD \cong \triangle CGD$, $\angle FDA = \angle GDC$. Since $\angle ADF + \angle FDC = 90°$, $\angle CDG + \angle FDC = 90°$; therefore $DF \perp DG$.

7.2 Statement and proof (2)

1 D **2** C **3** C **4** statement (or proposition), true statement (or true proposition), false statement (or false proposition) **5** is **6** true **7** a right-angled triangle, the two acute angles are complementary. **8** $a \parallel b$ and $b \parallel c$, $a \parallel c$ **9** two lines are parallel to the same line, the two lines are parallel **10** (b) If each pair of the corresponding sides of two triangles are equal, then they are congruent. (c) If the two sides of a triangle are equal, then the opposite angles of the two sides are equal. (d) If two angles have the same complementary angle, then they are equal. **11** (a) Since $DB \parallel EC$, $\angle AHC = \alpha$ (When two lines are parallel, the corresponding angles are equal). $\angle \beta = \angle AHC$ (Vertically opposite angles are equal.).

Hence $\alpha = \beta$ (property of equality). (b) Since $DB \parallel EC$, $\angle ABG = \angle C$ (When two lines are parallel, the corresponding angles are equal.), $\angle C = \angle D$ (given), so $\angle D = \angle ABG$ (property of equality). In $\triangle FDG$, $\angle F + \angle D + \angle DGF = 180°$, and in $\triangle ABG$, $\angle A + \angle ABG + \alpha = 180°$ (The angles in a triangle add up to 180°.), $\alpha = \angle DGF$, therefore $\angle A = \angle F$.

7.3 Practice and exercise in proof (1)

1 B **2** D **3** γ, the angles on the same side are equal. Vertically opposite angles are equal. property of equality **4** 80° **5** 40° **6** 50° **7** Since $AB \parallel CG \parallel EF$, $\angle B = CGF$ (When two lines are parallel, the corresponding angles are equal), and $\angle CGF + \angle F = 180°$ (When two lines are parallel, the interior angles on the same side are supplementary). Hence $\angle B + \angle F = 180°$ (property of equality). **8** Since $AB \parallel CD$, $\angle BAE = \angle AEC$ (When two lines are parallel, the alternate angles are equal). Since $\angle M = \angle N$ (given), $\angle AON = \angle EOM$ (Vertically opposite angles are equal), $\angle NAE = 180° - \angle N - \angle AON$ and $\angle AEM = 180° - \angle M - \angle EOM$ (The angles in a triangle add up to 180°), and $\angle NAE = \angle AEM$. Therefore, $\angle BAE - \angle NAE = \angle AEC - \angle AEM$, thus $\alpha = \beta$. **9** Given: In $\triangle ABC$, $AB = AC$, BE and CD are the medians on AC and AB respectively. Prove: $BE = CD$

Proof: From $AB = AC$ (given), D and E are the midpoints of AB and AC (given), which means that $AD = \frac{1}{2}AB$, and $AE = \frac{1}{2}AC$, $\angle A$ is common, so $AD = AE$, therefore $\triangle ABE \cong \triangle ADC$ (SAS). Therefore $BE = CD$.

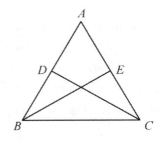

7.4 Practice and exercise in proof (2)

1 D **2** D **3** $\angle DBE$, CA **4** $\triangle ACE$, SAS, $\triangle ACD$ **5** 65 **6** 3 **7** Since $FC \parallel AB$, $\angle ADE = \angle EFC$ (When two lines are parallel, the alternate angles are equal). Since $\angle ADE = \angle EFC$, $DE = FE$ (given), $\angle DEA = \angle FEC$ (Vertically opposite angles are equal), $\triangle DEA \cong \triangle FEC$ (ASA). Hence $AD = CF$ (The corresponding pairs of sides in congruent triangles are equal.). **8** Since $AC \parallel DE$, $\angle ACB = \angle DEC$ (When two lines are parallel, the corresponding angles are equal) and $\angle ACD = \angle D$ (When two lines are parallel, the alternate angles are equal). Since $\angle ACD = \angle B$ (given), $\angle B = \angle D$ (property of equality); $AC = CE$ (given), $\triangle ABC \cong \triangle CDE$ (AAS); therefore $AB = CD$ (Corresponding pairs of sides in congruent triangles are equal).

7.5 Practice and exercise in proof (3)

Note: In the proof problems below, reasons are indicated only for some selected steps. **1** D **2** B **3** $180°$ **4** $45°$ **5** $55°$ or $125°$ **6** CEF, DCE **7** Since $MA = MD$, $\angle MAD = \angle MDA$. Since $AD \parallel BC$, $\angle AMB = \angle MAD$, and $\angle DMC = \angle ADM$, so $\angle AMB = \angle DMC$. Hence $\triangle ABM \cong \triangle DCM$ (SAS). **8** (a) Since $\triangle ABC$ is an equilateral triangle (given), $\angle ACB = 60°$ (property of equilateral triangle). Since $CE = CD$ (given), $\angle E = \angle EDC$ (In a triangle, angles opposite equal sides are equal). Since $\angle ACB = \angle E + \angle EDC$ (An exterior angle of a triangle is equal to the sum of the two non-adjacent interior angles); therefore $\angle E = 30°$. (b) Since $\triangle ABC$ is an equilateral triangle, $AB = CB = BC$ and $\angle ABC = 60°$ (property of equilateral triangle). Since D is the midpoint of AC, i.e., $AD = DC$, $\triangle BAD \cong \triangle BCD$ (SSS), so $\angle ABD = \angle DBC = \frac{1}{2} \times 60° = 30°$. Since $\angle E = 30°$ (proved), $\angle E = \angle DBC$ (property of equality), therefore $DB = DE$ (In a triangle, sides opposite equal angles are

equal). **9** Since $AE = DE$, $BE = EF$ and $\angle AEB = \angle DEF$, $\triangle AEB \cong \triangle DEF$ (SAS); so $AB = DF$ and $\angle A = \angle ADF$. Since $AC = 2AB$ and $AD = CD = \frac{1}{2}AC$, $AB = AD = CD$; so $DF = AB = DC$ and $\angle ADB = \angle ABD$. Hence $\angle BDF = \angle ADB + \angle ADF = \angle ABD + \angle A = \angle BDC$ (An exterior angle of a triangle is equal to the sum of the two non-adjacent interior angles). Since $BD = BD$ and $DF = DC$, we get $\triangle DBF \cong \triangle DBC$ (SAS). Thus $BC = BF = 2EF$ and $\angle F = \angle C$.

7.6 Practice and exercise in proof (4)

1 B **2** A **3** two angles are supplementary to the same angle; the two angles are equal **4** $90°$ **5** $50°$, $65°$ and $65°$ or $130°$, $25°$ and $25°$ **6** 50 **7** Since $AB \parallel MN$ (given), $\angle BCD + \angle CDN = 180°$ (When two lines are parallel, the interior angles on the same side are supplementary). Since CG and DG are angle bisectors, $\alpha = \frac{1}{2}\angle BCD$ and $\beta = \frac{1}{2}\angle CDN$ (definition of angle bisector), so $\alpha + \beta = 90°$. Since $\alpha + \beta + \angle CGD = 180°$ (The sum of the interior angles in a triangle is $180°$), $\angle CGD = 90°$; therefore $CG \perp DG$. **8** Since $\alpha = \angle B$, $\angle A = 180° - 2\angle\alpha$ and since $\beta = \angle D$, $\angle D = 180° - 2\beta$. Since $AB \parallel CD$, $\angle A + \angle C = 180°$, so $\alpha + \beta = 90°$. Since $\alpha + \beta + \angle BED = 180°$, $\angle BED = 90°$; therefore $BE \perp DE$. **9** Since $AB = AC$, $\angle B = \angle C$. Since $BE = CF$ and $\alpha = \beta$, $\triangle BEF \cong \triangle CFH$ (AAS), so $EF = FH$. Since M is the midpoint on EH, $FM \perp EH$ (property of isosceles triangle). **10** Since BE and CF are the heights in $\triangle ABC$, $\angle ABP = \angle ACQ$ (Two angles supplementary to the same angle are equal). Since $BP = AC$ and $CQ = AB$, $\triangle ABP \cong \triangle QCA$ (SAS), so $\angle BAP = \angle Q$, therefore $\angle QAP = \angle QAB + \angle BAP = \angle QAB + \angle Q = 90°$. Hence $AP \perp AQ$.

7.7 Perpendicular bisector of a line segment

1 B **2** B **3** C **4** D **5** true

⑥ 25　❼ 45　❽ 50　❾ 8　❿ 70, 12

⓫ In the right-angled $\triangle ABC$, since $\angle C = 90°$ and bisector AD of $\angle CAB$ intersects BC at D, then $\angle DAE = \frac{1}{2}\angle CAB = \frac{1}{2}(90° - \angle B)$. Since DE perpendicularly bisects AB, we get $AD = BD$, so $\angle DAE = \angle B$, $\angle DAE = \frac{1}{2}\angle CAB = \frac{1}{2}(90° - \angle B) = \angle B$, therefore $3\angle B = 90°$. Hence $\angle B = 30°$.　⓬ (a) Since $AD /\!/ BC$ (given), $\angle ADC = \angle ECF$ (When two lines are parallel, the alternate angles are equal). Since E is the midpoint of CD (given), $DE = EC$ (definition of midpoint). In $\triangle ADE$ and $\triangle FCE$, since $\angle ADC = \angle ECF$, $DE = EC$ and $\angle AED = \angle CEF$, $\triangle ADE \cong \triangle FCE$ (ASA); therefore $FC = AD$ (property of congruent triangles). (b) Since $\triangle ADE \cong \triangle FCE$, $AE = EF$ and $AD = CF$ (Corresponding pairs of sides in congruent triangles are equal), BE is the perpendicular bisector of AF, so $AB = BF = BC + CF$. Since $AD = CF$ (given), $AB = BC + AD$ (property of equality).

7.8　Angle bisectors (1)

❶ D　❷ A　❸ C　❹ $\triangle OPF$, AAS, PF, corresponding pairs of sides of congruent triangles are equal.　❺ 4　❻ (a) 12　(b) 4　(c) 12　(d) 40　(e) 70　❼ Hint: prove $DB = DC$.　❽ Hint: prove $\triangle DEB \cong \triangle DFC$.　❾* Hint: Through point E, construct $EF \perp CB$ with F being the perpendicular foot, and prove $EQ = EF = EP$.

7.9　Angle bisectors (2)

❶ D　❷ A　❸ B　❹ C　❺ 3　❻ 4　❼ Since AD bisects $\angle BAC$, $DE \perp AB$ and $\angle ACB = 90°$, $\triangle ACD \cong \triangle AED$ (AAS), so $DE = DC$; therefore $\angle ECD = \angle CED$ (In a triangle, angles opposite equal sides are equal). Since $EF /\!/ BC$, $\angle FEC = \angle ECD$, so $\angle FEC = \angle CED$ (property of equality); therefore EC bisects $\angle FED$ (definition of angle bisector).　❽ Since OP bisects $\angle MON$, $PA \perp OM$ at A,

$PB \perp ON$ at B, and $OP = OP$, $\triangle OAP \cong \triangle OBP$ (AAS), so $\angle OPA = \angle OPB$; $\angle CEP = \angle CFP = 90°$ and $CP = CP$, therefore $\triangle CEP \cong \triangle CFD$ (AAS). Hence $CE = CF$.

Unit test 7

❶ C　❷ B　❸ B　❹ C　❺ If two angles are vertically opposite angles, then the two angles are equal.　❻ 50° or 80°　❼ 3, 90°　❽ 24　❾ 12　❿ 40　⓫ Given: $AB /\!/ CD$, EF intersects AB and CD at points O and P. Bisectors of $\angle BOP$ and $\angle DPO$ intersect at G. Prove: $OG \perp PG$. Proof: Since $AB /\!/ CD$, $\angle BOP + \angle DPO = 180°$. Since $\angle BOP$ and $\angle DPO$ bisect at G, $\angle GOP + \angle OPG = 90°$, therefore $OG \perp PG$.　⓬ Since $BF = CE$, $BC = EF$, and since $\angle A = \angle D$ and $\angle B = \angle E$, $\triangle ABC \cong \triangle DEF$; therefore $AC = DF$.　⓭ Connect BC. Since $BD = CD$, $\angle DBC = \angle DCB$. Since $\angle ABD = \angle ACD$, $\angle ABC = \angle ACB$; therefore $AC = AB$.　⓮ (a) diagram drawn as described　(b) Connect CE. Since DE is the perpendicular bisector of AC, $CE = AE$. Since $AE = BC$, $CE = CB$. Let $\angle A = x$, so $\angle ECA = \angle A = x$, therefore $\angle B = \angle CEB = 2x$. Since $\angle A + \angle B + \angle ACB = 180°$, $x + 2x + 120° = 180°$, the solution $x = 20°$. Hence $\angle A = 20°$.

Chapter 8　Right-angled triangles and Pythagoras' theorem

8.1　Congruence testing for right-angled triangles

❶ D　❷ B　❸ D　❹ C　❺ hypotenuse, one side, hypotenuse, corresponding side, RHS　❻ (a) AAS　(b) ASA　(c) RHS　(d) SAS　❼ Hint: First prove the congruence of two right-angled triangles, i.e., $\triangle ACB \cong \triangle ADB$ (RHS), so $\angle CAB = \angle DAB$. Since $AC = AD$ and $AE = AE$, $\triangle ACE \cong \triangle ADE$ (SAS); therefore $CE = DE$.　❽ Hint: Since $BE = DF$, $BF = ED$. Since $AD = BC$, the congruence of two right-angled triangles $\triangle AED \cong \triangle CFB$ (RHS) follows, so

$AE = CF$. Since $\angle AED = \angle CFB = 90°$, $\angle AGB = \angle CGD$, $\triangle AEG \cong \triangle CFG$ (AAS); therefore $AG = CG$. **9** Hint: Join AN and CN; and prove the congruence of two right-angled triangles, i. e., $\triangle AND \cong \triangle CNE$; therefore $AD = CE$.

10 (a) Hint: First prove the congruence of two right-angled triangles, i. e., $\triangle ABF \cong \triangle CDE$ (RHS), then prove in the right-angled triangles, $\triangle DEO \cong \triangle BFO$ (AAS). (b) The conclusion is true.

8.2 Properties of right-angled triangles (1)

1 A **2** C **3** 65, 25 **4** 45 **5** 2
6 20 **7** 145 **8** Hint: Proving $\triangle DBE \cong \triangle DCA$ leads to $BE = CA$. Since M and N are the midpoints on hypotenuses BE and AC, $DM = DN$.
9 Hint: (a) Connect DE, and you can prove $DE = DC$ (note $\triangle ADB$ is a right-angled triangle and E is the midpoint of its hypotenuse). As $DE = DC = \frac{1}{2}AB$, $\triangle EDC$ is an isosceles triangle, and $DG \perp CE$, therefore G is the midpoint on CE. (b) Since $\angle EDB = 2\angle BCE$, $\angle BDE = \angle B$; therefore $\angle B = 2\angle BCE$ **10*** (a) In right-angled triangle $\triangle ADC$, $\angle DEA = 2\angle DCA$ and in right-angled triangle $\triangle ABC$, $\angle BEA = 2\angle BCA$, then $\angle DEA + \angle BEA = 2\angle DCA + 2\angle BCA$; therefore $\angle DEB = 2\angle DCB$. (b) In right-angled triangle $\triangle ADC$, $\angle DEA = 2\angle DCA$ and in right-angled triangle $\triangle ABC$, $\angle BEA = 2\angle BCA$, then $\angle BEA - \angle DEA = 2\angle BCA - 2\angle DCA$; therefore $\angle DEB = 2\angle DCB$.

8.3 Properties of right-angled triangles (2)

1 C **2** D **3** C **4** 10 **5** 120
6 5, 50 **7** 60 **8** 6 **9** Hint: First by proving $AE = \frac{1}{2}BC$, you can get $AD = \frac{1}{2}AE$, so $\angle DEA = 30°$. Since $\angle B = \angle EAB$ and $\angle AEC = \angle B + \angle EAB$, you can get $\angle B = 15°$. Since $\angle CAB = 90°$, you have $\angle C = 75°$. **10** Hint: First prove $\angle ACF = \angle ABF = 30°$. Since $FD = 2$ cm and $FE = 4$ cm, $FC = 4$ cm and

$FB = 8$ cm, so $BD = 10$ cm, therefore $CE = 8$ cm. **11** (a) Take E on AC so that $AE = AB$. Connect DE. Since $AC = 2AB$, E is the midpoint of AC. Since AD is the angle bisector of $\triangle ABC$, $\angle BAD = \angle EAD$. Since $AD = AD$, $\triangle ABD \cong \triangle AED$; therefore $BD = DE$, $\angle B = \angle DEA$. Since $\angle C = \frac{1}{2}\angle BAC$, $\angle C = \angle DAE$, so $AD = DC$; therefore $DE \perp AC$, that is $\angle DEA = 90°$. Hence $\angle B = 90°$. (b) From (a), $3\angle BAD = 90°$, so $\angle BAD = 30°$, therefore in right-angled triangle $\triangle ABD$, $AD = 2BD$.

8.4 Properties of right-angled triangles (3)

1 A **2** B **3** 15 **4** 2 **5** 12
6 $\frac{5}{2}$ **7** 30 or 150 **8** Hint: Connect EM and CM. Since M is the midpoint of BD and $DE \perp AB$, we get $ME = \frac{1}{2}BD$, with the same reason we get $MC = \frac{1}{2}BD$, so $EM = CM$, hence $\triangle MCE$ is an isosceles triangle. Since N is the midpoint of CE, then $MN \perp CE$. **9** Hint: It is easy to prove that $\triangle AEF$ is an equilateral triangle, so $\angle C = 30°$; therefore $\angle BAC = 75°$. Hence $\angle BAE = 15°$. **10** Since $AB = AC$ and E is the midpoint of BC, $AE \perp BC$, $\angle BAE = \angle CAE$ and $\angle B = \angle C$. Since $\angle A = 120°$, $\angle BAE = \angle CAE = 60°$ and $\angle B = \angle C = 30°$. Since $DE \perp AC$ and $\angle CAE = 60°$, $AE = 2AD$. Since $\angle C = 30°$ and $AE \perp BC$, $AC = 2AE = 4AD$; therefore $CD = 3AD$. **11** Hint: first prove $\triangle ACD \cong \triangle CBE$, $\angle CAD = \angle BCE$, $\angle AFE = \angle CAD + \angle ACE = \angle BCE + \angle ACE = 60°$. Since $EH \perp AD$, $\angle FEH = 30°$ and $EF = 2HF$. Since $DG \parallel EH$, $\angle FGD = \angle FEH = 30°$ and $\angle FDG = \angle EHF = 90°$, so $FG = 2FD$, therefore $EG = EF + FG = 2HF + 2FD = 2HD$.

8.5 Pythagoras' theorem

1 C **2** B **3** D **4** C **5** (a) 20
(b) 24 (c) 9 (d) 3 (e) 9, 12 (f) 12,

$6\sqrt{3}$ **⑥** $1: 1: \sqrt{2}$ **⑦** $1: \sqrt{3}: 2$ **⑧** 2.5
⑨ 24 **⑩** Hint: It is easy to prove $BD =$
$\frac{1}{2}BC = 5$, so $AD = \sqrt{AB^2 - BD^2} = \sqrt{39}$, therefore
$S_{\triangle ABC} = \frac{1}{2}BC \cdot AD = 5\sqrt{39}$. **⑪** Since $\angle C =$
$90°$ and $\angle B = 60°$, $BC = 5$ and $AC = 5\sqrt{3}$. Since
$BD : DC = 2 : 3$, $CD = 3$, therefore $AD = 2\sqrt{21}$.
⑫ Hint: Since $\triangle ABC$ is a right-angled isosceles
triangle, it is easy to prove $\triangle AEF$ is also a right-
angled isosceles triangle, so $AF = EF$ and $AE^2 =$
$AF^2 + EF^2 = 2EF^2$. From the given, $\triangle ACD \cong$
$\triangle AED$, so that you can deduce $AC = AE$;
therefore $AC^2 = 2EF^2$.

8.6 Applications of Pythagoras' theorem

① D **②** B **③** B **④** $10\sqrt{3}$ **⑤** $\frac{\sqrt{3}}{4}a^2$

⑥ 12 **⑦** $2\sqrt{5}$ 8 **⑧** 4 or $\frac{\sqrt{119}}{2}$ **⑨** 5

⑩ Connect AC. Since $AB = 1$, $BC = \sqrt{3}$ and
$\angle ABC = 90°$, $AC = 2 = 2AB$, so $\angle ACB = 30°$,
therefore $\angle ACD = 120° - 30° = 90°$. By
Pythagoras' theorem, $AD = \sqrt{AC^2 + CD^2} = 2\sqrt{2}$.
⑪ (a) 24 m (b) 8 m

8.7 The converse of Pythagoras' theorem

① C **②** C **③** is **④** $2\sqrt{3}$ cm^2 **⑤** $\frac{168}{25}$

⑥ 26 **⑦** Hint: Connect AC to get $AC = 5$, so
$\triangle ABC$ is a right-angled triangle. The area of the
land $= S_{\triangle ABC} - S_{\triangle ACD} = 30 - 6 = 24$ m^2
⑧ Hint: Rotate $\triangle APC$ through 60 degrees
clockwise around point A, so that the image of
point C is the image of point B and the image of
point P is the image of point P_1. Connect AP_1 and
BP_1, hence $\angle BPA = 150°$.

8.8 Applications of Pythagoras' theorem and its converse theorem

① B **②** D **③** 25 **④** 4.8 **⑤** 13 or
$\sqrt{119}$ **⑥** $30 + \sqrt{34}$ **⑦** (a) $CD = \frac{12}{5}$

(b) $AD = \frac{16}{5}$ (c) $AB = 5$ (d) $\triangle ABC$ is a
right-angled triangle, since its sides are in the ratio
$3 : 4 : 5$. **⑧** Hint: From $\triangle ADE \cong \triangle AFE$,
$AD = AF = 10$. Let $CE = x$, then $DE = EF =$
$8 - x$. In right-angled triangle $\triangle ABF$, $BF =$
$\sqrt{AF^2 - AB^2} = \sqrt{10^2 - 8^2} = 6$, so $CF = 10 -$
$6 = 4$, therefore in right-angled triangle $\triangle EFC$,
$EF^2 = EC^2 + FC^2$, that is $(8 - x)^2 = x^2 + 4^2$, $x =$
3. Hence $EC = 3$. **⑨** In the diagram, inside
$\angle ECF$ construct $\angle ECG = \angle ACE$ and $CG = CA$.
Connect EG and FG. Since $CE = CE$, $\triangle ACE \cong$
$\triangle GCE$ (SAS), so $\angle 1 = \angle A$. With the same
reasoning, $\triangle CGF \cong \triangle CBF$, so that $\angle 2 = \angle B$.
Since $\angle ACB = 90°$, $\angle A + \angle B = 90°$, so that
$\angle 1 + \angle 2 = 90°$, $\angle EGF = 90°$; therefore the
three segments AE, EF and FB can form a right-
angled triangle with EF being the hypotenuse.
Hence $EF^2 = AE^2 + BF^2$.

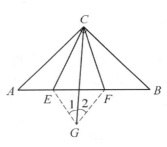

Diagram for question 9

8.9 The formula for distance between two points

① B **②** A **③** B **④** D **⑤** right-
angled **⑥** right-angled isosceles **⑦** $(-1,$
$3\sqrt{3})$ or $(-1, -3\sqrt{3})$ **⑧** $B(3, 3)$ or $(-7,$
$3)$ **⑨** $2\sqrt{5}$ **⑩** $B(3, 3)$ or $(-4, -4)$
⑪ $(4, 9)$, $8\frac{1}{2}$ or $(4, 1)$, $7\frac{1}{2}$ **⑫** Hint:
First find $AB = 5$ (using distance formula between
two points). Let the co-ordinates of point M be
$(x, 0)$. Since $\angle AMB = 90°$, $AM^2 + BM^2 = AB^2$.
From the distance formula between two points,

$AM^2 = (x - 2)^2 + (0 - 2)^2$, $BM^2 = (x - 5)^2 + (0 + 2)^2$, so $[(x - 2)^2 + 4] + [(x - 5)^2 + 4] = 25$. Simplified, this is $x^2 - 7x + 6 = 0$, the solutions are $x_1 = 1$, $x_2 = 6$. Thus the co-ordinates of point M are $(1, 0)$ or $(6, 0)$. ⑬ Hint: Consider this in two cases: point P is on the angle bisector in quadrant I and III, or point P is on the angle bisector in quadrant II and IV. (1) P is on the angle bisector in quadrant I and III. Let P be (a, a), then $(a - 2)^2 + (a - 4)^2 = (a + 1)^2 + (a - 3)^2$, the solution $a = \dfrac{5}{4}$, then $P_1\left(\dfrac{5}{4}, \dfrac{5}{4}\right)$. (2) P is on the angle bisector II and IV. Let P be $(a, -a)$, then $(a - 2)^2 + (-a - 4)^2 = (a + 1)^2 + (-a - 3)^2$, the solution $a = \dfrac{5}{2}$, then $P_2\left(\dfrac{5}{2}, -\dfrac{5}{2}\right)$.

Unit test 8

① D ② D ③ C ④ C ⑤ D

⑥ 40 ⑦ 60 ⑧ $\sqrt{5}$, $\sqrt{5}$, $\sqrt{2}$, an isosceles

⑨ 50° ⑩ $\sqrt{3} + 1$ or $\sqrt{3} - 1$ ⑪ 4

⑫ (a) $\dfrac{3 + \sqrt{3}}{4}$ (b) Since E is the midpoint of BC and $\angle ADB = 90°$, $DE = BE$, so $\angle EDB = \angle EBD = 30°$, therefore $\angle EDC = \angle EBC$, $\triangle EDC \cong \triangle EBC$, so that $\angle ECD = \angle ECB$. Hence $EC \perp BD$. ⑬ Since $BD \perp AD$, $\angle ADB = 90°$. Since $AD /\!/ BC$, $\angle CBD = \angle ADB = 90°$. Since points E and F are the midpoints of AB and CD, $DE = \dfrac{1}{2}AB$ and $BF = \dfrac{1}{2}CD$. Since $DE = BF$ (given), $AB = CD$. In right-angled triangles $\triangle ABD$ and $\triangle CDB$, since $BD = DB$, $AB = CD$, $\triangle ABD \cong \triangle CDB$, therefore $\angle A = \angle C$.

⑭ (a) Since $AD \perp BC$ and $\angle ABC = 45°$, $AD = BD$. Since $AD \perp BC$, $BE \perp AC$ and $\angle BFD = \angle AFE$, $\angle DBF = \angle DAC$, therefore the right-angled triangles: $\triangle BDF \cong \triangle ADC$. (b) Since the right-angled triangles are congruent, i. e.,

$\triangle BDF \cong \triangle ADC$, $BF = AC$. In right-angled triangle $\triangle BDF$, since M is the midpoint of BF, $DM = \dfrac{1}{2}BF$. With the same reasoning, $ND = \dfrac{1}{2}AC$, so $MD = ND$. Since $MD = BM$, $\angle MDB = \angle MBD$. With the same reasoning, $\angle MDA = \angle MFD$, $\angle DAN = \angle NAD$ and $\angle NDC = \angle NCD$. Since $\angle AFE + \angle FAE = 90°$ and $\angle MDF = \angle AFE$, $\angle MDF + \angle ADN = 90°$; therefore $MD \perp ND$.

Chapter 9 Statistics (I)

9.1 Organising and presenting data (1)

① D ② B ③ B ④ pictogram, block diagram ⑤ 6 ⑥ (a) From 2010 to 2016, the number of students joining CCAs in School A has increased more than that of students in School B. (Answer may vary.) (b) School A has more students joining art and sports than science. (Answer may vary.) (c) $2000 \times 38\% + 1105 \times 60\% = 1423$ (students)

⑦ (a) (i)

Year	2010	2013	2016
No. of students	600	1000	2000

(ii)

Year	2010	2013	2016
No. of students	600	625	1105

(iii)

Year	2010	2013	2016
No. of students	1200	1625	3105

(b) Yes

Year	2010	2013	2016
School A	600	1000	2000
School B	600	625	1105
Total	1200	1625	3105

9.2　Organising and presenting data (2)

① D　**②** D　**③** pictogram, bar chart, line graph, pie chart　**④** bar chart, line graph, pie chart　**⑤** (a) 25　(b) 32%　(c) pie chart correctly constructed.　**⑥** (a) 60　(b) The total number of tourists surveyed at exit A: $1 + 3 + 2.5 + 2 + 1.5 = 100$ thousand (people), and the total number of bottles of drinks the tourists surveyed at exit A bought: $3 \times 1 + 2.5 \times 2 + 2 \times 3 + 1.5 \times 4 = 3 + 5 + 6 + 6 = 200$ thousand (bottles), so the average bottles of drinks bought per person by the tourists surveyed at exit $A =$
$$\frac{\text{total no. of bottles of drinks bought}}{\text{total no. of tourists}} =$$
$\frac{200 \text{ thousand bottles}}{100 \text{ thousand of people}} = 2$ (bottles).　(c) Let the number of tourists at exit B be x ten thousand people. Then the number of tourist at exit C is $(x + 2)$ ten thousand people, so $3x + 2(x + 2) = 49$, the solution is $x = 9$. Hence the number of tourist at exit B is 90 thousand people.

9.3　Measuring central tendency of data: Mean

① B　**②** C　**③** C　**④** D　**⑤** 25　**⑥** 9　**⑦** 7　**⑧** (a) 22　(b) line graph correctly constructed　(c) Answer may vary.　**⑨** (a) $a = 50 - 15 - 20 - 5 = 10$　(b) The mean: $\frac{1}{50}(5 \times 10 + 10 \times 15 + 15 \times 20 + 20 \times 5) = £12$.　(c) vertical bar graph correctly constructed　**⑩** (a) The mode of scores that the judges gave Matt in the debate is 94.　(b) 20%　(c) His score from the debate: $(95 + 94 + 92 + 90 + 94) \div 5 = 93$, and the score from the opinion poll: $50 \times 70\% \times 2 + 50 \times 20\% \times 1 = 80$, so Matt's overall score: $93 \times 0.4 + 80 \times 0.6 = 85.2$　(d) Let Emmy's score from debate be x. From the question: $82 \times 0.6 + 0.4x \geqslant 85.2$, the solution is $x \geqslant 90$, so Emmy should score at least 90 from the debate.

9.4　Measuring central tendency of data: Mode and median (1)

① B　**②** A　**③** 90, 90　**④** 20. Since the number who donated £100 is 25% of the total number of paticipants, the total number who have donated is: $15 \div 25\% = 60$. Thus, from the diagram, the number who donated £20 is: $60 - 20 - 10 - 15 = 15$. If the amounts donated are arranged in order, from the greatest, then the median is 20.　**⑤** (a) The mean of the annual income of the 15 families: $(2 + 2.5 \times 3 + 3 \times 5 + 4 \times 2 + 5 \times 2 + 9 + 13) \div 15 = 43$ thousand pounds. If the 15 incomes are arranged in order from least to greatest, the middle number (the 8th number) is 3, thus the median is 30 thousand pounds. In this set of data, 3 is the most frequent number, so the mode is 30 thousand pounds.

(b) Answers may vary. For example, the mode is the most appropriate to represent the general annual income for the 15 families, because the most frequent number is 3 and it can represent the average income of the families.　**⑥** (a) 3, 5
(b) £260 000, £250 000, £240 000　(c) No, because at that time the mode is £260 000, which is greater than the median £250 000. (or: from the table we know that among the 20 staff members, only 9 of them can meet the target or beyond, which is less than half of the staff numbers.)

9.5　Measuring central tendency of data: Mode and median (2)

① C　**②** B　**③** 1　**④** Safe. The total sum of the items in the graph of the 2004 survey does not add up to 100%.　**⑤** (a) Let the number students who donated £15 be $5x$. From the question, the number of students who donated £20 is $8x$, so $5x + 8x = 39$, thus $x = 3$, therefore the total number of students in the sample survey is: $3x + 4x + 5x + 8x + 2x = 66$ (students). The percentage of the donations that are £20 or more is

$\dfrac{30}{66} = \dfrac{5}{11} = 45.45\%$. (b) From (1), the mode in this set of data is £20, the median is £15. (c) The students in the whole school have donated in total $(9 \times 5 + 12 \times 10 + 15 \times 15 + 24 \times 20 + 6 \times 30) \div 66 \times 2310 = £36\,750$. **6** (a) The mean is: $(163 + 171 + 173 + 159 + 161 + 174 + 164 + 166 + 169 + 164) \div 10 = 166.4$ cm; the median is: $\dfrac{166 + 164}{2} = 165$ cm; and the mode is 164 cm. (b) Choosing mean as the standard height: the height x satisfies: $166.4 \times (1 - 2\%) \leqslant x \leqslant 166.4 \times (1 + 2\%)$, that is, when $163.072 \leqslant x \leqslant 169.728$, it is normal height, so the heights of trees 7, 8, 9 and 10 are normal. Choosing median as the standard height, the height x satisfies: $165 \times (1 - 2\%) \leqslant x \leqslant 165 \times (1 + 2\%)$, that is when $161.7 \leqslant x \leqslant 168.3$, the heights of trees 1, 7, 8 and 10 are of normal height. Choosing mode as the standard height: the height x satisfies: $164 \times (1 - 2\%) \leqslant x \leqslant 164 \times (1 + 2\%)$, that is when $160.72 \leqslant x \leqslant 167.28$, the heights for trees 1, 5, 7, 8 and 10 are normal. (c) Choosing mean as the standard height, it is estimated that the number of trees of normal height is about: $280 \times \dfrac{4}{10} = 112$ (trees). When choosing median as the standard height, it is estimated that the number of trees of normal height is about: $280 \times \dfrac{4}{10} = 112$ (trees). When choosing mode as the standard height, it is estimated that the number of trees of normal height is about: $280 \times \dfrac{5}{10} = 140$ (trees).

Unit test 9

1 D **2** B **3** C **4** C **5** 260, 270 **6** 1 **7** 187 **8** (a) The mean is $\bar{x} = \dfrac{1}{6}(0 + 1 - 2 + 0 + 2 - 1) + 50 = 50$, the median is $\dfrac{50 + 50}{2} = 50$, and the mode is 50 (b) Line

graph correctly constructed. In March and June. (c) 20%, 72 **9** (a) fail, pass (b) 75% 25% (c) 240 (d) Not necessarily, because it is not clear how the 32 students were selected. (Answers may vary.)

End of year test

1 D **2** A **3** C **4** A **5** B **6** C **7** B **8** B **9** B **10** C **11** two, 5 **12** 1.47×10^8 **13** 10 **14** $\angle A = \angle D$ (for example) **15** 55 **16** $(-5, 7)$ **17** 12.4, 11, 12 **18** 6 **19** $(-3, 1)$ **20** 120 **21** 4 **22** second and fourth **23** 30 **24** 1 **25** 3 **26** Since $\angle BCE = \angle ACD$ and $\angle ACD = 25°$, $\angle BCE = 25°$; since $CF \perp DE$, $\angle ECF = 90°$, that is: $\angle BCF + \angle BCE = 90°$, therefore $\angle BCF = 65°$. **27** Since $AB = DC$, $AB + BC = DC + BC$, that is $AC = DB$. In $\triangle AEC$ and $\triangle DFB$, since $AE \parallel DF$, $AE = DF$, $\angle A = \angle D$ and $AC = DB$, $\triangle AEC \cong \triangle DFB$, therefore $EC = FB$. **28** (a) $\triangle ABC$ correctly drawn. (b) $A_1(3, 0)$, $B_1(-1, 3)$, $C_1(-1, -3)$ (c) right, 4 **29** Since $\alpha = \beta$ (given), $\alpha + \angle BDE = \beta + \angle BDE$ (property of equality), that is: $\angle ADE = \angle BDC$. In $\triangle ADE$ and $\triangle BDC$, $\begin{cases} AD = BD(\text{given}) \\ \angle ADE = \angle BDC, \\ ED = CD(\text{given}) \end{cases}$ so $\triangle ADE \cong \triangle BDC$ (SAS) and $\angle AED = \angle C$ (The corresponding angles are equal in congruent triangles); and since $\angle BED = \beta + \angle C$ (The exterior angle of a triangle equals the sum of the two non-adjacent interior angles), that is: $\gamma + \angle AED = \beta + \angle C$, so $\gamma = \beta$ (property of equality); since $\alpha = \beta$ (given), then $\gamma = \alpha$ (property of equality). **30** 90 cm^2 **31** In the equilateral triangle ABC, since $AB = AC$, $AD \perp BC$ (given), $\angle CAD = \dfrac{1}{2}\angle BAC$; and since $\angle BAC = 60°$, $\angle CAD = 30°$; since $AD = AC$ (given), $\angle ACD = \angle ADC$. In $\triangle ACD$, since $\angle ACD + \angle ADC + \angle CAD = 180°$, $\angle ACD = 75°$. In $\triangle ACE$, since $\angle EAC + \angle ACE + \angle E = 180°$, then $\angle E = 45°$. **32** (a) Frequency table correctly filled in; 12, 12 (b) Line graph correctly constructed. The conclusion may vary.

33 (a) Since $\triangle ABC$ is an equilateral triangle, $AB = AC = BC$, $\alpha = \beta = \angle BAC = 60°$; since $\alpha + \gamma = 180°$, $\beta + \theta = 180°$, then $\gamma = \theta$. In $\triangle CBD$ and $\triangle ACE$, $\begin{cases} BC = AC \\ \gamma = \theta \\ BD = CE \end{cases}$, then $\triangle CBD \cong \triangle ACE$ (SAS). (b) Guess that $\triangle AEG$ is an equilateral triangle. Since $\triangle ABG$ is obtained by the rotation of $\triangle CBD$ anticlockwise $60°$ around point B, $\triangle ABG \cong \triangle CBD$, so $AG = CD$, $\phi = \sigma$. Since $\triangle CBD \cong \triangle ACE$, $CD = AE$, $\phi = \mu$, $AG = AE$ and $\sigma = \mu$, therefore $\triangle AEG$ is an isosceles triangle. Since $\sigma + \lambda = 60°$, then $\mu + \lambda = 60°$, that is: $\angle GAE = 60°$, therefore $\triangle AEG$ is an equilateral triangle.

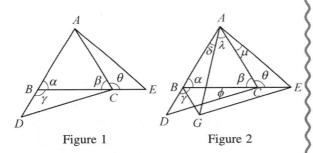

Figure 1   Figure 2

Diagram for question 33

34 (a) $(8 - 2m, n)$ (b) Since point C is on line $x = -2$, $-2m + 8 = -2$; therefore $m = 5$. (c) When $AP = AB$, $\angle A = 90°$, as shown in Figure 1, it is easy to prove $\triangle APH \cong \triangle BAG$, so $PH = AG = 1$, $BG = AH = 6$ and $P(-2, -1)$; when $PB = AB$, $\angle B = 90°$, as shown in Figure 2, it is easy to prove $\triangle AGB \cong \triangle BHP$, so $BG = $ $PH = 7$, $BH = AG = 1$, $P(-2, -8)$, which are the conditions that satisfy co-ordinates of point $P(-2, -1)$ and $(-2, -8)$.

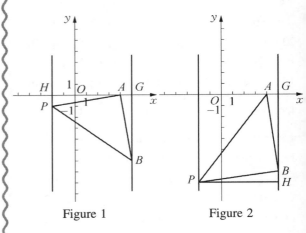

Figure 1   Figure 2

Diagram for question 34

35 (a) The area of $\triangle POA$ reduces gradually. (b) Through point P, construct $PC \perp OA$ with C being the foot of the perpendicular. Since $\triangle POA$ is the isosceles triangle and $OA = 2$, $OC = 1$ and $PC = \sqrt{3}$, that is the co-ordinates of point P are $(1, \sqrt{3})$. Substituting the co-ordinates of point P into $y = \dfrac{k}{x}$ leads to $k = \sqrt{3}$. Therefore the inverse proportional function is $y = \dfrac{\sqrt{3}}{x}$. **36** (a) 12 (b) 15 **37** (a) Since $BM \perp a$ at M, $CN \perp a$ at N, $\angle BMN = \angle CNM = 90°$, so $BM \parallel CN$, therefore $\angle MBP = \angle ECP$. Since P is the midpoint of BC, $BP = CP$. In $\triangle BPM$ and $\triangle CPE$, $\angle MBP = \angle ECP$, $BP = CP$ and $\angle BPM = \angle CPE$, then $\triangle BPM \cong \triangle CPE$. (b) Since $\triangle BPM \cong \triangle CPE$, $PM = PE$. In right-angled $\triangle MNE$, since $PM = PE$, then $PM = PN$.

Notes

Notes

Notes

Notes

Notes

Notes

Notes

Notes

Notes

Notes